The World Bank
and the Environmental Challenge

The World Bank and the Environmental Challenge

Philippe Le Prestre

Selinsgrove: Susquehanna University Press
London and Toronto: Associated University Presses

Associated University Presses
440 Forsgate Drive
Cranbury, NJ 08512

Associated University Presses
25 Sicilian Avenue
London WC1A 2QH, England

Associated University Presses
P.O. Box 488, Port Credit
Mississauga, Ontario
Canada L5G 4M2

The paper used in this publication meets the requirements of the American National Standard for Permanence of Paper for Printed Library Materials Z39.48-1984.

Library of Congress Cataloging-in-Publication Data

Le Prestre, Philippe G.
  The World Bank and the environmental challenge.

  Bibliography: p.
  Includes index.
  1. World Bank—Developing countries. 2. Development banks—Developing countries. 3. Environmental policy—Developing countries. 4. Economic development projects—Environmental aspects—Developing countries.
I. Title.
HG3881.5.W57L4   1989   332.1'532   88-42825
ISBN 0-941664-98-8 (alk. paper)

PRINTED IN THE UNITED STATES OF AMERICA

Contents

Acronyms

ADB	Asian Development Bank
AfDB	African Development Bank
BOISEA	Bureau of Oceans and International Scientific and Environmental Affairs (United States Department of State)
CCCE	Caisse Centrale de Coopération Economique (France)
CDB	Caribbean Development Bank
CEQ	Council on Environmental Quality (United States)
CIDIE	Committee of International Development Institutions on the Environment
CPP	Country Program Paper (World Bank)
CPS	Central Project Staff (World Bank)
DAC	Development Assistance Committee
DFC	Development Finance Company
EC	European Community
ECOSOC	Economic and Social Council (United Nations)
EDI	Economic Development Institute (World Bank)
EIS	Environmental Impact Statement
EPA	Environmental Protection Agency (United States)
FAO	Food and Agriculture Organization
GATT	General Agreement on Tariffs and Trade
GEMS	Global Environment Monitoring System
IBRD	International Bank for Reconstruction and Development
ICSU	International Council of Scientific Unions
IDA	International Development Association
IDB	Inter-American Development Bank
IFAD	International Fund for Agricultural Development
IFC	International Financial Corporation
IGO	International Governmental Organization
IIED	International Institute for Environment and Development
ILO	International Labour Organization
IMF	International Monetary Fund
IMO	International Maritime Organization
INGO	International Non-Governmental Organization
IRPTC	International Register of Potentially Toxic Chemicals

IUCN	International Union for the Conservation of Nature and Natural Resources
MAB	Man and the Biosphere Programme
MDB	Multilateral Development Bank
MIT	Massachusetts Institute of Technology
MNC	Multinational Corporation
NASA	National Aeronautics and Space Administration
NGO	Non-Governmental Organization
NIC	Newly Industrializing Country
NIEO	New International Economic Order
NRDC	Natural Resources Defense Council
ODA	Official Development Assistance
OEA	Office of Environmental Affairs (World Bank)
OECD	Organization for Economic Cooperation and Development
OED	Operations Evaluation Department (World Bank)
OESA	Office of Environmental and Scientific Affairs (World Bank)
OPEC	Organization of Petroleum Exporting Countries
OPS	Operations Policy Staff (World Bank)
OTA	Office of Technology Assessment (United States)
PCR	Project Completion Report (World Bank)
SAL	Structural Adjustment Loan
SCOPE	Scientific Committee on Problems of the Environment
SIDA	Swedish International Development Agency
SUNFED	Special United Nations Fund for Economic Development
TVA	Tennessee Valley Authority
UN	United Nations
UNCHE	United Nations Conference on the Human Environment
UNCTAD	United Nations Conference on Trade and Development
UNDP	United Nations Development Programme
UNEP	United Nations Environment Programme
UNESCO	United Nations Educational, Scientific, and Cultural Organization
UNIDO	United Nations Industrial Development Organization
USAID	United States Agency for International Development
WBG	World Bank Group
WHO	World Health Organization
WMO	World Meteorological Organization
WRI	World Resources Institute
WSS	Water Supply and Sewerage Sector (World Bank)
WWF	World Wildlife Fund

The World Bank
and the Environmental Challenge

Introduction

Famine, droughts, floods, desertification, chemical contamination, and deforestation in Asia, Latin America, and Africa during the 1980s all suggest that development strategies have proven economically and environmentally costly, as well as ineffective in improving the welfare of the people to whom they are directed. International organizations established to address these issues appear to have failed miserably, despite their significant contributions in specific instances. Seemingly incapable of responding to rapidly changing needs and perspectives, the future of these agencies is increasingly in doubt. Perceived as prisoners of anachronistic, narrow, irrelevant, or self-defeating quarrels, they are now considered to be unwilling or unable to lead or reconcile conflicting values. Diminishing rates of financial contributions, the emergence of new actors, and the development of more nationalistic and ideological policies have required considerable adaptive capabilities from International Governmental Organizations (IGOs). Consequently, their ability to cope with changing values, to identify and address global issues has become central to their continuing relevance. Must they remain in their roles as interstate cooperative agencies, or can they promote and implement the world-order values that individual states are unable to pursue?

IGOs are essentially schizophrenic institutions: they must adapt to their task-environment as well as transform it.[1] Adaptation and transformation are more than descriptions or interpretations of the role of IGOs, however. They tend to constitute expectations of their behavior and contribution to the international system. IGOs are castigated for not achieving their goals, while being required to function "in the interstices" of the Western State system.[2]

This apparent contradiction symbolizes the constraints that IGOs face in the formation of international public policy. Limits are set on their activities, but the successful achievement of goals requires, or implies, that these very limits be transgressed. Judged according to their ability to transform their milieu (such as solving ecological problems or improving the amount, quality, and impact of development aid), IGOs must nevertheless adapt to it by respecting a broad definition of sovereignty or by furthering the interests of the more powerful coalitions among their members. The task of international organizations is then to reconcile their need to adapt to the present system, while their objective is to transform it.

The World Bank[3] has traditionally been regarded as uniquely able to solve this basic dilemma. With the United States Agency for International Development, it has exerted the greatest influence on the contemporary Third World. It has been deeply involved in national policy making, and, perhaps more than any other international organization, it has been instrumental in creating new values and redistributing old ones. Its extensive resources and financial independence from governments has allowed it to bestow rewards or withdraw benefits to a much greater extent than any other IGO. Whereas UN resolution-based agencies seemed unable to shield themselves from disruptive external influences, the Bank had the means to define its goals and achieve them. In particular, at a time when the United Nations Environment Programme (UNEP) was searching for the best way to adapt to its milieu in the absence of a clear political and functional definition of its role, the World Bank's resources and value to international actors suggested that it should be a powerful instrument for the formulation and implementation of global ecological values. Its role in the formation of international environmental policy would then constitute a unique and best-case example of the potential contribution of IGOs to building a new global order.

Yet, however powerful it is considered, the Bank confronts a particularly diverse and unpredictable task-environment. Shortly after its creation, for example, the establishment of the Marshall Plan compelled it to modify its goal and turn its attention away from reconstruction, toward the development aspect of its mandate. It subsequently spent its early years trying to control specific parts of its task-environment. The main concern of its president, Eugene Black, during the 1950s was to gain the confidence of the financial community that forms the basis for the organization's relative autonomy. Having successfully established its financial trustworthiness with a superior rating for its bonds, the Bank turned its attention to the developing countries. It has been suggested, for example, that, to a large degree, the International Development Association (IDA) was created to secure a stable clientele for the organization.[4] Throughout the 1960s and 1970s, the Bank met with increasingly vocal developing countries seeking to establish greater control over its activities, while it witnessed a growing antagonism from its main contributor.

The Bank's task-environment evolved with the transformation of the international system in the last two decades, and with it, so did the organization's goals. Although the Bank's primary objective remains economic development, its scope broadened, and the definition as well as the methods to achieve it, changed. Greater emphasis was placed on the agricultural sector. The Bank also turned its attention to social sectors (education, health, water supply and sewerage, population), reflected in its adherence in the 1970s to the twin goals of meeting basic needs and redistributing income.[5]

Along with these new social concerns, the Bank included environmental criteria in the appraisal and implementation of the development projects it funds. This new value, however, met with wide opposition within and outside the organization. These antagonisms were exacerbated by the importance of the Bank as an international lender. Its control of large amounts of money (the IBRD and IDA authorized the lending of more than $16 billion in fiscal year 1986) renders its clients and creditors all the more eager to define the criteria governing their allocations. As a leader among Multilateral Development Bank Institutions, its potential contribution to building an effective international environmental regime is considerable at a time when environmental deterioration is causing developing countries serious economic losses and limiting their future. Yet fifteen years after the establishment of an environmental unit in 1970, the environmental record of the Bank came under heavy challenge.

Why was the Bank unable to play a more effective role in the protection of the developing countries' natural resources? What internal and external obstacles did its environmental policy encounter? How did the organization try to overcome them? How has its dual need to adapt to and transform its milieu influenced the definition and implementation of its environmental policy? These are the questions this study addresses using organization theory as a framework for understanding the Bank's behavior.[6] The first chapter outlines the genesis and major characteristics of the policy, while the next examines the internal constraints arising from the organization's mandate, technology, and structure. Chapter 3 describes the Bank's task-environment and the constraints it puts on the definition and implementation of the policy. Subsequent sections review the strategies that the organization has used to adapt and transform its milieu in the past, applying these to its environmental policy, and also reexamining that policy in light of two case studies and the criticisms the Bank has faced. The last chapter looks toward the future after the 1987 decision to place environmental protection at the center of the work of the Bank. With the gradual implementation of the 1987 reforms, any understanding of the potential role that the organization can play in that area and of its relative ability to reform itself must rest on an analysis of the factors that have shaped the definition an implementation of a contested policy and prevented OESA from playing a larger role in the past.

1

Defining an Environmental Policy

The Emergence of the Policy

On 13 November 1970, at the end of the first United Nations Development Decade, Robert McNamara, president of the World Bank, prepared himself to give his annual address to a session of the United Nations Economic and Social Council (ECOSOC), which was full of hopeful pessimists. The findings of the Pearson Commission, pointing to the failures of the first development decade and of the traditional strategies of economic development it embodied, were still fresh in all minds.[1] Despite steady growth and a few impressive successes, gaps were ever-widening between the developed and the developing countries, between the fast industrializing countries and the "fourth world," and between the rich and the poor within each poor country.[2]

Table 1.1 shows how impressive the aggregate economic gains of the poor countries had been in the 1960s. Their Gross Domestic Product (GDP) and industrial and agricultural outputs surpassed that of the richer countries, which themselves were experiencing remarkable growth at the time. Yet, given their low starting base and their staggering population growth, not only could they not entertain the hope of ever catching up with the developed countries, but they were falling farther behind them in relative terms. Furthermore, this record hid great disparities in performance. The inability of African countries to increase their agricultural output sufficiently to keep pace with population growth was worrisome. Clearly, greater multilateral efforts were needed in the 1970s, and development strategies had to be reexamined carefully. Foreign aid had to be increased and targeted more effectively, population growth slowed, education and research revitalized, and international economic relations made more equitable. The *Pearson Report* recommended these measures and assigned the primary role in implementing them to the World Bank.

Aware of the urgency of the task, the president of the World Bank had the year before identified four structural problems that presented "grave threats" to development: the population explosion, unemployment, uncontrolled urbanization, and misdirected and inefficient industrialization.[3]

Table 1.1.: Selected Average Annual Rates of Growth, 1960–1984

Year		1960–65	1965–70	1970–75	1975–80	1981	1982	1983	1984
Developed Countries (excl. non-market economies)	Total GDP	5.3	4.8	3.4	3.5	2.0	-0.5	2.2	1.8
	Per capita	4.1	3.8	2.4	2.7	1.2	-1.2	1.6	1.1
	Agriculture	1.3	2.0	2.0	1.4	3.8	1.6	-3.1	4.3
	Industry	6.3	5.5	3.3	4.5	1.4	-1.6	2.6	4.5
Developing Countries	Total GDP	5.4	6.3	6.2	5.0	2.3	2.4	2.1	4.3
	Per capita	3.0	3.9	3.6	2.8	0.2	0.3	0.1	2.2
	Agriculture	2.5	3.4	2.9	2.7	4.7	4.2	3.8	4.1
	Industry	8.8	8.9	5.8	4.9	-0.6	0.3	1.5	8.6
Africa (excl. South Africa)	Total GDP	5.2	6.0	5.0	3.7	-0.2	1.5	0.0	1.1
	Per capita	2.8	2.9	2.3	0.6	-3.3	-1.8	-3.0	-1.8
	Agriculture	1.8	2.1	0.6	-0.2	0.5	5.0	-0.3	1.0
	Industry	16.8	12.2	0.6	5.7	-7.1	-7.2	1.5	2.7
Latin America and Carribean	Total GDP	5.3	6.3	6.2	5.1	1.1	-1.2	-2.2	3.3
	Per capita	2.3	3.6	3.5	2.5	-1.1	-3.5	-4.3	1.0
	Agriculture	4.8	2.2	4.0	3.4	4.9	-0.2	0.9	3.7
	Industry	6.7	7.4	5.8	5.5	-0.8	-0.2	1.2	7.5
East & S.E. Asia (excl. Japan & North Korea)	Total GDP	4.6	5.6	5.2	6.4	5.5	5.4	7.2	7.6
	Per capita	2.2	3.4	2.8	4.5	3.7	3.6	5.4	5.8
	Agriculture	1.6	4.8	3.4	2.6	4.8	4.7	6.3	6.1
	Industry	7.1	7.8	5.9	7.7	4.8	4.6	7.1	9.2

SOURCE: United Nations Statistical Yearbook 1985, pp. 6, 8–11.

To symbolize and foster a continuing effort, the 1970s were proclaimed the Second Development Decade, the objectives of which McNamara redefined as follows:

What we need—and what we must fashion—is a more effective overall development strategy. . . . Progress in the solution of the problems of population planning, educational advance, and agricultural growth is fundamental to such strategy. But. . . no such strategy will be complete unless it provides for an attack on the interrelated problems of unemployment, urbanization, and industrialization.[4]

The delegates were therefore deeply interested in hearing a preliminary exposition of the new attitude that the largest international development agency was to adopt for the decade ahead. Indeed, President McNamara emphasized that the Bank was developing new policies. The urban sector would be given more attention. The Bank would also increase considerably its activities in agricultural development, expand its Economic Development Institute, and promote projects that would approach modernization more holistically.[5] It involved a new emphasis on meeting the "basic needs" of the poor, a change that the International Labor Organization (ILO) had pioneered within the UN system.[6] The *Pearson Report* eventually led to a reorientation of the lending pattern toward agricultural and "new style" projects, as well as to the development of new sectors such as population and health (see table 1.2). These "new style" projects were designed to benefit directly large numbers of the rural poor, take a comprehensive approach to small scale agriculture, and insert components that were both directly and indirectly productive (including infrastructure, the provision of services, and institution building).[7]

But another suggestion surprised his audience. The World Bank would also be interested in another aspect of the development process: "The problem facing development finance institutions, including the World Bank, is whether and how we can help the developing countries to avoid or mitigate some of the damage economic development can do to the environment, without at the same time slowing down the pace of economic progress."[8] This pronouncement responded to the growing international awareness of the state of the environment as it was threatened by pollution and exhaustion resulting from misapplied technology.[9] If implemented in the developed countries, a successful environmental protection strategy carried an implication that it might usefully be extended to the developing world as well. The interdependence and multinational aspects of many environmental issues necessitated international cooperation not only among idustrialized countries, but between developed and developing countries. Development strategies had to be reassessed to avoid irreparable damage to the biosphere. Numerous studies outlined the failures of traditional

18   **DEFINING AN ENVIRONMENTAL POLICY**

Table 1.2.: Trends in Bank and IDA Lending in Millions of US$ and Percentages

Sector	1964–68a $	%	1969–73a $	%	1974–78a $	%	1979–83 $	%	1984 $	%	1985 $	%	1986 $	%
Agriculture & Rural Development	124.2	12.5	502.8	19.8	2003.72	29.92	3303.98	26.9	3472.9	22.4	3749.3	26.1	4777.4	29.3
Development Finance Cos	b		b		656.2	10.1	976.54	7.9	918.3	5.9	565.3	3.9	1449.2	8.9
Education	31.4	3.2	143.5	5.6	267.7	4.1	549.14	4.5	693.8	4.5	927.8	6.5	829.2	5.1
Energy:														
Oil, Gas, Coal	0	0	0	0	0	0	609.02	4.9	864.4	5.6	1331.4	9.3	231.1	1.4
Power	287.2	29.1	448.8	17.6	864	13.4	1793.92	14.6	2649.4	17.1	2250.3	15.6	2786.9	17.1
Industry	120.2	12.1	362.7	14.2	587.8	9.1	750.48	6.1	590.8	3.8	644	4.5	821.1	5
Non-Project	91	9.2	137	5.4	311.1	4.8	923.28	7.5	1377.9	8.9	629.2	4.4	1321	8.1
Population, Health & Nutrition	0	0	13.2	0.5	37.6	0.6	84.78	0.7	243	1.6	191	1.3	419.5	2.6
Small Scale	c		c		c		278.28	2.3	672.6	4.3	560.6	3.9	274.5	1.7
Technical Assistance	0	0	2.8	0.1	18	0.3	59.8	0.5	135	0.9	111.7	0.08	137.9	0.8
Tele-Communications	30.3	3	133.5	5.2	146.5	2.3	204.6	1.7	166.5	1.1	121.6	0.08	50.4	0.3
Tourism	0	0	16.1	0.6	51.4	0.8	22.64	1.8	0	0	0	0	0	0
Transportation	278.5	28.2	647.4	25.5	1091.4	16.9	1593.76	13	2596.9	16.7	2138.7	14.9	1498.2	9.2
Urban Development	0	0	10.4	0.4	162.5	2.5	417.68	3.4	500	3.2	384.6	2.7	1117.5	6.8
Water Supply & Sewerage	23.8	2.4	117.8	4.6	265.9	4.1	687.32	5.6	640.8	4.1	780.8	5.4	604.8	3.7
Total	986.6		2536		6463.82		12255.22		15522.3		14386.3		16318.7	

a = annual averages; b = included in Industry figures; c = included in DFCs
SOURCE: Annual reports. Reprinted by permission of the World Bank.

appraisal and cost-benefit techniques to account for the negative side-effects of development projects.[10] To catalyze its concern, McNamara announced that the Bank had just created a small unit with the purpose of reviewing the environmental consequences of the development projects it funded: the Office of Environmental and Scientific Affairs.[11]

This evolution carried three implications. First, traditional methods of economic analysis would become more difficult to apply with meaning, and new project appraisal methods should be developed. Second, these projects could also provide a useful framework for studying the value of experimental components, such as environmental protection or rehabilitation. Finally, however, this reorientation suggested that the concern for the environmental consequences of industrialization and development that was emerging in the developed countries would matter insofar as it bore upon the welfare of individuals, or on the fulfillment of basic needs. As a Bank pamphlet later exclaimed: "Poverty is the worst form of pollution."[12]

Why Be Involved?

The creation of the Office of Environmental Affairs appeared a very significant departure of policy. To be sure, environmental aspects internal to the project, those affecting the short-term success of the project itself, had long been taken into account. But the issue in the early seventies was whether to expand the scope of project analysis to include aspects external to the project itself. At that time, "no systematic procedure existed to identify and examine those effects."[13] After all, many arguments militated against adopting this perspective. Concerns cited included the proper role of the Bank, the different priorities of developing countries, the difficulties associated with implementing this concern, or the "right" to impose it.

What accounted for this unprecedented decision of the Bank? Broadly speaking, three main types of influences induced the Bank's new awareness: economic, political, and intellectual.

Economic Arguments

In light of the traditional economic perspective of the institution, a proposal to include environmental considerations in development projects would have been heretical in the late fifties. Not so in 1970. By then, economic logic formed the basis for the Bank's justification for the development of the Water Supply and Sewerage sector:

> A major reason why the Bank Group has tried to encourage the development of this sector is that its benefits are so pervasive. It is generally accepted that the financial returns accruing to water and sewerage

authorities considerably understate the true benefits to the community, by no means all of which are apparent or easily quantifiable. Environmental improvement, a valuable end in itself, can also result in additional financial benefits by improving the community's production capacity through raising or safeguarding the level of public health.[14]

This link to public health concerns, itself justified by the argument that healthy workers are more productive, allowed for the approval of a 1971 pollution abatement project of the Tiete River in São Paulo, Brazil, to which the Bank contributed $37 million (out of $141.3 million).

Macroeconomics had also begun focusing on the problems associated with the failure to discount externalities. Mishan in 1967 discussed external diseconomies arising from the failure to take into account the social, environmental, and ultimately the economic costs of growth in the making of economic decisions.[15] The "free" exploitation of public goods, such as clean air or soil fertility, engenders high costs that present or future generations will be forced to assume. More and more project lending was sought in order to alleviate the adverse effects of previous development projects. The very success and long-term viability of many projects was hampered because environmental consequences had been overlooked. Dams silted up, modified the hydrology of whole watersheds, and disrupted human economic activities downstream. Air and water pollution threatened public health. Infrastructural projects needlessly destroyed precious top soil. Overgrazing followed the forced resettlement of nomadic peoples.[16] For example, by creating a favorable habitat for snails and black flies, both the Kariba hydroelectric project on the Zambezi, first funded in 1956, and the Volta River Project in Ghana, first funded in 1961, propagated bilharziasis and onchocerciasis (river blindness). The eighty thousand displaced Ghanaians found themselves in a worse economic situation, and fishing on the lower Volta was also greatly reduced.[17] Colombia's Anchicaya dam lost 80 percent of its capacity in two decades because of heavy sedimentation, and the expected life span of many other dams was considerably reduced. Moreover hydroelectric projects often flooded parts of the homelands of indigenous tribes or destroyed valuable ecosystems as would the Bayano Dam in Panama.[18]

With the new emphasis on agricultural projects, a large portion of which was irrigation development, the consequences of neglecting the environmental effects of the new development systems could be disastrous. The Bank often saw its irrigation canals silted, increasing salinity reduce soil quality, scarce water wasted, and new diseases, all affecting both crops and humans. New intensive methods of cultivation and the introduction of sophisticated technology would lead to a loss of fertility and to the pollution of aquifers.

Clearly, one needed new methods of appraising projects for their long-term social and environmental costs, as well as for their short-term economic benefits. This view was then in perfect accordance with the Bank's new concern with social welfare, which led it to develop the social cost-benefit analysis of projects to complement the traditional one. As James Lee, Director of the newly created Office of Environmental Affairs, said in 1972: "The issue of the environment provides a new imperative, a new opportunity, a new mandate to measure development assistance in terms other than growth of output—for man himself is the ultimate resource." [19]

Political Motivations

Economic reasons alone did not induce the change in policy. External diseconomies are often difficult to perceive and may not directly threaten the viability of a specific project. In fact, much of the economic rationalization evolved after a strong international environmental movement had emerged. Clearly, other influences were at work. A crucial impetus was given by political demands which had a triple origin: the United States Congress, the developed countries, and the preparation for the 1972 United Nations Conference on the Human Environment (UNCHE).

Late in 1969, Congress passed the National Environmental Policy Act (NEPA). In keeping with its strong involvement in environmental matters, it did not fail to review the activities of international organizations. Given the leverage that Congress has over foreign aid and especially over the American contributions to IDA replenishments, the Bank pays close attention to its opinions, even when it strongly criticizes them.

The promotion of environmental concerns by the Bank's American executive director and his Scandinavian and Canadian colleagues reflected an extension of this influence. To be successful and respond to the concerns of an active public opinion, national environmental policies had to be coordinated internationally so as to ensure the effectiveness of national pollution abatement programs and discourage a deterioration of commercial competitiveness. The developed countries which control the Bank were instrumental in prompting an examination of this issue, although some of them were either reticent (West Germany, Japan), or largely indifferent (France). This process corresponds to a general pattern. Kay and Jacobson, as well as M'Gonigle and Zacher, have emphasized the crucial role of country leadership in promoting global environmental values and policies. [20] The role of the United States in that respect has been determinant: in their review of eleven environmental areas, Kay and Jacobson found that U.S. leadership had been critical in fostering awareness, urging action and facilitating the implementation of policies among international organizations and countries.

The UN itself provided another strong impetus. Preparations for the United Nations Conference on the Human Environment (UNCHE) in particular, significantly prompted the Bank's awareness. This conference had been called in 1968,[21] and active preparations were taking place from 1969 to 1971 to define its scope and limit the political controversies surrounding it.[22] M'Gonigle and Zacher have described how, in the case of oil pollution, oil companies resorted to a preemptive strategy when faced with the prospect of a meeting designed to solve some specific pollution problem. They would try to dissipate the pressures by implementing, before the meeting, alternatives to the kind of restrictions they feared the conferees would impose. Likewise, the World Bank found itself obligated to evidence some recognition of the environmental limits of development in order to avoid being publicly denounced for its neglect. It needed a positive record and thus was forced to think about those problems, articulate and define a position, and present accomplishments.

International Governmental Organizations (IGOs) were then preoccupied with establishing themselves into the new environmental field in order to expand the range of their activities at the expense of other organizations, and to avoid the creation of a new agency with superordinate authority (e.g., an Environmental Council analogous to ECOSOC). Thus as "[a] number of UN agencies charged with aiding economic development felt threatened by the impact of the new interest in environmental protection, . . . internal measures were taken . . . to reorganize their programs in order to protect their budgets and preserve the integrity of their mandate."[23] This is especially true of the United Nations Educational, Scientific, and Cultural Organization (UNESCO), the Food and Agricultural Organization (FAO), the World Meteorological Organization (WMO), and the International Maritime Organization (IMO), but applies equally well to the World Bank.

Intellectual Influences

The decision to adopt an environmental protection posture originated at the top, with President McNamara. It did not spring from the staff's own appraisal. Rather it was strongly supported by elements of the senior management. Following the general environmental awareness of the time, McNamara was influenced by his contacts with prominent U.S. intellectual circles. Thanks to his close association with the Ford Foundation in the late fifties, he kept in close touch with the intellectual ferment of the U.S. community which was deeply environmentally conscious at the time.

More direct influence came from Barbara Ward (Lady Jackson) whose friendship with McNamara enabled her to express the concerns she would later so successfully dramatize in an influential book.[24] A student of development and environmental problems, her influence on the president of the Bank is said to have been profound:

> He would consult her on his speeches, submit his early drafts ("as shy as a 17-year-old about them," William Clark says) and somehow they matched, he the detailed quantifier and she the great generaliser. To him, as to so many other people, she gave the extra nudge, the touch of rhetoric that he needed. And all this time she had been nudging other people towards the Stockholm conference on the environment. . . .[25]

She went on to establish the International Institute for Environment and Development (IIED), over which she presided from 1974 to 1980. She strongly urged that the Bank take the leading role in reconciling the dual imperatives of environmental protection and economic development.[26]

Another set of powerful influences which reached staff as well as senior management, arose from attempts to develop "global models." The staff was familiar with both the 1970 MIT/SCOPE report on "Critical Environmental Problems" and the famous 1972 "Limits to Growth" report which it studied extensively.[27] Although experts from within the Bank criticized them on numerous grounds, the models pointed to the notions of limits and interdependence. The environmental concern had to transcend the frontiers of the developed countries to encompass the whole globe. This awareness of the existence of "Only One Earth" was embodied in new endeavors to model global environmental trends, and meant that developing and developed countries should address similar issues, albeit from different perspectives. For example, one senior manager learned that "the present economic order could [not] give even the basic human needs to six billion people in 20 years time."[28]

To be sure, the Bank was to proceed cautiously. Projects directly and primarily for environmental improvement were not be funded. Rather, an effort would be made to review projects for their environmental consequences and insert environmental components into selected operations. How such a review would be undertaken, what it would include, and which component was to be emphasized, was unclear. Projects were then reviewed "at the eleventh hour," when it was too late to modify them substantially and impossible to stop them.[29] Clearly, when James Lee took office as Environmental Adviser, the Bank was far from being totally and unconditionally committed to the idea. The staff strongly questioned its relevance and feasibility. Furthermore, the Bank's economists did not know how to conceptualize environmental issues in terms meaningful to their expertise. The Bank's early insistence on the primacy of development and the subsequent reorientation of its lending activities did not foster wide staff acceptance of the necessity of tackling a new and, for many, incomprehensible set of problems. Indeed, the staff initially moved into that area reluctantly, and then only as a result of developed countries' pressures and McNamara's overt support. The rationalization and justification of this move took place only gradually. For the moment, in 1971, it appeared as a distraction of the main goal of the organization: "the development business."[30]

The Development of the Policy

The Policy Framework

The environmental issue was raised at a time when the Bank was engaged in an all-out campaign in favor of population control. Despite the interrelatedness of population and environmental questions, specific environmental problems were neglected in official speeches. Population growth was not yet criticized for its impact on the environment (that would come later in the Bank's publications), but primarily because it prevented an increase in the per capita share of a nation's growing wealth and threatened to ruin all development efforts. Environmental problems were not perceived to be potentially detrimental to the Bank's overall development effort. While it could be argued that, with controlled population growth, development per capita—as seen through simple aggregate measure—would have improved, no such neat correlation could easily be advanced with respect to the protection and improvement of the environment.

The extreme difficulty of quantifying its characteristics and benefits precluded the Bank from raising the issue dramatically. Three months after the Stockholm conference (UNCHE), for example, McNamara failed to mention environmental issues at the 1972 annual meetings of the Board of Governors. Whereas *Finance and Development*, the quarterly magazine published by the Bank and the International Monetary Fund (IMF), devoted a special issue to the problems posed by population growth in 1973, no such publicity covered the environmental issue. A rubric on the Bank's environmental policy appeared for the first time in the 1973 *Annual Report* under an "environmental impact" headline. Six years elapsed before a second account of these activities was mentioned and a more complete description of the policy was given (in 1979 and again in 1985 and 1986). This lack of publicity reflected the Bank's perception of the political priorities that developed and developing countries had set on the issues that confronted them, which led to an inability to agree on a common definition of the problem and on acceptable solutions.

The extremism of many environmental positions of the time prevented the Bank from taking a strong stand in favor of the environment. Much of the early environmental discourse of the Bank was directed neither at the developed nor at the developing countries. Rather, the Bank chose to target its arguments against the primacy of environmental concerns at the advocates of a zero-growth economy who implied that development, as the Bank conceived it, could not proceed. Ignoring more balanced arguments, the early publications strongly defended the right to development, even at the cost of a "possible addition of misery to a few."[31]

Reflecting the concerns of the developing countries, the early years consequently saw a strong affirmation of the primacy of development: "There is no evidence that economic growth which the developing countries so desperately require will necessarily involve an unacceptable burden either on their own or on anybody else's environment."[32] Given the primary goals of the organization and the priorities of its clients, it was easy to conclude that environmental considerations had to take second place to modernization. For example, in the first official publication on that subject, there was no mention that ignorance of the environmental effects of development projects could be economically short-sighted in the long run. Environmental concerns were then seen only as a threat to the goals of the organization; a direct transposition of the experiences of the developed countries was in need of reexamination before their transfer to the developing world.

Indeed, not much thinking had been done about the specific environmental problems that developing countries faced. Since the movement was a response to the problems of industrialized countries, the focus was on pollution: "[to] help today's Underdeveloped Countries to avoid some of the undesirable consequences on the human environment of industrial and general economic development that are now identified in the advanced industrial societies."[33]

Having to reconcile both perspectives, senior management was thus led to articulate a different approach to the environmental problems of developing countries. The Bank now argues that environmental problems have a dual origin: poverty and economic development. Poverty is seen first as bearing on the quality of life and leads to pressures on the environment; poor housing, nutrition, health and sanitation; deforestation; loss of soil productivity; erosion; pollution of surface waters; and overgrazing. Life itself is eventually threatened. Economic development can directly damage the natural environment or disrupt societies mainly through rapid and unchecked industrialization.[34] The acute air and water pollution of São Paulo and Mexico city provide good examples of the latter.

This dual ascription leads to a very extensive concept of the environment. In contrast with the developed countries' experience, poverty, not wealth, is the problem and causes losses of natural resources. Raising the income of the poor, not lowering that of the rich, is the solution. Anything that helps the poor gain higher incomes and better facilities becomes "environmental." Thus, for the Bank, environmental problems are linked to the development process in three ways: they are caused by a lack of development; they arise from development activities; and they can impair the future development prospects of a country. The last two points give the Bank good arguments for considering this problem, whereas the first justifies the need for development in the first place. Concern for the environment becomes an integral part of the development process.[35] This three-pronged approach means that economic development need not be sacrificed on the altar of environmental protection, and that, because of the future internalization of current externalities into the projects, the incorporation of environmental standards makes acceptable good sense.

Indeed, the perception of a dichotomy between development and environment was to change slowly. Talks of "controlled" growth were omnipresent in the early 1970s. In his address to the 1972 United Nations Conference on the Human Environment (the "Stockholm Conference"), McNamara reaffirmed the necessity of growth on which "three-quarter billion humans" depend for "the achievement of a level of life in accord with fundamental human dignity." Then he added:

> But economic growth on the pattern of the past poses an undeniable threat to the environment and to the health of man. The question is not whether there should be continued economic growth. There must be. Nor is the question whether the impact on the environment must be respected. It has to be. Nor—least of all—is it a question of whether these two questions are interlocked. They are.
> The solution of the dilemma revolves clearly not about whether, but about how.[36]

Thus the principle of environmental protection and the respective responsibilities of the development finance institutions in that area are no longer questioned. The problem is to find a method to reconcile those twin goals. Clearly, environmental concerns are relevant to developing countries. The problem no longer lies in choosing between a polluting factory or no factory at all; rather, it is identifying the best way of eliminating the negative externalities engendered by its operation.[37] Yet, while there had been an evolution in the Bank's thinking, the choice, according to the Bank, was not whether to reassign domestic priorities toward a new pattern of development; rather, it was to keep the same one while avoiding its negative consequences.

The main problem therefore, was to minimize the disruptions that development projects could cause in the environment. Environmental review was not intended to question the very rationale behind a project. It would only ensure that project implementation would proceed normally and promote its success. The argument shifted away from principles to technical matters which the Bank could resolve internally. These questions, however, proved a far more powerful obstacle to the implementation of environmentally sound development policies than was expected, as will be discussed in the next chapter.

It is worth emphasizing these early concepts and attitudes to appreciate the evolution of the Bank's thinking since the early 1970s. The perception of an irremediable antagonism between environment and development has now largely disappeared. In fact, they are now seen as interdependent: economic growth may harm the environment, but it may also reduce pressures on certain natural resources. Conversely, neglecting the environment threatens the achievement of sustainable development. As the 1985 *Annual Report* emphasizes: "The environmental indicators of today foreshadow the economic trends of tomorrow."[38]

Furthermore, environmental problems specific to developing countries have been identified. The Bank chose to focus on access to safe water supplies and has belatedly isolated desertification and deforestation as key areas of concern. It is also clear that environmentally sound projects are necessary to achieve the long-term goals of the organization, although this is much more evident in agricultural and urban sectors than in industrial ones. It now makes economic sense to include environmental costs in the appraisal of a project. Nevertheless, the question of the relationship between environment and development, although no longer at the center of the Bank's rhetoric on the subject, has constrained its policy ever since its inception and continues defining much of it now. What did it translate into in practice?

The Content of the Policy

The initial strategy of the Office of Environmental and Scientific Affairs (initially OEA) was to focus on the following objectives:

1. Educate the Bank; render its environmental concerns legitimate to the staff
2. Educate the developing countries
3. Convince developed countries of the peculiar nature of the problems they face
4. Devise methods of appraising projects that would fit the intellectual framework of the staff, and research the true and full consequences of development projects
5. Incorporate its concerns into sectoral policies
6. Expand its activities from indirect to direct lending, to institution building
7. Improve the coordination of its programs and knowledge with other international organizations

The environmental policy of the Bank has evolved substantially since its articulation in 1970, but it has largely emphasized an indirect approach to environmental destruction. It first sought to internalize environmental concerns into the economic decisions to fund specific development projects rather than directly support environmental ones. The first step was to develop greater awareness within and outside the Bank about the ecological impact of development funding. The Bank was the first development agency to screen development projects on a systematic basis for their environmental and health effects. It is now an integral part of the appraisal of each project. A second step was to support specific components designed to protect or restore environmental quality. The final step was to decide to support environmental projects as such. This emphasis logically led it to search for a "feasible method for correlating ecological protection with effective cost-conscious development."[39] Various proposals for integrating these concerns into the appraisal framework familiar to the Bank are discussed in the following chapter.

The OESA faced considerable problems in implementing even the restricted policy the Bank adopted in the early 1970s, much less the specific objectives of its initial strategy. Since the developing countries were concerned with growth and development, environmental considerations were perceived as irrelevant, costly, and counterproductive. Since the Bank's staff economists focused on financial assessment of projects (rates of return, for example), environmental projects were perceived as non-amenable to "objective" criteria of appraisal, thus possibly endangering the Bank's credit with the financial community. Furthermore, whereas developed countries were concerned with pollution problems, the developing countries' environmental problems were of a quite different nature. Finally, as many United Nations agencies were moving into that area, the action or non-action of the Bank was seen as determining much of the success of their own policies.

In the absence of an objective method to determine the allocation of scarce resources (in the form of a modified cost-benefit analysis, for example), project appraisal had to be approached pragmatically. One possibility was to devise environmental guidelines drawn from experience. In 1973, for example, the OESA's first instructional document on environmental precautions was completed, later followed by more specific handbooks.[40] Environmental aspects were also more frequently mentioned, identified in detail, and discussed in sector policy papers.

Although environmental safeguards are project-specific, they now constitute a formal condition for lending. Measures the Bank deems necessary must be included in the project design if the loan is to go through. Thus, while projects were at first examined after the lending decision had been made, environmental considerations were progressively introduced into the project cycle itself. In practice, halting disbursements is so drastic a measure that it was not used until 1985, after strong pressures to do so. The first cancellation of an on-going project on environmental grounds occurred the following year over the same case.[41] To be sure, the Bank's leverage is often strong enough to convince borrowers to adopt and implement the environmental safeguards formally agreed upon. Yet, examples abound of the Bank's failures to implement these safeguards effectively. It claims to have often rejected loan proposals on environmental grounds until modifications of the design were made, although this is difficult to substantiate. By 1985, more than 1,500 projects had included environmental safeguards or components (or 45.7 percent of all operations approved).[42]

Table 1.3 summarizes the early performance of the environmental review process. It is difficult to see any definite evolution between 1971 and 1978. No firm conclusion can be drawn about the evolution of the lending because the criteria for acting or not acting on projects may have changed in the interim. For example, with time, environmental standards as well as their scope were improved and strengthened, which could account for the increase in the number of projects needing outside appraisal. On the other hand, the number of projects acted upon remained the same, which could mean that with the spread of an environmental awareness, the Bank selected fewer projects presenting dangers to the environment. But it could also mean that neither the scope nor the environmental criteria expanded, and that simple manpower problems prevented the OESA from reviewing projects in greater detail. Nevertheless, this table gives an idea of the scope of the OESA's involvement. It shows that such a policy was needed since about 37 percent of all projects selected and funded between 1971 and 1978 had immediate negative environmental consequences.

Table 1.3.: Environment Screening of Bank Group Projects 1971–1978; IBRD, IDA, IFC.

Results of screening	7/1971 to 12/1973			1/1974 to 6/1978		
	per year	total	percent	per year	total	percent
No problems apparent when reviewed	92	275	64	114	570	63
Problems handled by others prior to Bank Group involvement	1	4	0	4	18	2
In-house disposition	44	133	31	46	232	26
Consultants and special studies required	7	22	5	18	88	10
Total	145	434		182	908	

The annual figures and the percentages are rounded.

SOURCES: The World Bank, *Environment and Development*, 1975, 1979. Reprinted by permission.

This table reflects only one aspect of the Bank's action, the mitigation of the adverse environmental consequences of its development projects. That is, these projects originally did not contain specific provisions for environmental improvement, but, typically, anti-pollution or alternative designs were suggested after the project had been proposed and appraised. Thus, they were measures which were *added* to the cost of the project.

In the case of industrial projects for example, environmental hazards occur both within the plant (occupational safety and health) and outside it (effluents). In practice, two considerations led the Office to emphasize internal environmental effects: (1) occupational safety and health laws in developing countries are rare, whereas broad environmental laws, however weak, often exist; and (2) these matters are less politically sensitive than other environmental issues which affect a greater part of the population. Since many countries tend to ignore the first, the Bank's involvement is most advanced in industrial projects. It includes the issuance of general and specific industry guidelines. It requires that, as a condition of lending, specific precautions be taken. A training program is instituted whenever possible, and medical examinations of workers are requested.

Other projects may have specific components that not only alleviate the harmful impact of modernization but also include environmental protection or restoration. Many "new style" rural area development projects conform to this type where irrigation schemes, roads, and the provision of services are mixed with flood control or reforestation components.

In 1974, the Bank's Executive Directors gave the environmental sector a new boost when they adopted the principle of a new environmental lending sector. Projects in this category have largely focused on urban pollution rather than on the rehabilitation or conservation of natural ecosystems. Changes have taken place, however, in the 1980s with the growing realization that economic catastrophes often were rooted in ecological ones. Africa has been singled out as an example of what happens when the environmental support system breaks down; and both the Bank and recipient countries are now more open to projects designed to arrest environmental deterioration.

But what does the environment encompass for the Bank? Following the Stockholm Conference (UNCHE) and the position of the United Nations Environment Program (UNEP), the World Bank adopted a very broad definition of the environment. A desire to reconcile different political perspectives set forth during the preparatory work for UNCHE, led to a definition which transgressed the narrow scientific aspects of the ecological problems, to focus on patterns of resource use, on modified ecosystems, and on a better quality of life in general. The Bank's Office of Environmental and Scientific Affairs could therefore concern itself with any factor which would influence the short-term productivity or long-term benefits of development projects.

In fact, the notion of what constitutes environmental concerns has fluctu-
ated. In the beginning, the Bank's environmental unit functioned largely as
a catalyst: pointing up potential problems and trying to integrate their solutions into the project approach. OESA progressively assumed a more
directive role that placed it at the project identification stage where environmental concerns become part of the notion of development itself.

Not only is its domain broad; it is also dynamic. If for example, there is
enough external and internal support for the creation of a new unit, this
area may be taken away from the environmental unit itself. That is what
happened with health care delivery projects. The early Office of Environmental and Health Affairs lost its health component (OEA), then became
OESA, but retained some oversight over environmental health components. OESA was then attentive to the use of pesticides, which lies at the
core of the agricultural development strategies promoted by the regional
offices of the Bank, although the dangers of such products as DDT and
Dieldrin are well-known and their use banned in the United States. Indiscriminate use of pesticides even destroyed a nascent cotton industry in
several areas by causing environmental damage, destroying natural pest
predators, and raising production costs.[43] When the regional and agricultural sector offices take these factors into account, the pesticide issue will
virtually disappear from the concern of the environmental unit.

In 1981, Alden Clausen included population planning and energy conservation as central environmental concerns. By 1986, however, health,
population, and energy issues had disappeared from a list that included
pollution, management of natural resources, sustainable productivity, conservation of unique habitats, and protection of mankind's aesthetic and
cultural heritage. In essence, the notion of "environment" came to include
any issue that did not fit clearly within any existing unit or that was barely
accepted as legitimate by others.[44]

The interest OESA developed in the late 1970s in the welfare of involuntary displaced populations provides a salient example of the broadening of
the concept of "environment." The Bank is concerned that a development
project does not adversely affect the indigenous culture that the country
wishes to perserve. For example, if a project required the relocation of
people, the Office of Environmental and Scientific Affairs tried to ensure
that any injurious disruptions of their socio-economic life were avoided in
the resettlement. Accordingly, guidelines for involuntary settlements were
formally incorporated into the *Operations Manual* in 1980. Various problems of acculturation enlarged the scope of this concern two years later.[45]
The record of the Bank has, however, been very poor in this area and has
fueled sharp criticisms of its general environmental performance in the
1980s, as will be discussed in chapter 5.

The new emphasis upon the importance of meeting basic needs contributed to the broad definition but narrow involvement that the Bank gave

the environment. In practice, most funded environmental projects have overlapped the six areas of basic needs: nutrition, basic education, health, sanitation, water supply, and housing. Many environmental projects are funded, not because they are good in themselves, but because, it is argued, they further the achievement of basic needs. This is particularly true of water-pollution projects which enhance access to potable water and reduce infant mortality, of projects to combat environmental diseases which raise the life expectancy at birth, and of sewerage projects which increase the percentage of people with access to sanitation facilities.

Although the Executive Directors' 1974 pledge to lend for strict "environmental projects" referred to projects designed to protect or restore natural ecosystems, a broad definition of the environment allows the Bank to point to efforts in many non-traditional sectors when describing its contribution to this concern. If population growth is the problem as Alden Clausen stated in his 1981 and 1985 addresses to the Board of Governors, then population planning projects become positive enhancements of the environment along with sewerage treatment, solid waste removal, and energy conservation.[46]

For a general overview, let us combine the United Nations' conception of the environment as including general amenities with the Bank's neo-malthusian approach that stresses the detrimental impact of population growth on natural systems. Table 1.2 clearly shows that the "environmental" work of the Bank began early. Lending for the Water Supply and Sewerage sector (WSS) began in the early sixties, Population and Urbanization soon afterward. The Bank can argue that it was concerned with the "quality of life" of its clients long before the issue was raised. Moreover, these three sectors grew more rapidly relative to any of the other eleven sectors. Their share of IBRD and IDA funds increased from about 2.4 percent of total lending in the 1964 to 1968 period to 13.1 percent in 1986. The WSS and urban sectors accounted for most of that increase, while lending for population remained quasi stable at about one percent (2.6 percent in 1986). The figures for the WSS sector even underestimate this growth since they leave out the amount spent as components of other projects.

But lending for the environment refers in practice to a more specific area. Following the legitimization of the environment as a sectoral object of loans in 1974, "environmental" projects in this study refer to projects mainly directed toward the protection, rehabilitation, or enhancement of the self-regulating capacities of natural ecosystems. This includes water pollution projects, certain forestry projects, soil conservation and anti-desertification projects, air pollution, wildlife and range-management projects, as well as solid wastes disposal projects.

Funded projects in this category have been rare in recent years. The

WSS sector expanded rapidly in the 1970s (table 1.2) with increasing attention paid to water pollution and solid waste disposal capabilities as well as access to potable water. Funding has, however, considerably diminished since the height reached in 1979, with a major part of current resources devoted to the rehabilitation of existing water supply and sewerage systems.

Environmental projects have focused primarily upon urban water pollution and forestry. Five in particular have been heavily cited in the Bank's literature or in conversations with Bank officials. These first five projects dealt with water, air pollution and waste disposal and involved large urban areas. (Four loans were made to control São Paulo's pollution problems, three to Yugoslavia for Dubrovnik and Sarajevo.) This underlines the political overtone of the implementation of an environmental policy (a point developed in subsequent chapters, especially Chapter 4).

There are still some indications of a movement toward the rehabilitation of ecosystems. Loans to Kenya in 1977, Nepal in 1980, India and Zimbabwe in 1983, Pakistan in 1984, Indonesia in 1985, and Mauritania in 1986 involved primarily the protection or rehabilitation of biomes. These were intended to preserve the tourist industry in Kenya and prevent further erosion of farm lands in other countries. (Zimbabwe's concerned afforestation policy development.)

Finally, environmental components—that is, aspects of the projects for which the Bank was willing to lend and its clients to borrow—have involved mostly water supply, the rehabilitation of irrigation systems, and flood control. Health and soil conservation components were not as prominent, and others (protection of animal and plant species, reforestation, pollution abatement), were rare.

The Bank created an environmental unit in 1971. Its Executive Directors approved environmental projects in 1974. By the early 1980s, the Bank had assumed a leadership role among multilateral development agencies in promoting environmental awareness. Lending did increase. Upon assuming office as presidents, both Alden Clausen in 1981 and Barber Conable in 1986 stressed the extent to which the Bank's emphasis on the concept of "sustainable development" rested on a firm ecological foundation. The depletion of mineral resources, urban air pollution, deforestation, and erosion were singled out as the most pressing environmental problems.

Yet, the Bank's environmental policy was strongly attacked in the 1980s for its failure to mitigate the environmental destructiveness of many development projects, for supporting virtual ecological and human catastrophes, and for failing to expand environmental lending. The Bank was pressed to stop financing certain projects, meetings were picketed, and critical reports written. The United States Congress devoted seventeen hearings between 1983 and 1986 to these questions.

The rest of this study addresses the constraints and the degree of success the Bank has encountered in its role as the legitimizer of a new concern, and looks into the reasons why the Bank failed to do more until a bold initiative in 1987 sought to squelch the critics and give the environment center stage. (The last two chapters discuss these developments and assess their significance.) Let us first turn to the internal constraints that influence the definition and implementation of the Bank's environmental policy.

2

Internal Determinants of the Policy

This chapter seeks to identify the organizational determinants of the environmental policy of the World Bank by looking at the formal constraints that its founders placed upon it, by examining the ideology and techniques its staff uses to carry out its mission, and by exploring the relations between the units entrusted with the conduct of this policy and the rest of the organization.

The *Articles of Agreement* which established the Bank stipulated various procedural requirements for lending. The Bank is to lend only for productive purposes, for specific projects, and for the financing of the foreign exchange components of these projects. Moreover, borrowers have to be creditworthy and ineligible for market loans to receive funds. Other constraints are not linked to the formal definition of the Bank's activities found in the *Articles of Agreement*,but relate to the functioning of the Bank. Thus, the methodology used to appraise projects, the definition of new means to achieve development goals (the so-called "new style" projects and new "social" concerns, for example), and the redefinition of the notion of development itself also greatly influence the context and nature of the Bank's environmental policy.

The discussion of these procedural constraints will be logically followed by an examination of the process of environmental review of development projects. Many of these constraints evolved as measures to control the uncertainty of the organization's task-environment. But these very safeguards which are intended to reduce the organization's vulnerability to its milieu, may also deny its environmental units (OESA in particular) enough flexibility to enable them to achieve their goals fully, and may force them to adopt an approach which will ultimately diminish their effectiveness.

Methodological changes also create internal dissent. Lending for new "social" sectors in the early 1960s, and a focus on "basic needs" and income redistribution a decade later led to sharp internal debates. The nature of the bureaucratic opposition the OESA has faced, its ability to overcome it, and the presence of an internal consensus about the goals and content of the environmental policy of the Bank will be concerns taken up in the last part of this chapter.

Although remarkable progress has been made, numerous obstacles remain. Associated with the lending requirements and the methodology used to appraise projects, they can lead to serendipitous results and severely constrain the scope and efficacy of the Bank's environmental policy. Organizational consensus is a prerequisite for successfully dealing with a turbulent milieu. If procedural as well as bureaucratic factors prevent the organization from building a strong unified attitude about the environmental imperative, how likely is it to be able to transform its milieu?

Procedural and Ideological Constraints

The Formal Goals of the Organization

The *Articles of Agreement* specify the formal goals as well as the essential norms and regulations of the organization they set up; that is, they regulate the fundamental aspects of its internal and external life. In particular, they specify the purpose and conditions of lending, which in turn constrain the capacity of the organization to move into new areas, such as the environment.

Article I(i) states that the principal objective of the institution is to contribute to economic development: "To assist in the reconstruction and development of territories of members by facilitating the investment of capital for productive purposes, including. . .the encouragement of the development of productive facilities and resources in less developed countries."

Thus, in principle, only projects which contribute to economic development can be funded. The flexibility of the lending scope of the Bank will depend on how it defines economic development, and projects have to be appraised and justified according to their contribution to that goal.

Until the time of the Green Revolution, the development doctrine of the Bank remained centered around capital investments in export-oriented and infrastructure projects, overlooking agriculture. But the dangers of a dual economy, a modernizing industrial sector and an agricultural sector left behind, became increasingly evident.[1] It was also clear that, despite rapid growth, the majority of the poor in these countries were not better off than before. With a redirection of lending to agriculture came an awareness of the negative elements that could ensue, such as income and job losses for poorer farmers.[2] The failure of the earlier trickle-down strategy led to an emphasis on basic needs and income redistribution which helped the organization focus on the social aspects of development projects and on elements pertaining to the quality of life of the poorer segments of those societies.

Thus, after a first generation of development projects centered around capital accumulation, a second generation more concerned with allocation led to an expansion of the social sector and "reoriented the theory toward . . . the quality instead of the quantity of investment."[3] The Bank, however, still believed that growth could come only from an inflow of capital and the expansion of exports—precisely the strategy it recommended for China in the late 1970s.[4] The new focus was intended only to *complement* earlier approaches, not replace them. This reorientation influenced new methods of project appraisal but also weakened the organization's adherence to many of its lending requirements.

It is no coincidence, therefore, that interest in the ecological context of development arose at a time when the purposes and methods of attaining economic development were being redefined. Without this evolution in development theory and the prior experience of the Bank with "social" projects such as water supply or education, the adoption of a new environmental criterion would have been much more difficult.

Despite the evolution in Bank thinking, the scope of its environmental policy is still constrained by the organization's goal: the problem is no longer to deny the importance of environmental question. Rather, one asks how can environmental considerations contribute to economic development. Furthermore, although the abandonment of the trickle-down approach and the focus on basic needs helped emphasize the quality-of-life aspects of development projects (like health), it also excluded environmental concerns which are not part of a definition of basic needs (such as aesthetic pleasure). Notwithstanding Streeten's definition of a basic-needs approach to development as "[the provision of] opportunities for the full physical, mental, and social development of the individual,"[5] basic needs are in practice narrowly defined as vital amenities such as access to food, shelter, clothing, and clean water. This definition is centered around material needs, a consequence of the general income approach the Bank takes, and overlooks the importance of "non-material" needs.

The Bank's 1981 endorsement of the concept of sustainable development helped broaden the scope of legitimate environmental projects. "Sustained development" is a catch-all phrase which can mean different things to different people. Developing countries see in it the need to maintain a growth momentum in their region. This entails adopting measures that minimize the turbulence of the financial markets, maintain or increase development aid, reduce the threat of protectionism in developed countries, or manage the debt problem. To the business community and donors, it means ensuring that investments will not be wasted and will have a multiplier effect. To environmental groups and to the United Nations Environment Programme (UNEP) which started promoting it in the mid-1970s, it means making sure that the ecosystem and natural resources are not exhausted quickly, thus leading to future misery. The World Bank's proposed program of action for sub-Saharan Africa draws attention to the long-term constraints on development, notably population growth and the erosion of natural resources: "Unless these long-term issues receive continuing and increased attention, whatever the short-term problems, development in Africa will continue to be frustrated, leading to . . . a political, social and economic 'nightmare' by the turn of the century."[6]

Speaking along the same lines, President Conable in 1986 emphasized to the governors of the Bank and IMF the need to keep development in harmony with natural forces. The role of the Bank is to "provide leadership for sustained development" which means "to balance growth with environmental protection" and "to restrain overpopulation." Of course, the World Bank has always been interested in sustainable development. But using a term that is widely promoted by environmental organizations indicates a change of attitude and a recognition that ecological considerations must help define the goal and method of development, and not be limited to remedying its most negative consequences. It opens the door to projects that rehabilitate or enhance the natural environment.

Financing for Productive Purposes

To prohibit loans for consumer goods, debt repayments, or government salaries, the founders of the World Bank imposed upon it an obligation to lend for productive purposes only (IBRD, I[i]). The Bank was to develop "the productive resources of members, thereby assisting in raising productivity, the standard of living and conditions of labor in their territories" (I[iii]). This in turn led to efforts to devise appraisal methods which would show gains in productivity or high rates of return.

One can approach the notion of productivity from either a narrow or broad perspective.[7] On the one hand, it has a financial aspect where it is equivalent to the concept of rentability. Thus it forces the Bank to finance only self-liquidating projects. For example, it implies setting charges for public services at a high enough level for the project to be self-sustaining. In certain cases, however, economic circumstances can be so bad that, whatever the charges, the project will never be self-liquidating. Should it then be abandoned, thus foreclosing long-term benefits?

To define productivity in terms of an acceptable rate of return in principle does not constrain projects whose negative internal environmental consequences have been taken into account. To demonstrate, however, that additional costs arising from the incorporation of anti-pollution devices, for instance, lead to an increase in economic productivity is more problematic. Although OESA argued that the rate of return of anti-pollution projects was as high as the average return on a typical project, the lack of an acceptable rate of return has been a standard argument against environmental components and projects. This requirement naturally led OESA to emphasize, and the Bank to approve, projects which could so be justified, namely anti-pollution ones (especially within factories), rather than projects whose short-term benefits to productivity could not be easily demonstrated (such as environmental protection).

Not only are strict environmental projects likely to be rejected below a rate of return of 10 percent, but many environmental components (such as environmental training or soil conservation techniques) are easily left out since their inclusion often diminishes the overall rate of return of the project. Environmental conservation does not pay. On the contrary, it is costly to the borrower since the latter is likely to incur short-term economic and political opportunity costs.

The adoption of a new environmental concern was not the first instance in which that problem arose. Lending for education and health projects (at the request of the developing countries) posed similar problems of reconciling the purpose of lending with definite procedural requirements. Lending for population control was even harder to justify on productive grounds. How can birth control be productive?

The Bank solved this difficulty by adopting a broader definition of productivity which can also refer to any activity contributing to economic well-being as measured by the gross national product. For Adam Smith, only work that increased the amount of material goods was productive. For modern economists, any work which directly or indirectly creates wealth is productive.[8] In this larger sense, any project with or without an acceptable rate of return, could be justified so long as it contributes to the economic well-being of the country. Education becomes a good investment because, given the LDCs' chronic shortage of skilled manpower, its beneficiaries are bound to improve national economic productivity in the long run even if short-term gains are unlikely.

Similarly, projects that help reduce future expenses can also be said to enhance productivity. This approach indeed formed the basis for the justification of population and health projects. The 1980 Health Sector Policy Paper recognizes that no tangible monetary gains can be expected from the adoption of health components, but it also justifies this involvement by pointing out that healthy workers are more productive workers. The same reasoning applied to environmental projects: as McNamara already explained in 1970: ". . . a small investment in prevention would be worth many times over what would have to be expended later to repair the damage."[9] But not all the benefits of environmental components can be defined this way. This approach tends to favor urban pollution projects, watershed protection, and health components. Other conservation measures (protection of species diversity, for example) are harder to justify from this perspective.

Nevertheless, a basis for bypassing the narrowly-construed productivity requirement exists. If, then, the fundamental obstacle does not lie with this criterion, why oppose projects on these grounds? Why not finance environmental education, for example?[10] Part of the answer lies with the Bank's clientele. Most developing countries have put a low priority on the environment, although this situation is changing, as discussed in chapter 4. The Bank must also take into account the interests of the financial community which must be convinced that the money it lends will generate acceptable rates of return that will ensure repayment. Adherence to a narrow definition of productivity also allows the Bank to reject projects which developing countries may find politically or economically expedient, but which would only worsen their financial position and development prospects. It is clear, however, that this method of guarding itself against its milieu can have detrimental consequences for the promotion of the Bank's environmental concern.

Financing Foreign Exchange and Local Costs

Another procedural constraint on the Bank's lending is the provision that, barring exceptional circumstances, it can only finance the foreign exchange components of projects, leaving out local financing (IBRD, IV, 3[b]; IDA, V, 2[e]). This requirement has been somewhat relaxed since 1964, and the Bank Group now seems more favorable to financing local costs. Exceptional circumstances were defined under President McNamara to refer to three conditions:

1. If the borrower has an adequate development program and fiscal policies
2. If the program requires funds in excess of that which can be raised locally or borrowed externally
3. If there are not enough projects identified whose foreign exchange components the Bank could finance, or if projects involving local costs financing would further the development program better

Since the first two requirements hold for every project, the only real condition is the third one. Thus, the Bank increased lending for local costs from $49 million in 1968 to $297 million in 1972 (about 10 percent of total lending or 20.5 percent of the disbursements for that year).[11] Through the end of FY 1980, local procurement disbursement accounted for $9.8643 billion (22.6 percent of total disbursements), increasing to $35.761 billion (or 35.1 percent) by the end of FY 1986. In that year alone, $4.8171 billion (or 42 percent of total disbursements) went to finance local procurement.[12] Like the other procedural provisions of the charter, constraining local-costs financing is a means which allows the developed countries some control over the use of their funds and over the activities of the organization.

Several countries (Japan, West Germany, France) have opposed local-costs financing on the grounds that they needed to get back in export orders all or more of the money lent to the Bank either by permitting it to borrow on their markets and from their central banks, or by their subscription and replenishment of IBRD and IDA capitals.[13] However, the Bank has shown flexibility in limited instances. Some population loans granted to India, for example, were almost entirely for local costs.[14] Likewise, IDA credits to some very poor countries have financed 90 percent of local costs.

In practice, the Bank mandates international competitive bidding, but gives a 15 to 25 percent preference margin to local manufacturers. This provision has been criticized elsewhere for promoting dependency, wasting scarce resources, and impeding the development of the local manufacturing sector.[15] Restrictions on local-costs financing cannot but limit the Bank's involvement in environmental projects, and increases the need to tie such projects to larger ones. Environmental protection and rehabilitation projects are likely to use local resources. Since, by definition, local capital is scarce in developing countries, failure to finance local costs can turn governments away from such projects and components, or limit the Bank to a narrow appraisal of the environmental impact of its development projects. Many forestry projects for example, have a small foreign exchange component (25 percent of less), which adds to the local financial burden.

Furthermore, the Bank's insistence on incorporating environmental safeguards into its projects adds to the total foreign exchange debt that the country assumes for a particular project. This reduces the likelihood that the government will easily adopt these provisions, even when local financing could be found. In the early 1980s, higher interest rates made it even more difficult for governments to justify such expenses which always tend to look like extra options. Finally, this provision tends to favor only a certain type of environmental safeguards, namely industrial anti-pollution devices, since the industrialized countries possess the technology and are ready to promote their costly importation financed through the foreign exchange provisions of the loans and credits. Consequently, more labor intensive aspects of environmental protection tend to be overlooked and institution-building neglected.

The flexibility in implementing this procedural requirement enhances the Bank's discretion. Since other areas of Bank lending (such as population or agriculture) compete for these "special circumstances," the negative incidence of this provision for environmental lending remains. Thus, although this requirement enables the Bank to control part of its task-environment, it also impairs the promotion of a concern whose importance it has acknowledged, and presents difficulties to countries willing to promote environmental conservation.

Project Versus Program Lending

Although silent about program lending, the *Articles of Agreement* of the IBRD and IDA specifically require that "[l]oans made or guaranteed by the Bank shall, except in special circumstances, be for the purpose of specific projects of reconstruction or development" (IBRD, III, 4[vii]) and "[f]inancing provided by the Association. . . , except in special circumstances, shall be for specific projects." (IDA, V, 1[b]).

Three reasons account for this preference. Firstly, the developed countries wanted to avoid repeating the mistakes of the pre-war program lending to East European nations. The Bank's reluctance to expand program aid until the mid-1970s stemmed from the fear that it might be used to finance short-term payment deficits rather than being invested for productive purposes, thereby endangering the achievements of the organization's primary objective.[16]

Secondly, program loans also give the organization little oversight in the use of its funds. Naturally, borrowers value them more for the same reasons (especially if they are IDA credits). And finally, the extensive experience of the project departments now gives the Bank a comparative advantage over other development institutions. This can only reinforce the organization's dedication to the project-by-project approach, even restrict its scope of activities: "Why mess around with non-project lending when there are still electric power projects to be financed?"[17] Again, this provision seems to be designed to protect the Bank without jeopardizing its flexibility. The introduction of "special circumstances" gives the organization additional leverage over the borrower.

The project focus has been an important element in the way environmental policy has been formulated. On the one hand, a specific project requirement enables the organization to control the use of its funds better. It is therefore possible to evaluate the environmental impact of the projects and supervise their implementation to ensure that environmental guidelines are respected. Given the developing countries' initial low commitment to ecological values, a project-by-project approach best enabled the Bank to ensure the initial implementation of its concerns.

On the other hand, this approach leads the Bank to consider projects in isolation of one another. This implies that the organization will be reluctant to condition a country's total investment program on a particular project. What Brazil does with respect to Amazonian land settlements, deforestation, Indians, or cattle ranching should not, according to this approach, and does not affect disbursements on hydro-electric projects. Actual disbursements on one project are not formally linked to the observance of conditions related to general policy performance, only to the observance of conditions attached to this specific project. Thus, at most, the Bank will stop lending for projects which destroy the environment "needlessly," without publicly condemning the policy, or without stopping lending for other sectors in the same country.

Not only are projects politically and financially limited in application, they are also geographically self-contained. The lack of a regional approach, that is the failure to analyze the impact of a single project on the regional ecosystem and the neglect of the impact of any concurrent project, also constrains policy.

Finally, and more fundamentally, the Bank's leverage depends on the existence of projects which justify its involvement in the first place. As Hayter points out: "It may happen that the Bank would particularly like to have an effect on policy at a time when there is no project loan pending."[18] The expansion of program loans may enable the organization to free itself from this constraint.

More program aid would give developing countries greater control over their own development programs, a concern echoed by the Pearson Commission.[19] Program lending has indeed increased since the early 1960s. The first program loan to a developing country (of $75 million) was made to Iran in 1957 to cover foreign exchange expenditures. Table 1.2 showed that non-project lending increased from an average of $91 million between 1964 and 1968 to $235 million in 1974 and $1.321 billion in 1986 (although its share of total lending diminished). Program loans were made for reconstruction after a war (Lebanon, Nicaragua) or natural disasters (Rumania, Guatemala, Mexico), for alleviating a sharp fall in export earnings (Guyana, Peru, Zambia, Jamaica), or the effects of higher oil prices (Korea, Tanzania).

The Bank started lending for sector-adjustment in 1979. Rather than loans designed to respond to unforeseen catastrophes, sector-adjustment loans are designed to support policy and institutional changes in particular areas so as to increase the efficiency of committed resources (for example, increases in agricultural production and non-traditional exports). They are means for the Bank to palliate the limitations of project lending which does not lend itself easily to changes at the policy level, and enables the Bank to reconcile its project focus with its concern for the context of their identification and implementation over which it traditionally had much less leverage. Sector adjustment loans accounted for 14 percent of total Bank lending in FY 1986.[20]

In 1980, the Executive Directors approved a Bank request to lend for "structural adjustment." These loans are similar but more comprehensive than sectoral loans and are designed "to provide support for member countries already in serious balance of payments difficulties, or faced in the year ahead with the prospects of unmanageable deficits arising from external factors which are not likely to be easily or quickly reversed."[21] Structural adjustment lending was expected to account eventually for about 10 percent of total lending. The Bank committed $777.2 million for structural adjustment in FY 1986, or 4.8 percent of its lending. Policy-oriented loans thus accounted for 18.8 percent of total Bank lending in 1986.

Clearly, "special circumstances" are becoming the norm. Both types of adjustment loans indicated a significant evolution in Bank policy toward policy-focused lending, and allowed it to (1) protect its investments and the ability of the recipient to service its debt, (2) shield a national development program from temporary disturbances, and (3) ensure that national policies are adopted that will increase the success of the funded projects. It also enables the Bank to influence macro economic policies more significantly, on a par with the IMF.

The influence of the Bank and of its major donors in a specific country is then no longer conditional on the identification of specific projects for which to lend. Thus, the $200 million loan granted to Turkey in 1980 is also explainable on political grounds. This country had recently benefited from extensive loans from the European Community and the IMF in order to enable it to overcome its economic difficulties and strengthen it in the face of its international strategic importance.

Although the Executive Directors upheld the project-by-project approach in 1979, and the Bank does not claim a shift away from this traditional approach, it is clear that the organization is pressured to evolve in that direction. Indeed, some observers have argued that there lies the future of the Bank. These loans enable the organization to press for urgent policy reforms, to side-step the issue of project implementation when policy changes agreed to in the convenant are often ignored, and enable the Bank to maintain a continuous policy dialogue with recipient countries.[22]

Policy-oriented loans would therefore nicely complement the project-by-project approach to the protection of the environment. They could give a country greater flexibility in determining what kind of environmental policy it wants to adopt and where it would like to channel its environmental funds (for example, toward the development of national and local institutions, training programs, experimental stations, or expertise for environmental rehabilitation or protection schemes). They can also be used to influence countries and develop a coordinated approach to national programs of envrionmental rehabilitation and protection, an approach discussed in the last chapter. They are, therefore, new instruments that give the organization more powerful means to implement this new concern. Whether it would be legitimate for the Bank to use them in this manner is another question altogether.

We now proceed from the procedural requirements that the Bank Group puts upon its operations to those which must be met by the borrowers. These external constraints concern the borrower's capabilities, namely its creditworthiness and whether it is eligible for market funds.

Creditworthiness and Market Eligibility

Creditworthiness and market eligibility form the lower and upper limits of the Bank's authorization to lend. Creditworthiness is another means of protecting investments and constitutes an important tool for reducing uncertainty: "[I]n making or guaranteeing a loan, the Bank shall pay due regard to the prospects that the borrower . . . will be in position to meet its obligations under the loan;" (IBRD, III, 4 [V]).

This is a judgment that the Bank alone makes. It gives it the right to scrutinize the borrower's economic and financial policies. It can demand policy changes and organize its task environment so as to secure maximum predictability when it eventually lends. The failure of the borrower to give the Bank satisfaction on some thirteen items could jeopardize its access to low-interest funds.[23]

Although this provision effectively protects the Bank from some elements of risk, it leads to the exclusion of countries with a weak balance of payments. Environmental problems, however, do not correlate with creditworthiness. A relatively rich country which possesses an extensive industrial base and important development programs, can still lack creditworthiness. Since projects are the main vehicle the Bank uses to implement environmental concerns, its refusal to lend to countries that lack creditworthiness precludes its influence on those matters.

The Bank may lend only when it is ". . . satisfied that in the prevailing market conditions the borrower would be unable otherwise to obtain the loan under conditions which in the opinion of the Bank are reasonable for the borrower" (IBRD, III, 4 [ii]). The picture of the Bank as a "lender of last resort" that this provision paints became rather fictitious in the 1970s as the organization competed with many other development funds for the financing of a restricted number or project.[24] This provision was initially intended to accomodate the limited amount of funds that the organization had at its disposal. Capital increases, growing borrowing on capital markets, organizational pressures to increase lending targets, and competition among lenders led to its relaxation during the 1970s.

From an environmental point of view, a strict application of this provision has adverse consequences. Indeed, the harder lending terms demanded by private international lenders work against environmental projects (or environmental components which add to the cost of the project) when a borrowing country is not strongly committed to environmental protection. Since many projects of this type are not self-liquidating, the money to repay the loans would have to come from elsewhere in the borrower's economy. Further, since multilateral development banks have a much lower environmental awareness than the World Bank, access to these funds could also jeopardize the Bank's efforts in that area.

Creditworthiness and market eligibility constitute, therefore, two other uncertainty-reducing requirements of the Bank. But, as in other examples, they may also impair the organization's achievement of a development strategy based on a close awareness of its ecological determinants.

The Terms of Lending

Because the Bank is theoretically a lender of last resort, it has endeavored to control the borrower's use of funds as much as possible. Lending terms have been an important vehicle through which the organization has tried to induce changes in its task-environment, as discussed in chapter 4. These terms mainly refer to three attributes of the loan: whether it is an IBRD "loan" or an IDA "credit," its maturity, and the interest rate.

Perhaps the most important decision is whether the loan will come from the IBRD or IDA. With their grace period of ten years, maturity over forty years, and no interest rate (except for a 0.75 percent annual charge to cover administrative expenses), IDA credits are virtual grants, and therefore much prized by the borrowers.[25] Only the poorest developing countries are entitled to these credits, while slightly richer ones can benefit from a mix of IBRD and IDA funds. Loans carry a shorter grace period and flexible interest rates. Obviously, since developing countries have other development priorities, environmental costs covered by IDA credits will be more acceptable.[26] Countries which experience both pollution and resource depletion are likely to concentrate on development-originated environmental problems since their effects are more visible and their mitigation is achieved through components of productive projects (such as emission standards for a newly-built plant) rather than through outright environmental rehabilitation projects (such as reforestation).

Although its loans and credits include a grant component, the Bank is not a fund, in that it expects all its transfers to be repaid sooner or later. This limitation again puts its environmental policy at a disadvantage. Even though environmental rehabilitation can influence the success of development strategies, the Bank's inability to make direct grants for environmental projects hinders the adoption of this concern by government leaders unwilling to deny their industries scarce capital in favor of projects whose results are often intangible.

Grace periods and maturities are typically determined not only by the borrower's strength, but also by the type of projects financed. The grace period, during which only interest is due, is usually decided in relation to the expected lapse time between the date of commitment and the time at which the project will come into operation.[27] Education projects, for example, have been given a longer grace period than road-improvement projects. But the desire of the organization to shield itself from the volatility of international markets by reducing the average grace period and maturity would deny it the chance to use them effectively to promote environmental projects.

Unlike maturity and grace periods, interest rates are uniform for all loans, whatever the project or the country. But another provision designed to protect the organization from unstable market rates may be detrimental to the promotion of environmental conservation. In 1982, the Executive Directors approved a proposal to adjust the interest rate during disbursement proportionally to the variation of market rates at which the Bank has to borrow. Since many environmental components of development projects are part of the "new style" projects that typically take much longer to disburse than more traditional ones, the introduction of some volatility into the borrowers' costs deters them from readily accepting such measures.

The Bank possesses numerous instruments to protect itself from the uncertainty stemming from its milieu. The criteria of productivity, foreign exchange, project loans, creditworthiness, and lending terms present powerful constraints to the implementation of the organizations' concern with the environmental impact of development projects. Except for the project-by-project approach, the organization's advantages can be self-defeating and impede the implementation of ecological concerns among its clients. These procedural requirements hinder the adoption and implementation of this new value, or complicate attempts to influence the behavior of its targets, or both. Experience has shown, however, that in each case, the Bank has developed a growing flexibility in the application of these criteria. But to retain this power, the Bank cannot routinely claim special circumstances, which, given the number of "social" projects, puts environmental considerations at a disadvantage.

This discussion of the various procedural constraints relevant to environmental policy leads us naturally to consider the policy process. How are the environmental concerns integrated into the work of the Bank?

The Policy Process: The Project Cycle

As a set of rules and procedures, the project cycle describes every stage of the project review, and constitutes the main instrument through which the Bank implements its environmental policy.[28] One of the goals of the Office of Environmental and Scientific Affairs was to instill an environmental ethic into this cycle which governs daily practice. As figure 2.1 illustrates, the cycle comprises six stages: identification, preparation, appraisal, negotiations, implementation and supervision, and evaluation.

Figure 2.1. The Project Cycle

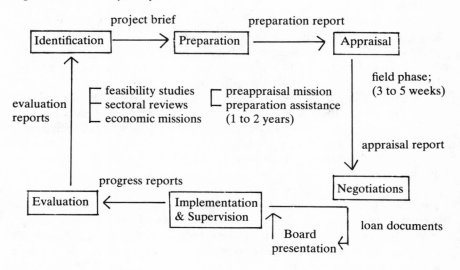

Identification

At its inception, the Bank thought that its volume of lending would be linked and determined by available funds. Rapidly, however, it realized that lending was also constrained by the number of well-conceived and competent proposals. During the 1950s, for example, Bank management argued against the Special United Nations Fund for Economic Development (SUNFED) on the grounds that it was not a shortage of finance, but a shortage of projects, which impeded a greater flow of aid to developing countries.[29]

Thus, although projects must be formally proposed by a country, they now are as much the products of the Bank's identification as of the borrowers' own determination of their needs. Shortages of skilled manpower in poor countries have forced the Bank to become intimately involved with project identification and preparation, so that the organization's technical requirements would be satisfied.[30] As a lending agency required to make a profit, the Bank must find projects worthy of investment. By sending country economic missions, by encouraging the creation of planning institutions, by following-up on past projects, by looking at countries' sectoral policies, and by cooperating with other UN organizations, the Bank is able to control the flow of projects it needs to carry out its mandate.

The first survey mission was sent to Colombia in 1949, and even at that time, the Bank "stimulated" the Colombian request.[31] These missions which substitute for the national bureaucracy's lack of expertise, also tend to supersede existing bureaucracies in order to assess the development needs and creditworthiness of the borrower. The Bank has since expanded on that concept. The larger developing countries, where much of the Bank's resources have been invested, are now "surveyed" every year, while smaller countries are visited every two or three years.

The resulting country program papers outline the problems a country faces and specify the basic development strategy to be followed. Typically, these papers pay little attention to the ecological constraints on the country's development strategy or on the success of its development projects. No attempt is made at this level to try to organize some kind of regional ecological planning. This is regrettable since these teams have ample access to relevant national data when the latter exist.

Country program papers are useful instruments for communicating with the rest of the staff and with the borrower. As Stein and Johnson suggested, efforts were needed to integrate environmental limits into their financial and economic discussions.[32] OESA therefore insisted that environmental experts accompany economic missions, or at least that such missions also include individuals aware of the ecological dimensions of their work. If successful, its subsequent workload would be eased, and irreversible detrimental environmental consequences minimized early.

Instead of belatedly trying to modify or adapt itself to a design whose guidelines have already been accepted, the OESA could influence the very design of the project and the decision to proceed to the next stage. As one OESA staff member emphasized: "If I have failed to incorporate my preoccupations at that stage, it will later be too late." He added: "The best way to minimize the environmental impact of a project is very often to change its location." Once the site is chosen, environmental influence can only aim to minimize the consequences. Clearly, the value of any input will also depend on the type of projects. For example, the major environmental impact may derive from the decision to build the project itself, and not from its operation.

In practice, however, these missions rarely included experts with any awareness of environmental issues, thus excluding ecological considerations from the definition of the development problems. This lack of involvement reflected the OESA's status within the organization as well as the content of its policy. The staff was kept small and its role was limited to minimizing adverse environmental impacts at a minimal cost. Therefore it could not and did not have to be included in the early decision-making process. OESA's function was to *review* projects for their environmental consequences, not identify them, influence their design, or question their rationale.

The absence of environmental specialists in economic or sectoral missions ensured that (1) strictly environmental projects were not identified unless the recipient suggested it, and (2) Country Programme Papers (CPPs) would not integrate ecological limits into their definition of the development problem of the borrower. This failure led to the schizophrenic behavior of an organization that funds environmental components and a few rehabilitation projects and also keeps supporting ecological catastrophes in the same country, a situation that was strongly denounced in the 1980s, as discussed in chapter five.

Preparation

Project preparation can take one to two years. It involves close collaboration between the lender and the borrower to consider all technical, financial, institutional, and economic conditions necessary to achieve the objectives of the project. Since it is an extensive undertaking which demands detailed expertise, many countries have encountered difficulties in achieving the Bank's standards and in submitting adequately prepared projects. This can create problems for the organization for it slows down the flow of projects that it can fund. Aspiring to a leading position among development agencies in terms of intellectual authority and financial turnover, "the Bank must have an active role in ensuring a timely flow of well-prepared projects."[33] Like the firm which expands vertically to control its environment in order to ensure a steady flow of resources, the Bank also involved itself in the preparation of projects, even though formal responsibility for preparation rests with the borrower. The Bank tried to do so in different ways: by training future LDC officials in its Economic Development Institute established in 1955; by providing loans or credits for technical assistance; by establishing a special project preparation facility; by ensuring the cooperation of other UN specialized agencies (UNDP especially); or in special circumstances, by preparing the project itself.[34] The need to expand vertically has increased with the complexity of the new style projects whose technicality drains the poor countries' manpower resources. By one estimate, the Bank prepares 40 percent of its projects through its own teams.[35]

This stage sets the basic frame of reference of the project, but OESA's involvement was still informal. Project briefs prepared after identification could alert it to potential environmental difficulties, allowing informal consultation with the borrower and the regional staff. Lack of involvement made it more difficult later to question a project and forced the OESA staff to work with what was submitted to them for review at the next stage. The Bank uses consultants extensively at this stage, but their environmental performance is not easily monitored either, nor would their recommendations necessarily be followed.

Appraisal

Appraisal is the Bank's sole responsibility. It is actually a technical, institutional, economic and financial review of the project preparation report. It was at the *conclusion* of this stage that OESA normally reviewed every project for its environmental consequences. It then decided whether additional safeguards should be included, a consultant sent in the field, or a partial environmental impact study undertaken. This stage involved close cooperation with other units of the Bank, and OESA could be part of an appraisal mission sent for four or five weeks to the future borrower.

Several constraints impeded OESA's action at this stage. A project may be modified only at the cost of extensive delays. A lack of manpower forced it to focus on projects which had the most obvious and largest detrimental impact on the natural or social environment, casting aside minor problems that were easier to solve. OESA's lack of information-gathering capabilities hindered notice of negative consequences that were hard to forecast. OESA often relied on its own experience with past projects, which created a considerable lag from the implementation and introduction of new projects to the time it could ensure reasonable account of environmental problems in subsequent projects.

Another constraint pertains to the place of environmental review within projects appraisal. Since environmental considerations tend to be taken into account only insofar as they influence the success of the project, or from a mitigation perspective, no separate environmental appraisal was conducted. Finally, the low degree of environmental awareness on the part of the staff of the regional offices also constrained the effectiveness of the Bank's review. Too often, OESA had to rely on reports of project failures after completion to drive home the importance of an environmental review. But, since ecological consequences are diffuse, spread over time and space, and incremental, a direct causal link between the source and the consequence is often hard to show. Simply relying on experience will not assure an adequate consideration and protection of the national and social environments.

Environmental projects and components must satisfy the general appraisal requirements which apply to any other project. Before lending, the Bank thoroughly investigates the various economic, technical, financial, organizational, managerial, and operational aspects of the project.[36] Appraisal methodologies do not form the single basis for decision-making, but serve as a supplementary tool particularly useful for assessing the relative merits of various project alternatives. Since they are only tools to help decision-making, they can be modified to accomodate new lending objectives. Thus, when it was decided to pay more attention to basic needs and income redistribution, existing appraisal methodologies had to be adapted to these goals. And since the Bank is a financial institution peopled by economists, the aim was to try to quantify the new concerns and modify the main tool for decision-making, the cost-benefit analysis.

THE COST-BENEFIT ANALYSIS

Cost-benefit analysis is a standard decision-making tool of the Bank. It has also been extensively used in environmental regulatory decision-making in the United States.[37] Three advantages are associated with attempts to devise a suitable environmental cost-benefit analysis. The Bank can (1) compare the relative merits of each project; (2) ensure that the economic consequences of environmental protection are taken into account, thus avoiding jeopardizing the organization's main goal; and (3) use its expertise in economic analysis.

Cost-benefit analysis is especially useful since the organization must balance conflicting goals and requirements: economic efficiency, redistribution, mitigation of adverse environmental impacts. On the one hand, it must show financial analysts and creditors that projects contribute to economic growth. On the other hand, it must also be an instrument for integrating political and environmental objectives into the appraisal of projects. These concerns led to attempts to broaden the scope of the appraisal process beyond strict financial criteria: "Project analysis attempts to ensure that the chosen option for a project is the best possible— not only in terms of its size, technology, and location, but also in terms of the ultimate beneficiaries and the quality of output."[38]

Although the addition of social goals to the traditional maximization of the total income of the economy enables the reconciliation of project-appraisal methods and policy objectives, it also complicates the analysis. The addition of yet another component, environmental costs and benefits, is therefore extremely difficult. Several methodological problems are associated with the development and use of cost-benefit analysis techniques for achieving environmental goals.[39]

First, it is often difficult to estimate with confidence the probable impact of a project on the ecosystem, either because of a lack of previous research, or because of the diffuse nature of the consequences of that action. Moreover, different parties may characterize attributes differently: what may be seen as a cost for the Bank or units of the Bank, may be seen as a benefit to the recipient or other units of the organization. A technique that would try to synthesize the social goal of poverty alleviation and the ecological objective of environmental protection is particularly vulnerable to that problem.

Second, many costs and benefits, when identified, are extremely difficult to measure. Their determination is, in fact, a function of the values held by a particular society at a certain time. While it is not hard to measure the cost of pollution-control projects, assigning a monetary value to their benefits is more problematic. The difficulty becomes more intractable in the case of environmental rehabilitation and conservation projects such as the protection of tropical forests.

"Willingness to pay" is a concept designed to remedy this situation when it is not possible to assign a market value to the environmental consequences of a project. The problems associated with this technique were clearly identified in the 1974 *Environment and Development* booklet. Willingness to pay is a function of a country's resource endowment, the number of available alternatives to the project, cultural preferences, the ecological scarcity of the resource destroyed, and the existing distribution of income.[40] This concept can only be applied to localized problems, where the polluters are also the polluted. Although this procedure has been used experimentally in Switzerland, practical difficulties abound. Given the low administrative capabilities of many developing countries, conducting polls on their constituents' willingness to pay might be far from the top of their priority list.

The main objective of devising and promoting such measures as "willingness to pay" or shadow prices as an approach to cost-benefit evaluation is to internalize the environmental costs of development projects. This approach, however, defines environmental values as relative ones, basically functions of a country's wealth and of the standard of living of the specific groups affected.

A third problem pertains to the discount rate to be used, whose determination is typically very arbitrary. The poor will highly discount their future welfare and neglect present hazards in favor of their immediate well-being or survival. The willingness of Bolivian mine workers to inhale dangerous and ultimately fatal dust for the sake of immediate employment (a case the Bank encountered) underlines the precarious usefulness of this concept. What rate is the Bank to use: one favored by those miners, by their government, by the Bank, or by the donors?

Finally, the costs and benefits must accrue to the same borrower if cost-benefit analysis is to form the basis for a lending decision. It is otherwise difficult to justify.[41] This approach therefore leaves out problems associated with shared resources and the international transfer of pollution.[42] It also ignores damages done to the "common heritage of mankind."

Even though one observer exclaimed that ". . . the social cost-benefit analysis can be seen as the most important practical application in development of theoretical welfare economics,"[43] it has not been universally accepted within the Bank or among developing countries because it could lead to the acceptance of unprofitable projects. Projects may be socially desirable but lack a positive rate of return. Thus, this analysis tends to be used as a complement to the traditional cost-benefit analysis to help choose among different alternatives on the basis of both financial and social value criteria.[44]

In light of these various difficulties, assigning a magic value of 10 percent to the desirable rate of return of a project, as is usually the case, becomes meaningless. Either it stems from a procedure that ignores all social and environmental costs and benefits, or it embodies the particular values of those who use a technique designed to compensate for these shortcomings. But the decisions relative to the identification of costs and benefits, their quantification, the discount rate to be used, or the distribution of costs and benefits among various groups, can be made to support any preferred decision. Certainly, this technique cannot be used as a substitute for political decisions as to which values should be pursued and how.

To say that an environmental cost-benefit analysis lacks meaning or is inappropriate is not to say that it is useless. Once the basic decision has been made actively to support environmental values, this procedure will be organizationally and politically useful in gaining acceptance for them. Faced with conflicting objectives, competing demands from its various clienteles, and uncertainty as to the economic and environmental effects of its actions, cost-benefit analysis becomes an indispensable tool for shielding the organization from greater pressures and uncertainty.

OTHER APPRAISAL METHODOLOGIES

Given the difficulties of internalizing environmental objectives into a standard cost-benefit analysis, the Office of Environmental and Scientific Affairs was forced to turn to more practical approaches such as the preparation of checklists and guidelines, the evaluation of completed projects, and the adaptation of environmental impact statement techniques (EIS).

Rather than attempting to assign monetary values to costs and benefits, one could try to catalogue the impact of a project by using natural units. Such a collection of facts is often what is crucially needed.[45] One of OESA's early actions was to put together, publish and disseminate environmental checklists for projects. Later, detailed handbooks offered an excellent methodological introduction to the evaluation of the environmental incidence of specific industrial activities.[46]

A related approach has been the evaluation of completed projects. The Bank performs a few case studies of this kind in order to identify environmental effects and remedy possible deficiencies in future appraisals. Performed immediately after completion of the project, however, these studies tend to circumscribe environmental analysis to a local dimension and limit themselves to the identification of the short-term and direct negative environmental impact of the project. They are not a systematic attempt to collect information on the project's ecological significance. More thorough and broader evaluations need to be undertaken. Although manpower may be scarce, these studies can and should be contracted out, and some of them performed in the Bank's own Research department.

A third possible approach consisted in using environmental impact statements (EIS). The Bank rejected the idea of mandating automatic impact statements on the American model for five reasons:

1. EIS are costly. Who would finance them? Since developing countries might not be willing to do so, EIS would work against small projects.
2. OESA does not have enough manpower to either prepare or review statements. If automatic EIS were required, about 250 would have to be conducted each year.
3. EIS are often too general to be useful. The strict regulations of NEPA would be irrelevant for very specific projects such as those funded by the Bank.
4. They would involve considerable delays which the organization tries to avoid desperately.
5. Finally, to be useful, they need to be conducted within a national institutional or policy framework which is often absent in developing countries. What good is an EIS if a country does not have an environmental policy?

Instead of being systematically required, EIS are performed on an ad-hoc basis and for a specific aspect of a project. Neither the developed countries, nor the developing countries (many of which have rejected it at home), the staff or the financial community favored this approach. Had OESA proposed it, it would never have been implemented and would have destroyed the credibility of the office.

An EIS has a double function. It serves to instill project identifiers and appraisers with an ecological awareness, and it serves to identify those areas of potential problem. Given the various costs associated with the requirements of such a procedure and the lack of shared values on this issue, OESA's reliance on handbooks and partial EIS for fulfilling these two functions seemed far more preferable.[47]

Standards to be used in assessing the environmental impact of development projects also provided OESA with some flexibility. The nature, type, and extent of the environmental problems of developing countries differ not only from those of the developed countries where standards were devised, but also among themselves, and even according to local circumstances. Moreover, many developing countries lack monitoring capabilities or efficient enforcement of the strict standards they have themselves adopted. Thus the OESA adapted them to local circumstances. The project-by-project requirement favors the implementation of flexible standards and minimizes the costs associated with unwarranted and strict ones. In practice, standards are either raised or lowered by the engineers in charge of the project and are negotiated with its sponsors.

Chapter 4 addresses this point further. Questions remain regarding how

liberal standards should be and how this latitude is determined. Furthermore, the adoption of standards does not preclude the need for a long-
term analysis of the ecological impact of these projects. The use of standards is also largely limited to industrial projects. Thus, focusing on
whether standards have been adopted and implemented may give a dim
idea of the real environmental impact of a project.

Negotiations

Next, the Bank and the borrower endeavor to agree on the technical
aspects of the project and on the financial or political conditions attached
to the loan. These conditions are then transformed into legal obligations in
the loan documents. They can cover such items as effluent charges and
standards, pricing of services, or the creation of new institutions.

Negotiations also make sure that both the Bank and the borrower agree
upon the environmental provisions which will result from compromises.
Effluent standards which industries must observe will be set relative to the
characteristics of the project and the borrower, and correspond to what the
recipient, the Bank's regional offices and the environmental unit think is
reasonable. Although the Bank is often able to impose its will, borrowers
have many resources they can use to influence the decision of the Bank. It
is impossible at this stage to question the value of a project itself in light of
its environmental impact, for the country and the regional units are already
committed to it. The experience of a consultant charged with reviewing the
impact of Brazil's POLONOROESTE project on Indian populations is in-
structive in this regard.[48]

Controversies surrounding the impact of Bank-funded projects on native
populations emerged in the 1970s. After David Price and other anthropo-
logists had started mobilizing public opinion, the Bank charged Price in
1980 with assessing the consequences of a massive highway and settlement
project in western Brazil, and with recommending what might be done to
mitigate its adverse impact on the people in the area. His experience led
him "to question the sincerity of that institution's commitment to safeguard the welfare of people affected by the projects it supports."[49] He
found that compromises had already been reached with Brazilian authorities over the treatment of the Indians when the Bank called on him. His
review of the agreement showed misinformation, misleading statements,
and unexplained manipulation of financial appraisal data to show greater
rates of return. Finally, his report was circulated only among three staff
members within the Bank.

Despite the particular perspective of a strong critic of Bank policy, this
experience illustrates the divorce that can exist between rhetoric and practice, the sensitivity of the organization to outside criticism, the frequent use

of consultants to defuse it, and the difficulties that the Bank has in balancing the various goals it pursues and its organizational interests. The OESA drafted a paper in 1982 recommending measures that should be taken in favor of native populations which were later incorporated into the *Operations Manual*.[50] This issue, however, has remained controversial, as will be discussed in chapter 5.

After the completion of negotiations, the project is sent to the Executive Directors for formal approval. Detailed review is impossible at that stage and they would not reject a project on environmental grounds alone. Rather, they tend to be concerned with broad issues or whether the project will accomplish its purpose. Given their lack of expertise and the skillful way management can present a loan, it is difficult for directors to raise detailed issues about the document itself.

Once formally adopted, a project is implemented pending the borrower's fulfillment of the negotiated pre-conditions.

Implementation and Supervision

The borrower implements the project as the Bank supervises. The first reason behind supervision is, of course, to give the Bank a means of ensuring that its money is being used for the purpose negotiated. This concerns especially the supervision of the procurement of goods and works financed under the loan through adequate international competitive bidding.

Environmentally speaking, supervision is crucial. Only constant supervision during construction or operation will ensure that negotiated guidelines are being observed. It is also important because of the nature of ecological knowledge. Implementation encounters problems which cannot be identified in advance. Thus, there is a need to review project implementation to ensure environmental safety and the provision of adequate information for future projects. Unidentified in the appraisal report or the loan documents, unforeseen environmental damages, however, could not stop the project unless they directly endangered the implementation of the project.

The Bank has allocated few resources to supervision, preferring to focus its attention on the identification of new projects. A gradual change in the 1970s can be partly attributed to the different types of projects funded. Isolated projects, such as road construction or telecommunication, undoubtedly need less supervision than a very complex rural development project with multiple objectives. The growing importance of the human variable in the determination of the success of projects, and the need to gather experience have helped strengthen the implementation stage.

The degree of involvement of environmental officers during implementation depends both on the individual's conception of his role and on the nature of the project. For example, whereas the impact of agricultural and infrastructural projects can be dealt with more efficiently in the early stages of the cycle, the impact of industrial projects depends more on their operation than on their construction. Yet, supervisory missions may rely solely on the progress reports that the borrower prepares. And agreed safeguards (standards, anti-pollution equipment) are often ignored. Moreover, these missions are primarily composed of economists, financiers, and sometimes engineers. Ecologists are not involved, although OESA staff could join if they so desired. This narrow composition tends to work against an effective enforcement of environmental standards and precludes the identification of unexpected environmental problems. The dispatch of progress missions itself depends on the type of reports the borrower sends back, and on the complexity of the project. OESA had to go itself in the field to ensure that its guidelines were respected.

If the environmental unit notices that environmental guidelines are not respected, it can use the Bank's extensive enforcement capabilities. In such a case, the regional office may support its finding and halt disbursements until the problem is corrected. Threatening not to lend for other projects is a less credible threat because it supposes that the environmental concern supersedes all others, which is most often not true. This enforcement capability can work as long as the project is not completed and paid for; after completion, the direct leverage of the Bank through supervision, and consequently its enforcement role, ceases.

Evaluation

The sixth and final stage of the project cycle, evaluation, follows the final disbursement and involves a completion report and an independent audit.

It was only under U.S. congressional pressure that this stage was included in normal Bank activities in the early seventies. There was little concern until then for determining whether the promises of the project were fulfilled and, if not, why not.[51] A special unit, the Operations Evaluation Department (OED), entirely separate from the operating staff of the Bank and reporting directly to the Executive Directors, was created in 1973 to undertake these audits.

The project completion report (PCR) produced as part of the regular supervisory function of the Bank's project staff, constitutes the basis for the OED's annual review. The reports do not typically assess the impact of the project on the environment, but tend to focus on implementation. This small unit mostly performs a simple desk review of the reports filed by the supervision missions, or of all material pertaining to the project. Borrowers are asked to comment on the OED's report and file their own. There are no environmental specialists in the OED, which relies mainly on reports submitted by the staff. It is therefore unlikely that it will uncover problems that were not identified earlier. The failure to use current standards as well as the standards existing at the time of appraisal also minimizes the learning function of the evaluation.[52] Moreover, evolving ecological and environmental knowledge precludes definitive assessments upon what worked and what did not, or heavy reliance on those assessments.

What PCRs do, however, is identify trends and regularities among projects which would affect the preparation, appraisal or implementation of future projects. But, since evaluation is undertaken so early after completion, it cannot, by definition identify the long-term environmental consequences beyond the end of the disbursement period. Thus, there must be a system of further evaluation, not only to appraise the environmental soundness of projects, but also to assess their relevance to overall economic and development strategies.

"Throughout IBRD history," van de Laar emphasizes, "the primary concern of its lending activities has . . . been to generate projects and to influence, shape and control many stages of the project cycle."[53] In fact, vertical integration enhances control over each stage of the cycle, reducing the uncertainty attached to the economic, financial, and developmental success of the projects. The Bank has the capability of playing an important role in implementing "soft" concerns. Since it cooperates closely with the local administration, it can foster a continuing concern for its goals provided that the borrower perceives them to be legitimate. This influence depends in part on the perception that the organization unanimously endorses this goal. Without a strong internal consensus behind the promotion of the environmental perspective, the Bank will lack the legitimacy it needs to convince other actors of the sensibility of its policy. The last part of this chapter addresses this question.

Organizational Interactions

To respond to the widening scope, complexity, and rapid growth of its operations since 1968 while maintaining a speedy decision-making process, the organization of the World Bank was modified in 1973. Six regional offices were established at the Bank's headquarters, each planning and supervising the projects and development programs of its assigned countries and employing most of the specialists needed to carry out these responsibilities. Another reorganization, in 1987, is discussed in chapter six.

After 1973, an Operations Policy Staff (OPS) included advisers for every sector as well as specialists engaged in new types of activities. There were separate departments for agriculture and rural development, education, population-health-nutrition, transportation and water, and urban development. The Energy and Industry departments were separate from OPS under their own vice president. OESA and the adviser on Women and Development belonged to the Projects Advisory Staff of OPS. OPS provided support for the regional offices, assured quality and consistency in the Bank's operations, and promoted technical innovation. It established project guidelines and standards and dealt with sector policy issues in areas which were not decentralized, such as the environment. Thus it contained both specialists who were not present in the regional offices and specialists with counterparts in the project units of the regional offices.

The Office of Environmental and Scientific Affairs

Rather than transform its administrative structure, the World Bank opted for adding an Office of Environmental and Scientific Affairs as the least disturbing organizational solution for coping with the new value. This response was typical of agencies whose activities were challenged on similar grounds in the early 1970s. As Caldwell remarked regarding the American experience, it was "[a] structural response that most agencies could make with the least amount of disruptions over the shortest period of time."[54]

The position of environmental adviser was created in 1970 and later organized into an Office of Environmental Affairs. Health issues were included in 1973 after an active promotion by the developing countries and the environmental adviser who was trained in that field. OEHA became OEA again after the creation of a separate Health sector, and finally became OESA when Science and Technology was incorporated in the early 1980s. One explanation of this fluctuation lies in the political interest that member countries have in these areas, and reflects the importance that the organization as a whole gives them. The creation of a separate health sector was a response to diffuse pressures from the Bank's constituency. Thus, many sectors or aspects of the environment did not fall under OESA. Like Health, the Population, Nutrition, Water Supply and Sewerage, and Urban sectors were also independent of OESA. Forestry, including conservation, was found in the Agriculture and Rural Development Department.

From the outset, the office was given few powers and a small staff charged only with "advising" the operations-policy vice-president. It employed from five to seven professionals, with the review of projects falling on three of them. (At the same time, Information and Public Affairs had at least twenty five professionals and the speech-writing unit had five.)[55] While the staff entrusted with reviewing the environmental impact of projects and disseminating findings remained limited, the staff of the Bank itself expanded considerably in the 1970s and 1980s: from 1,348 professionals in 1971, to 3,617 in 1986.

The small staff size demanded an extensive individual workload. One staff member claimed he reviewed between 200 and 300 projects a year, eighty to 100 of which may have been acted upon. This high number, given travel days and vacations, left very little time for an extensive analysis of the project or for the improvement of the staff's knowledge. It also gave staff members little time to communicate their concerns and perspectives to other units of the Bank, or to promote strictly environmental projects.

This scarcity of personnel would not have been troublesome if environmental specialists had been scattered throughout the organization. But the 1973 decentralization of sectoral expertise also put a heavier burden on the regional units ill-equipped at first to handle that load.[56] There were no environmental specialists as such in the regional offices, only specialists who, at best, may have had some awareness of these issues but few incentives to heed them. Given the important role that these units play in the project cycle, the lack of environmentally trained personnel weakened the capacity to make the necessary changes during the identification and preparation phases, and precluded the incorporation of environmental concerns into the country development plans.

Economists, Engineers, and Ecologists

The Bank is staffed by economists and engineers. Few general administrators are professional managers or "generalists" and owe their standing to their position in the organization. All the senior posts are held by accomplished economists who are also present everywhere, especially in operations policy and in the regional office where they are associated with engineers. The key positions in the Bank are held by economists. Since power is concentrated at the top, the ideology of the organization will tend to be dominated by traits typical of the economists.[57]

This professional orientation distinguishes the Bank and other international finance institutions from other development-oriented organizations; and the coexistence of two bodies of professionals, economists and engineers, differentiates it from the IMF. Conflicts will arise between the goals the organization may be asked to pursue and the preferences of economists who enjoy high professional standing in their respective fields.[58]

As an economic institution, the Bank can only tackle environmental problems from that perspective. This has two consequences. First, although the financial criteria used for appraising projects enable the Bank to shelter itself from the financial risks it takes in lending to developing countries, they also constrain its flexibility.

More importantly, economists will apply a particular perspective to the definition and solution of ecological problems in the developing countries. It has been widely argued that environmental protection does not challenge neo-classical economics if one assumes that everything of value can have a price. The Bank's economic approach to environmental problems assumes that more growth will enable societies to solve those problems, where environmental problems are quantifiable problems; and often that market mechanisms or the development of individual property rights will take care of most problems.[59]

The environmental and economic literature has identified many gaps between the economic and ecological analyses of environmental problems. It is argued, for example, that utility theory, and later its preference theory avatar (from which the willingness-to-pay concept derives), assume that individuals know what is in their best interest. Moreover, what is in the best interest of an individual may not be in the best interest of the environment. Conversely, individuals' preferences do not necessarily reflect the *real* benefit that they may derive from a healthy environment or from the protection of ecosystems.

Seeking to outline the basic shortcoming of the economic approach, environmentalists have questioned the fundamental assumption of economists that man acts rationally. The parable of the tragedy of the commons clearly illustrates the point that individual rational behavior can lead to collective catastrophe. Each herdsman seeks to maximize his gains from the use of a common pasture by adding animals to his herd. The situation is "tragic" not only because the result is erosion and ruin for all, but above all because economic logic compels each herdsman to increase his herd without limit. Economists have indeed refused to discuss how man's economic behavior affects the achievement of his ultimate goals.[60]

Thus, economists will assign the environment a value corresponding to its utility for the individual, whereas ecologists would argue that ecosystems have an intrinsic value, independent of what individuals wish to make of them. Furthermore, it is not, according to ecologists, because something has value that it should be for sale. So environmentalists are led to more normative questions about the right to pollute or destroy habitats, rather than to more technical questions of determining how much this right should be worth.

Market solutions (such as user charges) will be favored over reforms thay rely on state intervention, especially since many developing countries lack the administrative structure to regulate standards effectively. The solution to the tragedy of the commons will often lie in changes in land tenure, rather than in some form of regulation. Thus, desertification in the Sahel can be alleviated by changing property rights and settling the nomads. Many of these solutions also appeal to the governments. Settling nomads makes them more amenable to central control; user charges increase state revenues. Changing property rights, however, will not always work when it is more profitable to destroy a resource and invest the income than preserve it, as in the case of the tropical forests.

During appraisal, the staff focus on what can be quantified and tend to consider environmental problems insofar as they affect the economic or financial success of the project. The burden was then on OESA to demonstrate the extent to which failure to respect ecological limits may lead to future diseconomies or jeopardize the development prospects of a country. This may be particularly difficult in areas of uncertain knowledge or when different values are in competition (such as respecting native cultures versus promoting land settlements).

When economists jump from a micro-perspective that focuses on the short-term economic benefits of a single project to a macro-perspective that tries to integrate a project into an overall development policy, they can more easily adopt environmental safeguards. But the awareness of the social, macroeconomic, and environmental consequences of development projects must still take place within an economic intellectual framework. Ecologists and economists often hold dramatically different perspectives. A reduction in forest diversity (an ecological loss and possible danger), for example, can be extremely beneficial. It often makes economic sense to destroy tropical forests and replant fast-growing species. The country benefits from the sale of the tropical hardwood and then can establish a pulp and paper industry along with a fuelwood component that will benefit the local people. Several forestry projects in India illustrate this approach.

Further, economists tend to focus on the immediate consequences of projects rather than on the distant implications of their work. By tradition, they will discount the future more than ecologists will. Economists and ecologists, as Dahlberg pointed out, have different time frames: economists tend to restrict themselves to a policy time frame of a decade rather than adopt a development time frame of a century.[61] Given the economic situation of the developing countries, there are strong pressures to adopt the first perspective.

Finally, environmental economists have mostly focused their attention on pollution. Although pollution may prove costly and present grave constraints on development in certain areas, it still is not the most immediate and general threat to the future of the developing countries' environments. The economists' emphasis on production and consumption rather than on maintenance hinders their effectiveness in conceptualizing a comprehensive environmental policy, and impedes the integration of ecological variables into their work.

The opposition between economists and ecologists must not be construed as one between environment and development. Most environmentalists accept the need for development. But they often question the means and ends of the process. Because OESA was part of an organization which emphasizes this perspective, its environmental policy was fundamentally constricted. It is precisely to the extent that OESA tried to frame its objectives within the prevalent intellectual framework, that it was organizationally successful in having it accepted. OESA had to emphasize its contribution to the achievement of economic development as defined by economists, rather than question the rationale and objectives of Bank policies.

The influence of the economists' perspective on decision-making appears increasingly unclear. The adoption of more complex projects has favored the influence of the engineers on the definition of environmental problems and on the identification of appropriate solutions.

The limitations of a technocratic or technological approach to the solution of environmental problems, however, are well-known.[62] Technocrats are not known for their concern about the environment; and when they are, according to this approach, they tend to think that there exists a technical solution to environmental problems. Following the nineteenth century faith in progress through the conquest of nature, antipollution devices can always be invented, or new methods to exploit scarce resources found. For an engineer, there will exist one best way to solve a problem; one best way not marred by political or normative considerations. And the engineer tends to see his relationship to nature as adversarial: man must not adapt to nature, but nature to man.

A predominance of engineers in the areas of transportation, agriculture, energy, and industry in the regional offices predisposes environmental policy toward the mitigation of pollution and a concern for the means of achieving "unnecessary" destruction during modernization. One will try to fit a hydroelectric plant into nature rather than question the purpose and larger implication of its construction in the first place.

Engineers and economists are utilitarians at heart. Conservation becomes "the orderly exploitation of resources for the greatest good to the greatest number over the longest time."[63] A corollary to that position is their disregard for the social and political consequences of their actions (but not for the economic ones), as long as they are limited in time or to isolated populations.

The adoption of a basic needs strategy, the evolution of development thinking, and the concern for social justice in the 1970s reflected yet a third orientation that grafted itself on the other two. According to this humanistic perspective, the policy-maker's chief concern is the welfare of the mass of the people. Centered upon man, this orientation will also tend to view the environment in a utilitarian perspective.

According to Caldwell, three principal beliefs regarding man's relationship to natural resources and the environment characterize this orientation, two of which are particularly relevant here:

1. "The well-being of presently living people takes precedence over all other considerations including the survival of the species." Thus the

Bank is primarily concerned with the welfare of the present generation, which means that, in principle, short-term relief is preferred, though it may entail long-term misery. Economists will translate this approach into higher discount rates in the cost-benefit analysis of projects. Of course, it also is a very expedient means to garner political support from its third world clientele.

2. "The global environment and its resources are the common heritage of all mankind (but not of all living species)." Again this can translate into a right to exploit living resources and ecosystems, within a country, or with other countries in the commons.[64]

The Bank's environmental rhetoric and policy reflect the assumptions and training of economists and engineers in association with a humanistic ideology promoted by the UN system. Here again, the organization faces internal contradictions. But although it has made it more impervious to the influence of OESA or external organizations devoted to environmental protection, professionalism also filters demands, fosters political neutrality, and functions as a barrier against threats from the task-environment.

Bureaucratic Conflicts

Conflicts among Bank units are not new. At the time of the promotion of the Green Revolution strategy, for example, other units of the Bank had second thoughts about the policy.[65] These misgivings eventually contributed to the concern for income redistribution, basic needs, and rural development.

The Bank's rapid expansion since 1968 has much influenced the operation of the Bank. On the one hand, the influx of younger staff members has made it more receptive to new concerns like the environment. McNamara's introduction of limited planning in the form of the establishment of five-year country programs also provided a framework for a coordination over time of environmental projects and studies. It is potentially a better instrument for identifying the likely environmental spill-over of an integrated program than would an incremental development approach which looks at environmental dimensions from isolated points in time and space.

On the other hand, informal working-level contacts became more difficult. More importantly, soon after taking office, McNamara announced an effort to double the volume of lending and the number of projects within five years. Consequently, the performance of the regional offices came to be judged according to these two criteria, and they will regard anything that slows down the project cycle very critically. Environmental review inherently delays projects especially when design modifications are incorporated late in the cycle. OESA's performance on the other hand was not formally linked to the number of projects acted upon or to the cost of additional safeguards it required, although its effectiveness depended on the expressed cooperation of the regional offices. Because the regional offices perceive their reward system to be dependent on the behavior of an external unit, they will tend to resent any extensive involvement or zeal from the environmental unit. Likewise, OESA's performance was not be judged according to the soundness of its environmental analyses and requirements, but according to the degree to which it hindered the pursuit of the organization's goals. As one OESA officer once exclaimed: "Nobody can accuse me of having slowed down a project."[66] This task-interdependence has promoted conflict, led to bad morale, and prevented full cooperation.

Equating organizational effectiveness with the speed and amount of lending encouraged OESA to focus selectively on submitted projects. Problems that required further study suffered. Large, multi-purpose projects thus acquire an irresistible momentum. Negotiations under way with the borrower cannot be impeded lightly. The staff is strongly tempted to avoid anything that detracts from well-trodden paths. Innovation in project design and conception is quelled. Pilot projects which demand more time to prepare are neglected. Many environmental projects have been pilot projects, not specifically intended to achieve a certain rate of return or fulfill a specific development strategy, but simply designed to accumulate experience or demonstrate the benefits associated with an awareness of environmental variables. Obviously, this situation will transfer more of the burden of initiating these projects to the recipient which may have to ask specifically for them.

Pressure to increase volume of lending favors infrastructural, capital-intensive projects about which the Bank has much experience, at the expense of complex "new style" projects. It may be easier and more rewarding for the Bank to become involved in expensive dam building or in the modernization of the steel industry, than in labor-intensive agricultural projects that will use "appropriate" or light capital technologies. The latter also require more staff time per dollar lent than the former. The bureaucracy tends to develop a bias against simple, inexpensive, labor-intensive projects. For example, a regional vice-president of the Bank indicated that administrative reasons made it impractical to consider projects costing less than \$20 million to \$30 million.[67] Often, the borrower cannot afford the maintenance of the large scale project with high operating costs. This pressure to move money which affects many international development agencies[68] comes from creditors and borrowers as well as from management.

Finally, the regional offices, closer to the recipient countries, tend to minimize the importance of ecological considerations that are of little concern to Third World economic development bureaucracies. The contributions of OPS were therefore often seen as being made at the wrong time, in the wrong way, or with the wrong perspective. Collaboration existed; but it was informal and depended on individual rather than institutional links.

The identification of conflicts arising from task-interdependence or status inconsistencies does not necessarily imply that these conflicts are destructive. The confrontation of divergent ideas may clarify issues, produce better ideas, and strengthen innovation. There is little evidence of a dialectical process at work, however. Rather, different units continued with their traditional tasks, without overall integration. A few environmental projects were undertaken and many environmental components funded. Knowledge about the importance of environmental safeguards accumulated. Yet, traditional destructive projects continued. This situation was reflected within the recipient countries as well (such as Indonesia, India, and Brazil).

Chapter 4 discusses some of the means that the OESA and other officers conscious of the importance of environmental issues have used to enhance the legitimacy of this new concern within the Bank. OESA formulated its preoccupations in economic language, promoted environmental education among the staff (with little success), and hired consultants.

It also attempted to gain active support from senior management and the Executive Directors. The departure of many senior managers in the early 1970s, coupled with the administrative reorganization of the Bank, brought in a new generation more open to social problems in general, and possessing greater awareness of the importance of the environment. OESA's director and other senior managers sought to enlist the support of the directors who became the object of a power struggle among the staff. When OESA obtained that support—either actively from the US, Canada, and Scandinavia, or passively from Western Europe—it used it to sustain its activities against other factions of the Bank. This initial success, however, did not mean that senior management was unanimously supporting an active involvement of OESA in policy or in project appraisal. As the next chapter shows, even Mahbub ul Haq, the "resident radical" who supported an adoption of this concern, sought to limit the scope of the policy dramatically. The Office was later more successful in pressuring the organization in alliance with non-governmental organizations, as discussed in chapter 5.

Although dramatic changes in the organization's definition of its goals, scope, and even methods have taken place in the 1970s and 1980s, organizational inertia is considerable. As Mason and Asher emphasized, it generally required outside pressure for the Bank to change its strategies. Such was the case with the volume of lending, the appraisal techniques adopted "long after they had become standard practice in the business world," or the use of shadow-price accounting which came "slowly and haltingly." The Bank was "slow to break away" from its early emphasis on capital infrastructure to social needs, or to human resources development. Likewise, its interest in the ecological dimension of development was somewhat "belated" and came, as we have seen in chapter 1, after external pressure.[69] Even when the Bank has had direct experience with the shortcomings of a narrow approach, it was slow in organizing its activities on the basis of what it had learned. The mere fact that it took it twenty-five years to concern itself with an evaluation of its activities underlines its inertia, its concerns for moving money and not offending any party, rather than a commitment to learning. Escott Reid, a former senior Bank official, echoes this phenomenon and the concomitant gap between advocacy and practice that it creates:

> The Bank has an image of an institution predominantly concerned with financing capital goods. Changing this image may in practice be much harder than it sounds. Thus, most of the Bank's official pronouncements emphasizing such aspects as employment, income distribution and nutrition have been more in the nature of general exhortations, and have often been loosely related to operational reality.[70]

Development agencies should be innovative and capable of learning.[71] But the Bank's dependence on its creditors and borrowers, and the professional characteristics of its staff, have prevented it from taking what could be interpreted as long-term risks; they have indeed led to a bureaucratization of the organization with a limited capacity to learn from its errors.

Organizational inertia is restrained by the use of outside consultants who work on a temporary and task-related basis. This gives them considerable freedom of thought and an undeniable influence. Associated with official advisers, they act as a sort of brain-trust that generates ideas for the Bank. They are disproportionately drawn from the United States, or countries which have had a close association with certain developing regions (like France in West Africa, for example). Having a brain-trust, however, does not mean that many of the ideas or criticisms will be readily accepted by the organization; but they serve to strengthen a unit in its bureaucratic battles.[72]

As an organization, the Bank is often more a follower than a leader. It may be a leader among international organizations, but it is more often a follower in terms of awareness of critical problems. The Bank takes few risks. It is a conservative organization which never initiates changes but builds upon the experience of others.[73] Its real contribution is often the development of an economic rationale and of a methodology to tackle new concerns. It has tried to do so in the context of the environment, albeit with little success.

The Role of Leadership

The organization's inertia and bureaucratic resistance, which has plagued the adoption of environmental objectives, have put a premium on strong leadership capable of imposing this new value over a fractioned staff and a divided Board of Directors.

In practice, the World Bank is dominated by senior management. This top-heaviness is accentuated by the location of the Bank in a developed country, away from its clientele. The president and sixteen top managers made policy in the 1970s, a situation basically unchanged.[74] The decision to take environmental impact into account was not taken formally by the Executive Directors, but arose from a consensus between the president, several members of management, and a few individual directors.

With weighted voting giving developed countries a majority on the board (and the U.S. holding a dominant position), one would assume that a few directors would at least exert considerable influence and could easily pressure the Bank into seriously implementing this value.[75] The directors' input, however, is restricted to broad orientations. Their vote on the budget is probably their strongest avenue of influence. When the budget for agriculture comes up, for example, France can ask for more credits for forestry. There is no budget line for the environment, which means that "environmental projects" have to be tacked on to another budget line.

From a broad policy perspective, the directors have significantly influenced the operations of the Bank. Although, as Reid indicates, "[u]ntil about 1970 they did very little to alter the Bank Group in any positive way . . . [f]rom about 1970 on, directors representing donor countries have been reflecting much more the views of their national aid agencies, and they have been playing an increasingly liberal and positive role."[76] This influence was translated into the adoption of social concerns. The expansion of the Bank's activities and of IDA's lending induced its creditors to take a more active interest in its operations. The United States itself has played crucial roles in modifying Bank procedures and in determining the nature of the loans or the recipients targets. This will be discussed in chapter 3.

But the concerns of the directors tend to be diverse and transitory—from financial soundness, volume of lending, and levels of aggregate economic indicators to basic needs, energy, women, and debt—so it is incumbent upon the staff to keep an active role in these areas after their directors' interest has been superseded by other priorities. But not only do the various demands of the directors make it difficult for the organization to pursue consistent goals, the directors also tend to impose on the organization a short-term perspective that is often at odds with the perspective required for the development and implementation of a development strategy.

As in other international bodies, decision-making is based on consensus more than on formal voting. The chairman can determine the sense of a meeting and avoid a vote (unless one is needed for domestic consumption).[77] This often gives the directors power to determine policy without consulting with member states.[78]

But the directors' relationship to the Bank creates difficulties with respect to overseeing the details of the Bank operations. Their short tenure precludes a thorough familiarity with the intricacies of the Bank's development activities. Many staff members believe that it is extremely easy to get anything past the Board—a perception shared by the directors themselves who often have difficulties assessing projects as presented by the staff. These documents are developed in such a way that controversies that might have arisen during appraisal or negotiations are hidden. It is then difficult for the directors or national bureaucracies to identify shortcomings in what they perceive to be "sanitized" reports. One aide even went so far as to say, "McNamara controls the directors and could put anything past them."[79]

Directors do not have access to many of the Bank's internal documents about borrowers (with some exceptions for the American executive director) and consider only those matters which are formally presented by the staff. Their review of a loan takes place toward the end of the cycle, after the negotiations with the host country are completed. As a U.S. Treasury deputy assistant secretary admitted in 1984: ". . . by the time we know about the real guts of a project—which is when the project documents come to us at Treasury—the loan is put together, the negotiations between the country and the bank are over with, and we are in a final yes or no position in terms of economics of the loan and commenting on it after the fact."[80] It is therefore difficult for a single executive director to identify and propose remedies at this late stage of the project unless they are so compelling that a strong economic and environmental case can be made against it and allies found among other directors.[81]

Treasury departments which hold exclusive authority over national executive directors are likely to be more concerned with the financial aspects of the loans than with their environmental impact:

Treasury departments bring to their consideration of MDB [Multilateral Development Banks] loans and policy a primarily financial perspective. They are concerned with rates of return, interest rates, cost overruns and collateral economic policies of the host government such as price controls or tariffs relating to the project. Treasury is likely to favor projects whose financial costs can be projected with greatest certainty. Only secondarily are development objectives considered, and then usually in the economic and financial context of whether the proposal will achieve stated goals. Treasury has traditionally viewed loans for building or creating specific, identifiable things with tangible end-products such as roads, ports or hydro-electric plants as more desirable than loans designed to change social conditions such as population control or health or sanitation programs.[82]

This problem is compounded by the failure of the director's instructions to represent the views of all national agencies concerned. U.S. AID has claimed that there existed no agreed U.S. inter-agency position on environmental issues and on several other matters as well, although coordination has improved under congressional pressure. The French executive director has no contact with the French ministry of the Environment and the latter has no input into his position. The same holds for the United States: the Environmental Protection Agency (EPA) and the Council on Environmental Quality (CEQ) have no contact with the American director. An environmental position can only be articulated through the Bureau of Oceans and International Environment and Scientific Affairs of the Department of State which then must discuss it with Treasury.

Whether it remains true that the staff possesses the initiative, that "[t]he President proposes and the Board accepts, amends, or rejects,"[83] is now more open to question. To be sure, important decisions are still made by the president and influential individuals forming the establishment. But economic retrenchment, an openly active United States, and a turbulent international system tend to dictate the agenda for decision making. The tenure of McNamara, who enjoyed considerable latitude and autonomy, may have been exceptional. Under his successors, the agency has not so highly reflected "the ambitions, objectives, personality, and prejudices of its presidents more than most other institutions."[84] Yet, the role of the executive head remains important.

Successful control of the milieu of the international agency requires that the leadership develop an ideology that "binds and fires the organization's staff in support of objectives." Organizational decisions should "reconcile conflicting interests and perspectives on the basis of upgrading common interests" and result in "an extension of the organization's power and objectives."[85]

Cox and Jacobson and Kay[86] have emphasized how crucial a dynamic organizational leadership is to the success of an international agency and to environmental protection. It ensures internal consistency and cohesiveness and enables the organization to respond quickly to changes in its milieu. Such a function requires great sensitivity to external demands: the leader must be sensitive to opportunities as well as to trends and changes. The expansion in scope and volume that McNamara engineered in the 1970s responded to demands from the main creditors and donors of the organization. Chapter 1 described the important role that McNamara played in putting the Bank at the forefront of all multilateral development banks on the environment, but he and the unit he established could not overcome constraints originating in the staff, the states, and the international system that limited the Bank's effectiveness.

When bureaucratic conflicts over the environment arose, the president became the target of influence, and was forced to mediate. Instead of an initiator, he became the referee among different interpretations of the scope and implementation of the policy. The compromise McNamara reached was translated into the limitations of OESA's size and role. Clausen, who took over at a difficult time in 1981 and faced numerous external challenges, could not change this pattern and was limited to pious rhetoric.

Conclusion

The World Bank shares problems with many other organizations. Like AID, it is subjected to a pressure to commit resources and to the generation of projects by units anxious to increase lending.[87]The bureaucratization of the organization which followed its recent growth, and the increased scrutiny of its operations by creditors, led to distaste for risk which precluded innovation. To fulfill this first objective, the Bank has devised methods of conducting the appraisal and supervision of projects designed to guarantee a predictable milieu.

Does the organization's quest for investment certainty or predictability preclude the achievement of other goals, such as environmental protection? On the one hand, the project approach, centralization tendencies, or lending terms, can impair the promotion of national environmental policies. The rigidity of the organization's rapport with its clientele precludes a successful dialogue, which in turn impedes the Bank's flexibility to respond to the local needs of its borrowers. On the other hand, the refusal by the organization and OESA to consider strict standards reflects the domain of flexibility that it wants to keep for itself in the face of what was first an educational and missionary assignment. Such flexibility encourages compromises with the regional offices or the borrowers, thus developing a more receptive audience for future initiatives.

Yet, the various bureaucratic elements which govern the behavior of the staff ensure that only projects which are likely to materialize in due course as approved loans or credits are likely to benefit from staff efforts. Environmental projects, which are bound to be controversial, are not likely to come from the staff's initiative, but will depend on a strong demand from the borrower. If, in addition, the scarcity of IDA funds means that these projects will only be funded through loans instead of credits, a borrower will be less likely to be willing to brave the multiple clauses that a project should fulfill in order to receive financial support.

Indeed, one of the biggest impediments to growth in the Bank's lending for environmental purposes is not so much the scarcity of environmental support, as it is organizational factors which prevent the successful initiation and completion of the project cycle. The type of projects favored and the different training of the staff made it harder for OESA to have its concerns adopted into the routine tasks of the organization. The tendency to economize on the early identification and preparation stages of the project[88] (a concern which followed a demand for greater efficiency) compounded this problem since these stages are the most crucial for a successful inclusion of environmental concerns into the work of the Bank. Its procedures, OESA's limited manpower, and the absence of environment officers in the regional offices often made it impossible to generate the information needed to make environmentally sound decisions, even when the staff was aware of the importance of these questions.[89]

"What is uncertainty to the organization is sovereignty to the borrower."[90] The following chapter focuses on the attitudes of external actors regarding the Bank's support of environmental concerns because many internal constraints derive from external ones. The Bank has faced conflicting demands from its milieu which it had to reconcile without losing its autonomy. Yet, its history and pronouncements show that it sees itself as a missionary, benefactor, mediator, and educator among international agencies and states. Developed countries are perceived to be unaware of the "true" problems that developing countries face, or oblivious of their legitimate concerns, and to lack generosity. Developing countries are castigated for their short-sightedness, for their inability to develop the political will which would ensure a successful development strategy, and especially for being incapable of developing a needed concern for the environment. The rise in the influence of international non-governmental organizations is viewed suspiciously, while support from the financial community is courted assiduously.

3

External Constraints on Bank Policy

In this chapter, we turn from the internal dimensions of the World Bank's environmental policy to an examination of the international context in which the formulation and implementation of environmental policy takes place. With whom does the Bank interact? Which specific problems, or opportunities, did these actors present to the Bank's attempts to incorporate a new environmental dimension into its development thinking? In answering these questions, we will consider the nature of the Bank's organization-set, and discuss the attitude of these actors toward the Bank's policy.

The Nature of the Bank's Organization-set

The Bank's task-environment comprises essentially two sets of interactions: the "organization-set" of the Bank,[1] and the "causal texture" of the environment[2] (see figure 3.1). The first set (solid lines) is evidenced through the attitudes of the various actors in the Bank's task-environment toward its newly-found environmental concerns. It includes influential developed countries and sub-sets of them (the United States executive and legislative branches, Scandinavia, France, Japan, West Germany, United Kingdom), developing countries (expecially the largest borrowers: India, Brazil, Bangladesh, Mexico, Indonesia, Pakistan), the financial communities of the United States, Japan, and Western Europe, key international organizations (FAO, UNESCO, WHO, ILO, UNEP), a few international non-governmental organizations (mostly American), and the most important bilateral aid agencies. Although the type of organizations that define the set remains constant, the specific actors will, of course, vary according to the issue-area in question.

The second set of interactions refers to the context of the policy (as shown by the broken lines in figure 3.1). Obviously, the Bank's activities do not take place in a vacuum: the relations that take place among the actors that compose the Bank's organization-set influence the definition and implementation of Bank policies. For example, did the North-South

Figure 3.1.: The World Bank's Organization-Set

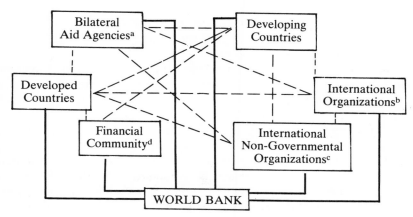

For example:

(a) Agency for International Development (U.S.), Caisse Centrale de Coopération Economique (France), German Technical Assistance Cooperation (West Germany), Overseas Development Administration (U.K.), and Swedish International Development Authority.

(b) Food and Agricultural Organization, International Labor Organization, United Nations Environment Programme, World Health Organization, United Nations Educational, Scientific and Cultural Organization, and United Nations Development Programme.

(c) Environment Defense Fund (U.S.), National Wildlife Federation (U.S.), International Institute for Environment and Development (U.K.), Sierra Club International (U.S.), Natural Resources Defense Council (U.S.), Resources for the Future (U.S.), World Resources Institute (U.S.), Survival International (U.S.), and Energy Probe (Canada).

(d) Developed countries' financial markets, international banks.

negotiations, the LDCs' debt problems, and conflict among LDCs impede the Bank's ability to predict the behavior of its task-environment and affect support for environmental issues?

In general, the various pressures that other actors put on the Bank called into question both the object and content of its environmental policy. To one degree or another, they took the position that:

1. this policy is irrelevant: developing countries do not have environmental problems, or if they do, their magnitude does not justify domestic action or external pressures.
2. it means a waste of scarce resources for developing countries to invest in environmental project.
3. Developing countries cannot afford the additional expense;
4. the Bank's business is development, not environmental protection; it should do what it knows how to do best;

5. countries are sovereign actors and therefore responsible for determining their own environmental policies;
6. the scope of the policy is too narrow, or too broad;
7. the Bank does not have the resources to devise, implement, and integrate this concern with its other goals;
8. the Bank is not doing enough to protect the environment or to maintain the conditions for "fair" trade and competition by harmonizing environmental standards.

The Developing Countries

The history of the developing countries' attitudes toward the environmental dimension of their development is characterized by scepticism mixed with a gradual recognition of the importance of this issue. This slow evolution from earlier antagonism was accomplished at some costs, not the least of which was a dilution of the issue. On the whole, they have largely succeeded in imposing their definition of the problem on the international community.

The developing countries' reaction to the environmental issue revolves around four major attitudes: defensiveness, formulation of demands, redefinition of the problem, and gradual recognition of its importance.[3] These four major themes correspond to stages in the evolution of developing countries' thinking, although, depending on the individual country, they can be found concomitantly.

DEFENSIVENESS

The initial attitude that developing countries held toward environmental issues was largely negative. The 1972 MIT Report on the *Limits to Growth*[4] was perceived as implicitly denying the foundations of the development creed. Its conclusions questioned two basic notions behind the development goal: a limitless availability of global resources, and reliance on technology for economic growth and the exploitation of resources. The analysis pointed to the rapid exhaustion of resources, a fall in food production, and increased pollution indirectly of directly resulting from development and population growth. Reacting against the implications of this report as well as to more extreme views, developing countries denied that any problem existed or that it applied to them. They denounced the issue as a ploy to thwart their own development prospects.

Thus, the developing world argued that environmental problems—which developed countries mostly defined in terms of pollution—only affected the industrialized countries since, by definition, the economies of developing countries were not advanced enough to engender similar problems. They also argued that environmentalism, born among Western middle classes, was a concept alien to the poor of the developing world who struggled for survival: "Aren't poverty and need the most important pollutions? . . . How can we talk to villagers and slum-dwellers of the need to protect the air, the ocean and rivers when their own life is contaminated? The Environment cannot be improved in conditions of poverty."[5] The fight against poverty must take precedence. Focusing on the environment would jeopardize a country's economic growth and condemn people to permanent and extreme poverty. This perception was encouraged by analyses such as the MIT simulations or *The Ecologist's* "Blueprint for Survival," which seemed to argue that developing countries should forgo rapid economic development and limit population growth drastically.[6]

In fact, developing countries would argue, environmental protection rests on economic growth: "The priority of developing countries [is] development. Until the gap between poor and rich countries [is] substantially narrowed, little if any progress [can] be made in improving the human environment."[7] In the early 1970s, they believed that growth only would enable them to afford costly anti-pollution measures that were bound to hurt their trade positions.

Environmental issues, therefore, should not provide developed countries with a pretext for diminishing development aid. On the contrary:

> Brazil's position is that economic development, in quantitative terms, conditions qualitative social development; it is important for developed countries to give priority to economic development, and to consider social projects only when their non-satisfaction would jeopardize development itself. In other words, development should not be negatively affected by the concern, exaggerated at times, for environmental protection.[8]

Thus, in 1971, not only was there "little awareness of environmental problems among the peoples of developing countries, or among their government administrators," but, preoccupied with the development of their resources, "there [appeared] to be apprehension that the social and economic costs of environmental protection [might] very well outweigh the benefits."[9]

Defensiveness, therefore, rests on what Boardman has called "the central dilemma of international conservation,"[10] the assumption that environmental protection and human welfare are mutually exclusive goals. This perception of a trade-off between economic growth and environmental protection derived from a perspective which lumped together all facets of the environmental problems of the Third World. Only by "splitting" the issue could a more balanced definition of the problem be achieved. This was to come later. At Founex (1971) and Stockholm (1972), the developing countries formulated demands in the hope of alleviating the consequences of this perceived trade-off.

DEMANDS

One set of demands sought to minimize the negative economic impact of environmental issues (the additionality and compensation principles, aid and trade relationships); a second set of demands sought to preserve the developing countries' opportunity for development by protecting their access to basic resources (asking developed countries to moderate their resource consumption, or stressing the concept of the "common heritage of mankind").

On the eve of the Stockholm Conference, their worries lay on three grounds: (1) environmental protection would prevent developing countries from externalizing the environmental costs of industrialization (although Europeans had been able to do so during their industrial revolution), thereby increasing the costs of production, which, in turn, would affect their trade prospect; (2) national environmental standards would be costly to implement; and (3) environmental standards set up by developed countries, to which most third world trade was directed, would impose discriminatory non-tariff barriers on their exports. The first two issues evolved into the "principle of additionality," the last into the "principle of compensation."

Originating at the 1971 Founex meeting, the additionality principle was formally included as Principle 12 of the Declaration of the United Nations Conference on the Human Environment adopted at Stockholm in 1972:

> Resources should be made available to preserve and improve the environment, taking into account the circumstances and particular requirements of developing countries and any costs which may emanate from their incorporating environmental safeguards into their development planning and the need for making available to them, upon their request, additional international technical assistance for this purpose.[11]

Additionality could therefore be interpreted as encompassing not only the additional costs of specific environmental measures introduced into development projects, but also additional funds for Official Development Assistance (ODA) to meet the environmental problems of the developing countries. This issue was prominent within the Bank: both its economists and the borrowers feared that adding the environmental safeguard to Bank projects would be costly: "These steps will increase the costs of development in our countries; and surely we have the right to expect assistance in meeting those additional costs."[12]

Since the Bank does not formally make grants, poor countries were reluctant to invest into a sector which would increase their debt without increasing their revenues and their ability to service their debt. Thus, Malawi was adamantly denouncing in 1970 ". . . advice, or rather lectures, for which we have not asked—What we do not want is to be told that money will be provided only if we take certain actions which we ourselves consider unnecessary and which involve expenditures we can ill afford." [13]

Considerations of sovereignty compounded the problem. Recipients objected to linking aid to environmental safeguards in development projects, and saw these attempts as interfering with their exclusive jurisdiction over their natural resources, a principle formally embodied in the 1974 Charter of Economic Rights and Duties of States. [14]

Thus, early opposition to the Bank's policy stemmed not so much from the Bank's decision to lend in this area (a decision made later in 1975), or from opposition to taking environmental parameters into account in development planning, but from making environmental protection an *additional* condition for lending. Araujo Castro, a former Brazilian ambassador to the United States, expressed the strong displeasure of developing countries with the Bank's decision. For him, the basic problem related to sovereignty:

> But each country must evolve its own development plans, exploit its own resources as it thinks suitable, and define its own environmental standards. The idea of having such priorities and standards imposed on individual countries or groups of countries, on either a multilateral or a bilateral basis, is very hard to accept. . . . Ecological policies should rather be inserted into the framework of national development. [15]

This position was shared by Latin American countries which, like Brazil, saw in the calls for environmental protection a plot to destroy a booming economy. Fifteen years after Stockholm, Latin America remains largely deaf to these concerns, although some evolution has taken place.

The compensation principle grew out of the non-tariff barriers issue. Reiterating a complaint that figured prominently in their call for a new international economic order, developing countries claimed they had to be "compensated" either financially or through trade advantages, for the diminished competitiveness of their products:

> The environmental policies of all States should enhance and not adversely affect the present or future development potential of developing countries, nor should they hamper the attainment of better living conditions for all, and appropriate steps should be taken by States and international organizations with a view of reaching agreement on meeting the possible national and international economic consequences resulting from the application of environmental measures. [16]

In particular, recommendation 103 proposed:

> . . . that where environmental concerns lead to restrictions on trade, or to stricter environmental standards with negative effects on exports, particularly from developing countries, appropriate measures for compensation should be worked out within the framework of existing contractual and institutional arrangement and any new such arrangements that can be worked out in the future.[17]

The Newly Industrializing Countries (NICs) feared further deterioration of their terms of trade, a declining demand for their products stemming from increased recycling or substitution, and higher production costs. The apprehensions of the developing countries centered around the fear that environmental measures could be sudden, arbitrary, discriminatory, and serve protectionist lobbies in the developed countries.[18]

This leads to the question of standards. On the one hand, developing countries argued for the development of common standards with respect to the product itself in order to avoid discrimination. On the other hand, they contended their own industry standards (related to the production process) should be laxer since their environmental conditions, technical expertise, and priorities, differed.[19] Third World countries maintained that they held a comparative advantage: they could become pollution havens precisely in those cases where their human and ecological absorptive capacities surpassed that of the developed countries.[20] The World Bank, therefore, should not promote industrywide standards. The resulting actions of the Bank gave them only partial satisfaction. The organization subscribed to the absorptive capacity argument but emphasized the working environment.

In addition to attempts to minimize the perceived costs of environmental protection by invoking the additionality, compensation, and sovereignty principles; developing countries attempted to turn the arguments about resources limits and global welfare against the developed countries themselves:

> It appears that the absorptive capacity of the world environment has reached or will soon reach the saturation point and that it is important that industrialized nations reduce or completely stop, their exploitation of natural resources (water, air, soil). A similar necessity does not apply to the developing nations. Industrialized countries should, however, reduce their own aggression against nature well under their historical share.[21]

Since there is unequal consumption of resources, there should be unequal liability over their use. An extension of that argument was found in the promotion of the concept of the "common heritage of mankind," promoted chiefly through the Third United Nations Conference on the Law of the Sea. Ecuador, for example, also called for the conservation of resources for *all* the parties to whom they belong, and not only for those who exploit them.[22]

A REDEFINITION OF THE PROBLEM

These arguments are linked to an attempt to redefine the problem of environmental protection in light of developing countries' situations, reacting to what they perceived as a strong bias toward the developed countries' definition of the problem chiefly in terms of pollution and resources exploitation. The landmark for such a redefinition was a 1971 meeting at Founex, Switzerland. Founex solved the perceived trade-off between environment and development by enlarging the scope of developing countries' environmental problems to include human welfare. Twenty-seven experts in the fields of environment and development met at the request of Maurice Strong, Secretary General of the Conference, to formulate guidelines for the inclusion of development concerns into the agenda and problématique of UNCHE, and prevent a split between developed and developing countries which would doom the conference.

The report concluded first that environmental factors could not be dissociated from any development strategy. Developing countries could not concern themselves with the "quality of life" as long as life itself was endangered. The environment only added another dimension to development; it did not substitute for it; ". . . environmental concern is only another dimension of the problem in the developing countries and cannot be viewed separately from their development efforts."[23]

Second, environmental problems, the report suggested, have a dual origin. They are the direct effects of poverty (leading to population pressure, soil erosion, deforestation, surface water pollution, shortage of arable land, and health problems), as well as the consequence of unchecked industrialization. For the developing countries, the first cause was more important and more prevalent than the second. Efforts should therefore be directed toward improving water sewerage and health, as well as increasing development aid. A corollary of the additionality principle was thus uncovered: development assistance should be greatly increased to cover the costs of a massive attack against the environment attributes of poverty;[24] "In their context, development [became] essentially a cure for their major environmental problems."[25]

Defining environmental problems as primarily resulting from poverty had one drawback: environmental ills were equated with the problem of human welfare. This redefinition was politically useful as it demonstrated to the Third World the relevance of environmental issues. While ensuring that not only upper class interests would be fulfilled,[26] it also diluted the meaning and object of environmental protection, complicated its implementation, and ensured that a whole series of environmental problems would be ignored. In practice, it made the environment divisible and forced the policy-maker to choose among what was redefined as competing environmental goals. Thus, according to the developing countries, rather than adopting strictly scientific or technical criteria—which would give politically insensitive experts inordinate influence over policy—environmental policies should reflect broader socio-economic concerns. This attempt to redefine the problem in humanistic terms was emphatically summed up by Araujo Castro: "From the point of view of man—and we have no other standpoint—Man, Pascal's 'roseau pensant', is still more relevant than Nature."[27]

The Founex report also stressed "The importance of establishing adequate safeguards and standards in project planning and preparation," while underlining demands for additional and compensatory financing and urging respect for the sovereignty of Third World nations.[28] The Bank policy of considering environmental impact as a condition for lending was thus upheld. In this context, the report announced two basic recommendations that should govern project appraisal. The first concerned environmental guidelines:

> The developing countries should formulate specific guidelines for project appraisal, taking into account environmental considerations. The social costs and benefits of projects, including their favorable and unfavorable impact on environment, should be fully reflected in these guidelines.[29]

Since the report emphasized national sovereignty, it was only natural that these recommendations be formulated with reference to the developing countries themselves. But since project appraisal is the prerogative of the Bank, this recommendation also pointed toward the need for Multilateral Development Banks (MDBs) to elaborate guidelines which would ensure a consistent implementation of this concern across projects.

The second recommendation sought to prevent an arbitrary imposition of environmental measures by stressing: "It would be undesirable that rigid guidelines for project appraisal from an environmental viewpoint be laid down by multilateral or bilateral donors at this stage, without consultations with the developing countries through various appropriate forums."[30] These forums would preferably be regional organizations where these countries' interests could permeate policy-making better.

The Founex approach was largely adopted at Stockholm as a compromise between the different concerns of the developed and developing countries and was incorporated into the Declaration, Principles and Recommendations issued by the conference.

This redefinition of the origins of the problem and of the object of environmental policies naturally identified the areas in which the developing countries would approve of the Bank's involvement. As Recommendation 1 of UNCHE underlines:

> All development agencies, such as . . . the International Bank for Reconstruction and Development . . . should in their development assistance activities also give high priority within available resources to requests from Governments for assistance in the planning of human settlements, notably in housing, transportation, water, sewerage and public health, the improvement of transitional urban settlements and the provision and maintenance of essential community services . . .[31]

These concerns were reflected in several global conferences, and developing countries became interested in projects involving air and water pollution control, reforestation, erosion control, disease vector control, natural disasters, and urban improvements. The Bank had already moved or was going to move into most of these areas. Responding to similar suggestions, USAID was also to place greater emphasis upon the environmental determinants of agricultural production, as the importance of this sector for development became clearer during the 1970s.

The basic analysis of the Founex report became the Bank's standard definition of the problem, often espoused by the adviser and largely reflected in Bank publications. There are two explanations for this.

The first relates to the Bank's organizational interests in its clients and goals. It had to demonstrate the relevance of environmental issues to nonindustrialized countries. Second, this analysis largely originated within the Bank. Mahbub ul Haq, then special adviser to President McNamara and later director for policy planning, had the prime responsibility for drafting the report and used its conclusions in his own book. Although he promoted environmental concerns within the Bank, he did so in the narrow perspective of direct impact on the success of the project itself. An irrigation project would always prevail over a national park.[32] Defining the problem in terms of trade-offs between development and environment, life and quality of life, basic needs and natural assets, present and future, Mahbub ul Haq always chose the first term, and thus articulated the opinions of many members of the Founex group who were ardent supporters of the developing countries' demands for a new international economic order.[33]

As in other policy areas, the definition of the problem remained the object of the greatest amount of controversy. The developing countries were successful in presenting their environmental problems as rooted in underdevelopment and in centering any environmental policy around humanistic and utilitarian concerns. The definition the Bank adopted was, therefore, an attempt to direct its environmental concern toward certain areas which could be reconciled with the organization's goal and basic needs objectives, and which could be assured of least opposition from its clients.

RECOGNITION

The recognition by developing countries of the environmental dimension of development stems from several factors. One is the gradual accumulation of evidence of the extent of their ecological problems. At the time of the Founex meeting, they were also beginning to analyze their environmental situation critically. Kenya, for example, stressed the distinction between growth and development, and, along with Trinidad, denounced the numerous side-effects of tourism.[34] Mexico and Kuwait emphasized the environmental costs of industrialization. Urban problems too were worsening: "We were skeptical two years ago. The Industrialized nations' concerns for pollution seemed another obstacle to our material progress. Now we recognize that all of us have a large stake in the matter, and we are committed to the search for a way out of the human predicament."[35]

Droughts, soil erosion, and food deficits placed a new emphasis upon agriculture and underlined its ecological limits. They uncovered problems of forestry, soil conservation, and genetic diversity, and provided the impetus behind global sensitization conferences on water or desertification. The negative impact of a strict engineering outlook was evident in well-known failures of large dam projects, such as the Colombian hydroelectrical project of Anchicaya where problems of sedimentation and extensive deforestation considerably decreased the lifetime of the project, while increased pollution, protests against flooding local municipalities, and settlement problems, made it dangerously politically sensitive.[36]

Another factor in the evolution of these countries, apart from the specific Bank measures and strategies used and discussed in chapter 4, stems from their realization that the environment could be used to further long-standing issues between them and the World Bank Group. Developing countries have traditionally asked for more soft loans through IDA, for larger financing of local currency costs, and for a greater share of procurements.[37] Arguing for environmental projects or components became an indirect means to achieve a positive resolution of these long standing issues without requiring the Bank to formulate a general policy on the subject.

Thus, the Founex report suggested that the environmental concern be used to bypass the strict requirements of the Bank and increase lending for social sectors. It would provide an opportunity "to escape from the tyranny of financial rates of return," "to seek broader international support for their social programs," and "to obtain a greater amount of local currency financing."[38] It is from this perspective that we can understand Mauritius' desire that more IDA funds be allocated to projects based on the "quality of life" concepts.[39] The earlier statement by the Governor of Trinidad and Tobago is also pertinent to this argument, since in his mind, the additional funds to which developing countries would be entitled for meeting their environmental problems would come in the form of local cost financing and on concessional terms. Thus, by tying the new environmental issue to old ends, the poorer countries were able to further both.

A third factor in the evolution and maturation of this attitude was the gradual recognition that many of the developing countries' initial fears would not materialize. The Founex report was written when international economic prospects were still good. The subsequent crisis forced countries to narrow the scope of their environmental concern to the direct environmental determinants of growth. This shift from protection or enhancement of the environment toward management and the need for sustainable development was also general among international agencies concerned with the environment (such as IUCN and UNEP).[40]

The gradual recognition that the compensation and additionality principles were losing relevance contributed to the alleviation of these fears. In 1976, an UNCTAD study reported that non-tariff barriers due to domestic environmental measures mostly affected trade among developed countries rather than developing countries.[41] Moreover, the worsening international economic situation also encouraged Western countries to lift or relax environmental restrictions. Two years later, a more political and informal meeting of mostly Southern experts on the trade aspects of environmental policies and measures identified some problems, particularly in the agricultural sector (pesticides, packaging, labelling, metallic and sulphuring content). The impact on exports, was nevertheless still deemed to be minimal.

On the contrary, the hope of benefiting from a redeployment of industrial opportunities from the North to the South materialized, in part, although on a limited scale. Developing countries gained a certain comparative advantage from the developed countries' anti-pollution measures which tend to be stricter or better enforced. But this advantage did not lead to a massive emigration of industries to the South for two reasons. First, environmental cost considerations are rarely prominent in corporate decisions to relocate. The operating costs and lower productivity of many industries in the South surpass the benefits that can be drawn from relaxed environmental standards. Secondly, developed countries have also tended to subsidize their industries for meeting those added costs through various tax incentives.[42] Relocation was therefore limited.

Not only has the compensation principle been defused, but the additionality one became less salient. To be sure, the developing countries still insisted on obtaining additional assistance for environmental measures.

The Strategy for the Third Development Decade, for example, reiterated the need for "bilateral and multilateral donors [to] consider, within the overall financing of projects in developing countries and at their request, meeting the cost of taking environmental aspects into account in the design and completion of such projects.[43] Current calls for increased assistance to meet environmental costs, however, are made amidst a greater scarcity of multilateral funds and new international efforts by the donors to harmonize their environmental policies, while developing countries realize that these expenditures will be necessary and are often cheaper than expected.[44] On the whole, the fears that the developed countries would divert funds from aid flows to meet their own environmental cost proved unfounded.[45]

Developing countries have come a long way on the environmental issue since Stockholm. Indeed, a "revolution in third world attitudes toward environmental protection" took place in the 1970s,[46] with UNEP ascribing most of this success to interactions between developing countries and national and international organizations concerned with development. Although great differences exist among them, awareness of the ecological parameters of development have grown as the Newly Industrializing Countries (NICs) became richer and more polluted, and as the relative impact of other countries' environmental catastrophes (floods, erosion, food deficits, health problems) increased while their own needs kept rising. Their governments' commitments to environmental protection were dramatized in their constitutions (India, Indonesia, Papua New Guinea, Pakistan, Madagascar) or were included in basic development plans (Nepal, Costa Rica, Botswana). Between 1972 and 1980, for example, the number of Third World government agencies with some sort of environmental responsibility rose from 11 to 102.

This evolution was finally reflected in the Strategy for the Third Development Decade which the UN adopted in December 1980. The goals and objectives of the strategy included the familiar subordination of environmental improvement to development, but also recognized the interrelationship between development, environment, population, and resources.[47] And it added:

> It is essential to avoid environmental degradation and give future generations the benefit of a sound environment. There is a need to ensure an economic development process which is environmentally sustainable over the long run and which protects the ecological balance. Determined efforts must be made to prevent deforestation, erosion, soil degradation and desertification. International cooperation in environmental protection should be increased.[48]

Health and nutrition problems were later acknowledged to depend on the "ecological soundness of development activities" and on the "integrity and productivity of the environment."[49]

This represented a considerable evolution since Stockholm. Although on the one hand, developing countries still tended to subordinate environmental protection to economic development, they now recognized the interdependence of these goals:

> The issue before us today . . . is not that of human well-being but of human survival. Through thoughtless projects of development and over-exploitation, worsened by consequences of mass poverty and infinite malpractices, havoc has been spread across the whole spectrum of the natural environment. There is no doubt whatsoever that continuation of the current trends will lead to total collapse. Those trends must be halted; and where possible reversed.[50]

Protection and rehabilitation are growing in importance. The developing countries could expect some help in agriculture-related environmental problems which, they acknowledged, could not solely be attributed to poverty, but also to bad practices.[51] For the first time, they recognized the needs of future generations. This was a far cry from Mahbub ul Haq's claim that they could not afford to think of future generations when the present ones were imperiled.

The notion of sustainable development points to the concept of ecodevelopment that UNEP has promoted since the mid-1970s. Ecodevelopment defines the problem not in terms of a trade-off between environment and development, but as the search for an appropriate pattern of development. Ecodevelopment means that "development should be ecologically sustainable; appropriate in terms of both the ecological relationships and constraints of a bioregion and its local cultures and energy resources; and should take account of and provide for nature conservation . . ."[52]

This rhetoric was adopted by the Bank. One of the first speeches of A.W. Clausen upon assuming office in 1981 focused on the environmental determinants of sustainable development—to which the Bank gives a broader meaning—and linked it to the goals of the organization he now headed: "Environmental spoliation is an international concern. It erodes hard-won economic gains and thus the hopes of the poor."[53] The "environmental" problems he identified were mineral resources depletion, population growth, urban air pollution, deforestation, and erosion. Continuing a persistent theme of McNamara's addresses, population growth was therefore considered to cause environmental degradation and thus constituted an "environmental" problem. Anything designed to alleviate it and its impact could be considered "environmental" projects, such as population planning, water sewerage and waste removal, and low-cost provision of energy.

Although recognition that population, resources, environmental, and economic questions were interrelated could justify undertaking environmental activities once considered low priority, it also further diluted and restricted the problem: reasoning in terms of environmental questions enabled the Bank and developing countries to justify much of their current actions as well as direct greater attention to long-standing concerns. Population growth causes poverty that in turn causes ecological damages. As the President of Kenya exclaimed: There is no doubt that poverty is a principal sponsoring mechanism of continued and desperate destruction of basic natural resources. . . . [T]he direct relationship between widespread poverty and environmental degradation cannot, and must not be, ignored."[54]

If positive feedbacks do exist among these four variables, so do trade-offs. Developing countries can therefore still define progress as dominance over nature. Their problem, as they see it, is to free themselves from the calamities they have endured for centuries and from their dependence on natural cycles. Per capita incomes and food availability in Africa have diminished since Stockholm. International development assistance has also become more scarce in the 1980s. Environmental programs were the first to be set aside or scaled down when these countries' resources diminished, or were abandoned in the face of domestic opposition.

The sheer number of new environmental agencies, just like the existence of standards, does not, of course, ensure results. Apart from the continuing subordination of the maintenance of critical environmental resources to short-term economic goals, a serious problem remains "the inability of government institutions to implement the more enlightened, environmentally sensitive policies which increasingly characterize current long-term development plans."[55] The adoption of unrealistic goals for political purposes compounded that problem. Coordination among governmental units and development projects is poor. Technical personnel is limited. Administrative resources and the authority and ability to enforce decisions are also limited, especially in Africa.[56] Laws and regulations designed to protect forests or manage parks and wildlife protection, for example, are rarely implemented in Asia where most of the people do not share the elites' perception of the need for better environmental management.[57] Nepal, which is facing grave deforestation problems, may be an exception.

Differences in environmental perceptions among developing countries are substantial. Africa's ecological catastrophes have forced many African countries to consider environmental constraints to development much more seriously than Latin America, which remains suspicious of the concept and is essentially concerned with preserving its economic achievements.[58] The tendency in developed countries to link concerns for Third World ecosystems to commercial issues has contributed to this perception. Halting the destruction of tropical forests, for example, also helps support the U.S. wood industry threatened by the availability of cheap wood pulp from the Third World. The same congressional panels still have a tendency to apply U.S. standards to the rest of the world out of commercial concerns.[59]

Yet, while developing countries may not have wholeheartedly endorsed the concept of environmental protection or rehabilitation when they face difficult political and economic choices, awareness of the adverse economic and social impact of environmental neglect has increased considerably. Even in countries which are strongly criticized for "needlessly" destroying their natural resources, a significant segment of the bureaucracy opposes these policies, as in Brazil or Indonesia. Indigenous organizations have sprung up in support of environmental protection and have developed ties with transnational non-governmental organizations to that end. But international support and endorsement of the political goals of these non-governmental organizations—which argue for "popular participation" in development decisions—associated with the protectionist overtones of some of the actions proposed, will create difficulties for the further implementation of this new value.

The Developed Countries

The developing countries' problem was to find a way to use the new environmental issue to protect their economic advantages and help them achieve the objectives of the Second Development Decade. For the developed countries, the problem was to minimize the negative impact of their own domestic environmental measures upon their international commercial positions, find a way to spread the costs of environmental protection, and respond to domestic pressures to take international actions to protect "Spaceship Earth." Until Stockholm, the developed countries had defined the environmental problem as an industrial pollution problem that required global cooperation.[60] They strongly supported data collection programs, such as UNEP's Global Environment Monitoring System (GEMS) and International Register of Potentially Toxic Chemicals (IRPTC), or international scientific undertakings, such as UNESCO's Man and the Biosphere program, which was carried out by researchers from these countries.

References to ecological problems in UN forums after Stockholm illustrated the diverging interests underlying the identification of the most pressing environmental problems. Table 3.1 shows that the developed countries were more interested in pollution control than developing countries, and especially more than the poorest countries which concentrated on food increases.[61] North America overwhelmingly emphasized pollution: of U.S. speeches in the United Nations General Assembly from 1968 to 1972 and in 1976 which mentioned ecological problems, 67 percent cited

Table 3.1.: Percentages of Speeches Mentioning Ecological Problems During Three UNGA Sessions: 1968, 1972, and 1976.

Geographical region	Environment (general)	Food	Population	Pollution	Resources, energy	Water, soil, etc.	Human settlements
North America	33	33	33	67	0	0	0
Western Europe	38	30	24	7	11	2	8
Soviet bloc	28	8	0	4	4	4	0
Latin America	25	16	16	16	10	8	3
Middle East	13	11	6	13	4	4	6
South Asia	26	26	21	11	5	11	11
Far East	15	19	16	3	6	0	3
Africa	16	16	10	11	6	6	7
Oceania	38	38	38	25	13	13	13
Level of Development							
Developed	30	29	20	11	10	5	7
Developing	19	14	13	13	8	5	5
Least Developed	14	20	9	8	2	6	6
World	21	19	14	12	7	5	6

SOURCE: Marvin Soroos, 1979: 15. © 1979, International Studies Association. Reprinted by permission of the International Studies Association, Byrnes International Center, University of South Carolina, Columbia, South Carolina.

pollution, whereas only 7 percent of Western European speeches did. On the other hand, the figures for food were 33 percent and 30 percent respectively. For the developing countries, food was the problem, although it was sometimes associated with population and pollution issues. Concern for pollution increased along with the level of development. Although the concerns of the industrialized world have since somewhat shifted toward natural resources and energy, the direction of environmental awareness would strongly favor agricultural ecosystems and related activities.

Stockholm, however, forced the developed countries to realize that gaining support for what interested them would require addressing the development issue and accepting the dual explanation of environmental problems in developing countries. They still strongly opposed the additionality and compensation principles, and claimed the latter violated the General Agreement on Tariffs and Trade (GATT).

The industrialized nations were concerned with transborder pollution and the effects of a lack of national environmental protection measures upon the global environment. They tended to agree that varying national assimilation capacities and political choices justified different national norms, but it was also clear that states could inflict external costs on others. The Organization for Economic Cooperation and Development (OECD) developed the "polluter pays principle" precisely as a means of assigning automatic liability for transborder pollution. These countries also shared the developing nations' concerns with trade discrimination based on environmental standards. Pollution control was therefore generally regarded as a potential source of tension among countries sharing natural resources.

Thus, whereas the environmental problems of the developing nations were defined nationally, the industrialized countries tended to define them internationally, as problems of cooperation and harmonization of norms. This focus on pollution and health, derived from the developed countries' perspective, was reflected in the first Bank loans for strict environmental purposes which dealt with water and air pollution control. The problems linked to overtaxed agro-ecosystems were only slowly identified and supported in separate projects.

Despite the promotion of environmental issues by several industrialized countries, discussed in chapter 1, only Japan mentioned this problem in 1970 and urged Third World nations to pay more attention to the improvement of the quality of life.[62] In fact, mention of the new environmental concerns of the Bank have been rare over the years. Several developing nations (Tunisia, Indonesia, Mauritius, Trinidad, Venezuela) voiced their interest in general terms, while few developed countries expressed their concern (Japan, Norway, Italy, the Netherlands did). This lack of reference to the environment in the annual meetings of the Board of Governors indicates that the organization was able to avoid controversy in this area and that tacit support existed for the Bank's careful approach.

The developed countries preferred handling the issue in the Bank quietly because, as Cohn suggests in reference to population problems, multilateral channels enable supporting states to be less easily identified with controversial issues.[63] The organization had apparently reassured both sides that its actions would not depart dramatically from past practices, and would be aimed primarily at improving its current activities. Above all, it had managed to keep the costs of added environmental measures down (between 0 and 3 percent of the total project costs),[64] so that Italy could openly support the Bank's environmental activities:

> Especially commendable is the concern shown by the Bank for the problems of the human environment and experience to date has shown that it is possible to reduce the dangers of environmental damages at a moderate cost. This has important implications for all countries, as it shows that the preservation of the environment is not incompatible with continued economic progress.[65]

This rhetorical neglect of environmental issues by the very countries which favored them also points to the relativity of their support. Several countries (West Germany, Japan, France), although not opposed to an inclusion of environmental criteria into the Bank's work, favored limiting the institution to its primary role of provider of capital for specific development projects appraised on strict financial grounds. The United States and Scandinavian countries were actively supporting this new value, while others remained more neutral, or less strident. The United States and Sweden, as in the population issues, initially adopted the most extreme positions, advocating conditioning funding upon the implementation and enforcement of strict standards. The U.S. government, however, quickly chose not to lead in pressing for institutional and multilateral arrangements. Other interests (population, energy) and diplomatic considerations explain this weakening of U.S. leadership which coincided "with a general decline and retreat of the U.S. from a leadership role across all of the UN system."[66]

Splits among developed countries were not restricted to environmental issues. There have been differences over the United States' bias against loans to public Development Finance Companies (DFCs) and to public manufacturing and mining industries, over American opposition to lending for the development and exportation of certain agricultural products, over specific borrowers, and over lending criteria (such as human rights).[67] On the whole, however, their role as donors impose certain positions which promote cohesiveness.

The five principal developed countries (the United States, United Kingdom, Japan, Federal Republic of Germany, and France) are the donors who provide the Bank with most of its financial capital. They account for nearly three-quarters of IDA's finances and contribute almost half of the IBRD usable paid-in capital. By forgoing dividends on this capital, they are also responsible for two-thirds of its reserves. Their citizens and central banks hold most of the outstanding bonds the Bank has sold. Almost all of the rest of its resources comes from other richer countries with a couple of exceptions (India and China). For example, four countries (France, Italy, Canada, the United States) contributed nearly 80 percent of the Sub-Saharan African Facility credits in 1986.[68]

Besides weighted voting (they possess over 40 percent of the voting shares), two other factors compound this dominance. First, the Executive Directors interpret the Article of Agreements, subject to appeals by the governors. Thus, the constitution of the Bank is what the governors, or more frequently the Executive Directors, say it is. This flexibility, from which the environmental sector has benefited, also gives final word to richer countries.[69] Second, the organization must negotiate IDA replenishments periodically:

> The Bank has been endowed by governments, and in consequence was relatively independent of governments. This is the great advantage of endowments: they foster autonomy and independence. But when IDA was founded, the Bank Group had to join the long line of agencies and institutions soliciting national governments for grants. This has made the Bank Group dependent, as it had not been before, on the good will of the governments which are the major contributors to IDA, especially the six largest contributors, who are responsible for 4/5 of IDA 's resources . . .[70]

This became a major source of uncertainty for the Bank. The American attempts since the late 1970s to influence more closely the operations of the Bank provide perhaps the most salient example of attempts to exercise leverage through IDA replenishments. The sixth replenishment of IDA (IDA VI), for example, was approved in December 1978 by the Carter administration and thirty-two other donors after months of negotiations, and was to have gone into effect on 1 July 1980. Congress, however, failed to authorize the U.S. share.[71] Although the Bank struck a temporary compromise whereby other donors tied the Bank over with a "bridging arrangement," the agreement could not go into effect without U.S. participation. Many Congressmen pushed for a renegotiation of IDA VI "to reduce the U.S. burden and force philosophical changes in bank lending policies."[72] Not only delays, but reduced appropriations beset IDA under the Reagan administration which also tried to influence the lending criteria of the Bank.[73]

In the mid-1980s, congressional committees and American non-governmental organizations used the same strategy in hopes of effecting changes in the Bank's environmental policy. The large number of hearings criticizing the policy, and the spill-over of these concerns into the debates of the Appropriations Committees threatened to hold IDA VIII hostage to tangible demonstrations of the Bank's willingness to heed the advice and criticisms of the American legislature. This will be further discussed in chapter 5.

Although IDA replenishments and negotiations over the Bank's capital increases are important avenues for United States' influence over the general policies of the Bank—or that of any developed country—policy toward the organization is also formulated and implemented at a number of different stages in the loan cycle, including overall policy and program planning, approval of individual loans, and evaluation of on-going or completed projects.[74] The process of review and approval of individual loans is a relatively more passive and incremental way of influencing Bank Policy, compared to the leverage held by donors when negotiating future contributions. The Executive Directors influence policy not when they approve or reject a loan—which rarely happens since negotiations with the borrowing country are completed at this stage—but through the comments and concerns they express.[75] Since the directors originate in and are controlled by their respective Ministries of Finance, however, they are likely to favor financial criteria over social ones.

The U.S. Executive branch will therefore constitute another potent source of uncertainty. Controversies erupted in the 1980s over the Office of Management and Budget's proposed foreign-aid cuts, and over American attempts to expand the institution's support for private investments and private enterprise in the borrowing countries, associated to a desire to limit the role of the state in the belief that "[i]n general, private ownership and free markets are the best institutions to avoid the 'tragedy of the commons' and to protect the interests of future generations."[76] Environmentalists have convincingly argued in favor of the "government imperative," that is, the idea that governments have a central role to play in remedying and preventing environmental damage.[77] The domestic political interests of Third World countries have encouraged their reliance on the state as an instrument of political consolidation and social and economic progress, a role that the Bank indeed has supported. To argue in favor of market solutions to environmental problems restricted the scope of the policy to a few industrial pollution problems, ignored the specific context of the implementation of such a policy, and ensured that the Bank's role in promoting environmental conservation through governments would remain secondary to its political and economic missions.

The formal requirement of the *Articles of Agreement* that finance ministries be the sole interlocutors of the Bank has become less relevant to the more diverse goals of the organization. The U.S. Treasury is still the dominant agency involved with Bank policies, although an inter-agency group which includes representatives of the State Department's Bureau of Oceans and International Scientific and Environmental Affairs (BOISEA), reviews each project.[78] Excluded are the Council on Environmental Quality (CEQ) and the Environmental Protection Agency (EPA), which have no official input into the U.S. executive director's position on environmental matters. BOISEA itself has access to the U.S. executive director only through Treasury and must cooperate with the State department's Bureau of Economic and Business Affairs which coordinates overall MDB policy with Treasury. Despite considerable change in the nature of the Bank in the last quarter century that has necessitated better inter-agency coordination, Treasury has retained exclusive authority to instruct the U.S. representative to that organization.[79]

The other executive directors have greater discretion in deciding to raise issues and approve a loan. Because of a lack of time and personnel, projects are not usually reviewed by an executive director's home office unless new instructions are needed. Furthermore, although named by their respective finance ministries, a few are instructed by their national economic cooperation ministry as well. Most national development agencies, however, do not share AID's dedication to the environmental limits of development.

Another set of constraints pertains to activities that developed countries would like the World Bank to emphasize or ignore. For example, the U.S. is opposed to projects designed to promote the production of goods which would compete with U.S. production on world markets. The Mathias Amendment, for example, prohibits the U.S. executive director from supporting palm oil projects.[80] The U.S. also opposes loans for citrus crops (the Bank has not made loans in that area), sugar (there is a surplus on world markets), or steel (unless it is for domestic consumption only). Although these loans can be approved over the objections of the U.S. director, the staff understands these conditions, and such loans rarely come up for approval.[81] As for more blatant political pressures, formally forbidden, the United States has preferred working informally with management rather than through legislative restrictions.

Despite the influence of its Third World clientele, the direction of Bank loans also reflects the dominance of the developed countries. The Bank was directed to use "appropriate technology," and pay attention to the role of women in development and to environmental issues. It was urged to increase lending for energy and mineral resources. To gain French support for IDA and the special sub-saharan African credit facility, for example, the Bank has had to pay special attention to West Africa, as well as consider forestry and desertification projects. Indonesia was favored in the 1960s as Japan and the United States wanted to support new non-communist regimes. According to Reid, the high level of lending to Thailand, Taiwan, and South Korea reflected the U.S. political interest in those countries at the time.[82] Various decisions announced in 1986 illustrated this tendency, ranging from massive loans to Mexico and Brazil to enable them to service their debt, to the commitment of $600 million for the economic recovery of the Philippines, and to reserving 45 percent of the expected IDA credits for the period 1987 to 1990 for sub-sahara Africa, and 30 percent for China and India.

The general organizational dilemma reflected in the receptivity of management to some political pressures was pathetically raised by the Chilean governor in 1972, before Allende's fall, when international financial institutions had canceled all loans and demanded immediate repayment:

> This dilemma with which the Bank appears to be confronted, between the desirability of not creating problems with any of its sources of funds, and on the other hand its obligation to pursue its fundamental purposes of cooperating in the efforts of the developing nations to achieve social change and economic growth, just has to be solved. . . . The World Bank cannot be an instrument of bilateral policy of any of its member countries.[83]

Other factors, some of them described in chapter 2, have tended to increase the autonomy of the organization. Lack of time and familiarity with the issues, lack of access to data held by the organization, conflicts among donors, and their propensity to seek contracts for their own national firms prevent then from micro-managing the institution. The United States can be very powerful, but it generally must form a coalition with the other important members of the organization to effect change. Although the Bank president has always been American, as has one third of the staff, and despite the size of the American voting share, other donors have become increasingly influential, especially Japan and oil-rich nations. The inability of the United States to use the Bank for blatant political purposes testifies to that trend. The various IDA replenishment and capital increase negotiations remain important vehicles for shaping Bank policy.[84] As the most important source of funds, the United States' support remains indispensable.

With the decline of America's relative dominance, however, U.S. administrations and the Congress are less willing to forego short-term economic gains for long-term political objectives, and so have tended to be more critical and impose more constraints on the institution.[85] Environmental issues have provided the U.S. Congress with an opportunity to raise again questions of "accountability."[86] But what is "accountability" to the Congress is "dependence" to the organization and subservience or political intrusion to its members.

The Financial Community

Although developed countries share many of the financial considerations of the financial community, their broader political perspective often forces them to rank strict financial criteria below political aims. In the case of the International Development Banks (IDBs), for example, the United States had been willing to subordinate short-term economic objectives to long-term political goals when its first goal was to use development against the spread of communism.[87]

The financial community which buys the World Bank's bonds, however, emphasizes strict financing criteria such as rates of return, low local financing, the overall economic policy of the country, or creditworthiness. Its main concern lies with preventing social concerns from diminishing the financial benefits of the projects. It tends therefore to emphasize with the developing countries the existence of a trade-off between a healthy environment and economic development, and to consider the latter as conditioning the achievement of the former. But the similarity between the their positions does not extend far, for the developing countries have not condemned all social projects or components. On the contrary, they have strongly pushed for more education, health, and water supply projects. The financial community, on the other hand, has preferred large infrastructural projects in more solvent countries, usually the NICs.

The financial resources of IBRD itself come from a few financial markets (excluding interests on capital and investments). Government subscriptions serve only to guarantee the Bank's solvency in case of major defaults. Consequently, one of the first objectives of the institution during the 1950s was to build the credit of its bonds in financial markets. President Eugene Black, through a policy of strict financial criteria, successfully achieved the best ratings for the Bank's bonds on the U.S. market. His task, as he characterized it, was to make "international development financing respectable."[88]

Conscious of its extreme dependence upon New York—where it raised most of its funds during the 1950s, the only major market then available—the Bank, as other countries' economies grew, endeavored to develop external markets for its securities with private and public institutions. Thus, the 1960s and 1970s saw a diversification of the Bank's financial sources. In the 1970s, for example, Germany, Switzerland, Japan, and several OPEC countries became important sources of funds. The sources of the Bank's outstanding debt as of 30 June 1986 are given in table 3.2.

The evolution is striking. No longer does the United States dominate

Table 3.2.: Sources of the World Bank's Outstanding Debt in percentages

Country	1971	1979	1986
United States	38.00	21.68	26.43
Japan	8.00	13.49	24.81
Germany	27.00	25.41	17.97
Switzerland	5.00	15.53	17.12
Other	22.00	23.89[a]	13.67[a]

SOURCES: E. Rotberg, 1979: 4; *Annual Reports*, 1971: 39, 1986, 172. Reprinted by permission of the World Bank.
[a] Includes OPEC members.

Bank borrowing. Germany and Japan have become important markets as well. As Rotberg emphasized, this policy of diversification consciously stemmed from the reluctance of the Bank to be in a position of relying on one particular market for the resources needed to support its lending program. For not only can domestic economic problems prevent Bank access to a particular market at any time (in cases of a shortage of capital, for example), but governments can easily bar it from borrowing on their own market.

To protect its sources of funds, the Bank must give substantial guarantees to potential investors. One of them is the government guarantee provided by its members. Another is its record. The Bank has never formally lost money on its loans, does not engage in debt rescheduling, and is profitable. Finally, it can insist on strict criteria to evaluate its projects and the borrowers' qualifications. The financial community, for example, has insisted that the Bank's credit be kept separate from that of IDA. The restriction of IBRD lending to creditworthy countries and for conventional loans is primarily designed to preserve the marketability of its bonds.[89] This, in turn, tends to prevent the presidents from responding very positively to developing countries' demands for more soft loans and for a relaxation of the conditions attached to them. We have seen in chapter 2 that these very conditions may also constrain the expansion of lending into the environmental sector.

The financial community has never supported the increasing attention paid to the environment which it considered and unproductive investment. The Bank avoided strong opposition by using their own financial language to justify this move, and introducing changes only gradually. Indeed, the expansion of social programs under McNamara made the financial community a bit uneasy, and private bankers wished to see this evolution somewhat curbed. McNamara's successor, A. W. Clausen—whose nomination represented a return to the private banking sector from which three of the four preceding presidents came—was criticized for sharing the broad "social orientation" of McNamara.[90] Nevertheless, his appointment signaled a period of consolidation in the scope of the activities of the organization. The selection of the head of the Bank of America responded to the need to gain the confidence of the financial markets where the Bank was going to turn for major future borrowings. His tenure saw the adoption of stricter lending terms and a remarkable expansion of the international financial role of the Bank in the form of structural adjustment lending and closer cooperation with the International Monetary Fund in the formation of international aid packages to the heaviest debtors.

The Bank's image must remain conservative. The real threat of defaults on the part of several large debtors compounds the constant need to reassure the lenders that it manages its financial affairs with great prudence. The importance of this support and the tightrope on which the president is forced to walk are illustrated by what happened early in McNamara's presidency: "When McNamara. . . announced that he wanted to shake up the Bank's operations, some of the underwriters to an envisaged Bank placement in Switzerland became nervous and withdrew, causing the borrowing offer to be withdrawn."[91] At the same time, it also helps steer its activities toward protecting its past investments. Lending for very large projects, for example, enables them to service past loans.[92] Halting disbursements on environmental grounds then becomes much more difficult.

International Governmental Organizations

Although the Bank and the United Nations now seem to have reached a modus vivendi, their relations remain tense. Though formally part of the UN system, the two Bretton Woods institutions have always kept their distance from the United Nations Economic and Social Council. In its early years, when the Bank was dominated by central banks and private investors to a greater extent than today, it viewed itself as autonomous from the UN system. Concerned with securing a stable source of funds in the capital markets, "the Bank felt that too close an association with the United Nations, regarded as a political body, might increase the difficulty of making itself known and trusted and thus adversely affect its ability to raise funds."[93]

As a new Third World majority came to control ECOSOC, the new independent countries sought to place the Bank under strict UN supervision to balance what they saw as undue Western influence in the working of an organization on which much of their future depended. The Bank's relatively autonomous source of financing and resources, its organization and its clear mandate, enabled it to resist those pressures successfully. On the other hand, these attributes also made it more vulnerable and open to attacks. It was criticized for being an agency of the industrialized countries, for being too narrow in its conception of development and of the needs of the developing countries, and for its agents' arrogance in their relations with its clients. The United Nations Development Programme (UNDP) and regional development banks were created in direct reaction to this perceived Western orientation. The same countries later raised many of the same issues under the call for a New International Economic Order. Pressures once again were geared toward giving the Bank's clients greater influence in the organization's decision-making process.

With the growth of the regional banks and bilateral aid agencies, competition entered the field of development assistance. Tendler, for example, described how the World Bank and the Inter-American Development Bank "have engaged in an informal competition with each other for project borrowers in Latin America by offering concessions to the potential borrower on financing terms and encouraging their own technicians to help get the borrower before the other bank did."[94] As mentioned in chapter 2, this had definite consequences for the Bank's environmental policy. On the one hand, it gave it an incentive for diversifying and expanding the scope of its activities into areas of interest to developing countries (such as education and health) which a client-oriented bank like IDB was already supporting. On the other hand, the Bank is pressured to soften its lending criteria when other banks do not apply similar ones, thereby stifling the expansion of its environmental activities.

IGOs have been involved in environmental protection from a very early stage and have even promoted these values independently of governments. Before Stockholm, various international bodies launched uncoordinated programs of research and cooperation on environmental problems. UNEP, starting in 1973, sought to provide some direction to these efforts but the competition for this new domain was keen. Given the breadth of the concept, nearly every agency of the UN system is involved with environmental matters in some way or another. UNESCO which emphasizes environmental research and education, sponsors the Man and Biosphere (MAB) program as well as numerous environmental studies and training programs. It ranked first in 1979 in total amount of funds committed by UNEP for implementing UNEP funded projects.[95] The Food and Agriculture organization (FAO), which ranked second, has great expertise in soil conservation, erosion, forestry, genetic resources, and pesticides. The World Meteorological Organization (WMO) monitors the global climate assessment program of UNEP, while the World Health Organization (WHO) is concerned with environmental diseases. For example, the United Nations Conference on Trade and Development (UNCTAD) performs economic studies and the International Labour Organization pays closer attention to working conditions. Among UN agencies, however, one of the least involved and cooperating with UNEP is the United Nations Development Programme (UNDP). It implemented only one UNEP project in 1979, and none in

1978. Given UNEP's focus on development and environment, this lack of cooperation may seem surprising and seems to derive from the lack of enthusiasm of UNDP and its clients.

This multiple involvement points up the tremendous pressures for task-expansion that these organizations encountered in the 1960s and 1970s. These pressures, of which the creation of UNDP and the expansion of the Bank scope and activities are but two examples, came not only from the developed and developing countries, but also from the organizations' own desire to appropriate new domains. As policy concerns diversified, more programs were set up, and more demands were made on the institutions. As FAO, UNESCO, WHO, and ILO began to turn to technical assistance and operational activities, they were brought closer to the Bank's area of activity.

The Bank, during that period, was also broadening its conception of development to encompass "special" projects. The evolution of the Bank into a broad-scale development agency, not only financing projects but providing technical assistance, intruded into other UN agencies' domains. The Bank's own involvement in the agricultural sector, education, water supply and sewerage, basic needs; in problems of the environment, water, desertification, food supply, population growth, human settlements, or employment maximization, attest to the diversification of the tasks of UN agencies. This general growth naturally led to jurisdictional overlaps, as well as to an intense competition among UN agencies.[96]

Many attempts to coordinate the activities of the system proved futile. The unification of a system's domain under a specific agency might be detrimental to the achievement of certain so-called "global values," since different international agencies are controlled by different coalitions. UNDP, being very much client-oriented, would be likely to implement a program that gives preeminence to these countries' short-term outlook. The same is somewhat true of the World Bank. The extremely broad scope of the environmental agenda coupled with a scarcity of resources would lead to the neglect of whole areas of concern or to the adoption of too broad a perspective (e.g., UNEP). Overlap ensures pluralism in the specific approach to development or environmental problems and is more conducive to an implementation of multiple values and perspectives which reflect the varied concerns and attributes of the international community.

The negative reaction produced by the new social concerns of the Bank also stemmed from its past record of poor relations with other IGOs. Both George Woods (with his promotion of the educational and agricultural sectors) and Robert McNamara (with his articulation of population growth and employment concerns) have greatly contributed to smoother relations with UNESCO, FAO, ILO, and WHO.[97] The Bank's move into sectors which are more remote from its expertise has forced it to cooperate more

fully with other agencies on whose domain it treads, and on whose expertise it often depends. As three international development strategies
emphasized the individual and collective contributions that these organizations could make to the welfare of humanity, and with the development of
cooperative programs since the 1950s and early 1960s, the relations between the Bank and other agencies improved somewhat. But much of the
Bank's negative attitude toward other agencies remains, and despite improvements in the Bank's relations with other international organizations,
the latter still perceive arrogance and contempt for organizations it deems
less knowledgeable and efficient:

> The [other agencies] believe that these officers are not really willing to
> share power or responsibility with the other agencies, but are constantly
> trying to extend the authority of the Bank Group over areas which are of
> primary concern to other agencies; and that when they talk to other
> agencies about aid coordination, they mean subservience to Bank Group
> Policies, enforced by the fact that the Bank Group has large resources to
> lend and the others have not.[98]

The existence of formal cooperation agreements does not necessarily
indicate smooth relations. Indeed, if these agreements exist, it is precisely
because these organizations could not informally agree on their mutual
activities. Agreements are more the outgrowth of conflict than the embodi-
ment of cooperation.

Rather than question the capabilities of these institutions and refuse any
relationship with them, the Bank has adopted a more missionary attitude
in its dealing with other agencies as they provide it with the opportunity to
spread its appraisal methodology across the system. It also realized the
benefits that it could gain from this cooperation: other agencies' studies
and experimental projects provided a basis for future Bank loans. The relationship with UNDP, for example, is centered around UNDP's role as a
pre- investment agency. Its experimental funding leads to the identification
of suitable projects which are then financed by the Bank.

When the Bank announced its willingness to consider environmental
criteria in its project appraisals and to fund environmental projects, many
of these organizations approached this new situation with mixed emotions.
On the one hand, the Bank would be competing with them using its greater
leverage effectively to displace them. But it could also provide them
with an opportunity to influence the work of the Bank and to associate it
with their own projects.

The main organizations with which the Bank is in contact with respect to
environmental matters are UNEP, FAO, WHO, UNESCO, and ILO. Despite the Bank's extensive field experience and operational scope, these
organizations co- finance few projects. In practice, their input resides most-

ly at the identification and preparation stages of the project. In short, they often run the risks in experimental projects that the Bank is not willing to take. The International Fund for Agricultural Development (IFAD), for example, which is administered by FAO, has co-financed several agricultural and rural development projects. On the other hand, UNEP does not use the Bank as its implementating agency. Their main relation lies at the technical level and at the preinvestment stages.

The Bank collaborates with WHO for the water supply and sewerage sector, with FAO for forestry projects, with UNESCO on education. The ILO is concerned with the factory environment as well as with basic needs. UNEP is interested in using the Bank to support its attempts to institute international environmental cooperation and gain acceptance for its rationale and goals, especially for the concept of ecodevelopment. But whereas other agencies are concerned with preventing the Bank from displacing them in the field, UNEP's wants the Bank to increase its environmental activities, such as protection of ecosystems, desertification projects, or forestry. UNEP also wants to influence the content of the projects themselves, the type of development being promoted, as well as convince the Bank to pay more attention to matters which concern it, such as pesticides. Its executive director has not hesitated to denounce publicly the Bank's limited efforts in carrying out its environmental pledges. Mostafa Tolba deplored the Bank's failure to hold a training course at the Bank's Economic Development Institute and the lack of meaningful action toward integrating environmental principles into development.[99]

UNEP's ecodevelopment strategy calls for developing specific solutions to local problems, using local technology or technology adapted to local requirements, and emphasizes self-reliance.[100] The ecological basis of this concept presumably puts it at odds with the Bank's model of economic development. For example, extensive export-oriented monoculture is condemned in favor of diversified subsistence agriculture. It emphasizes as well the anthropological limits to development change, where cultural preservation is often as important as environmental protection. These ideas were endorsed by many developing countries in the 1974 Cocoyoc Declaration[101] which called for the elaboration of new approaches to development, including "imaginative research in alternative consumption patterns, technological life-styles, land-use strategies, as well as institutional frameworks and educational requirements to sustain them." It became one of the chief goals of UNEP.

This concept also found a receptive ear among developing countries because it re-emphasized the primacy of *national* variables and national concerns over policies of internationalization, uniform patterns, and commercial openness promoted by the international development community. Since it draws upon more radical conceptions of development, there is a clear potential for conflict with the Bank. UNEP, however, has played down total reliance on this concept in favor of sustainability and environmental soundness. Cocoyoc also stressed the need to redirect development to the satisfaction of basic human needs, a milder version of a radical concept which the Bank adopted in the mid-seventies.

International Non-Governmental Organizations

International agencies have developed close relations with INGOs for two basic reasons. Either they wished to call on their expertise (e.g., UNESCO), or they wished to overcome their isolation and lack of clout by forming transnational alliances with organizations whose members could press for the agency's goals at the national level, or both. UNEP, for example, has a remarkably close relationship with a host of environmentally oriented INGOs with which it collaborates through the Environmental Liaison Centre.

The International Council of Scientific Unions (ICSU) through its Scientific Committee on Problems of the Environment (SCOPE) played a crucial role in mobilizing the international community behind environmental issues in the 1960s.[102] National and international scientific organizations have since collaborated actively with international organizations in this field. These organizations have continued setting much of the environmental agenda and have provided rival sources of information that national governments were often reluctant to research or release.

Compared to other agencies of the United Nations, the Bank historically has not worked closely with International Non-Governmental Organizations. The absence of close relations stemmed primarily from the Bank's activities: for a long time, few INGOs could provide it with expertise it did not possess.

Regarding broad development issues, a formal World Bank-INGO dialogue started in 1980, although there had been informal and project-specific collaboration in the 1970s. INGOs have thought to gain grants and be closely involved with the identification and implementation of projects. There has, however, been considerable resistance to closer collaboration with these organizations. The Bank was accused of "drawing out" a general dialogue for public relations purposes, and of remaining unwilling to discuss its own policies or use instances of happenstance cooperation in order to institutionalize INGOs' input and fund their projects.[103]

The Bank did not turn to INGOs when it started lending for water supply and sewerage, health, or education, since knowledgeable UN agencies already had extensive technical assistance in these areas. But when it undertook the task of evaluating the environmental impact of some of its projects, it had to turn to other organizations. UNEP and national environmental agencies lacked experience. The Bank thus turned to the International Union for the Conservation of Nature and Natural Resources (IUCN) and to organizations affiliated with the Scientific Committee on Problems of the Environment (SCOPE) of the International Council of Scientific Unions (ICSU). IUCN is an organization that emphasizes conservation, but its neglect of development issues prevented it from playing a larger role in the Third World.[104] Thus, it welcomed cooperation with the Bank since that provided it with an opportunity to learn how to reconcile conservation and development.[105]

More than IUCN or SCOPE, which provided scientific and technical assistance, the International Institute for Environment and Development (IIED) has influenced the Bank's objectives through Barbara Ward, its founder and first president. Her influence over McNamara ensured that the INGO perspective would be given consideration. As a non-profit foundation, IIED links the UN to other institutions, national governments, and INGOs. It thus functions as a useful intermediary among multiple organizations, facilitating a broad development-environment dialogue, while conducting its own research studies. IIED is both concerned with development and environment, and does not see any trade-off between the two.

The Bank supports a small part of the work of IIED to which it gives grants for specific projects—Earthscan, science and technology—or for unrestricted purposes.[106] The appointment of William Clark, former vice-president of the Bank for external affairs, as President in 1980, illustrated the close links between the two organizations. After having conducted a study of the environmental activities of multilateral banks in 1979,[107] IIED argued for greater environmental coordination among them and promoted the idea that environmental considerations must be brought early into the planning stages of development organizations. It was instrumental in convincing the Bank to try harmonizing the environmental activities of multilateral development institutions, which eventually led to the adoption of the 1980 Declaration of Environmental Policies and Procedures Relating to Economic Development, discussed in chapter 4.

Many older INGOs reflect the views of the scientific community. Others are activist organizations. All serve to mobilize popular support. As they are called upon by the Bank to study specific environmental aspects of its projects, they can influence its environmental ideas and practices.

Brian Johnson observed in 1972 that the scientific community was divided between those who believe that there is a most urgent need for action, and those asking for more knowledge first, in the form of data collection, research, and monitoring.[108] The Bank's environmental policy has clearly emphasized the former perspective. This is partly due to its requirement to fund specific projects, partly due to its bestowing loans and not grants, and partly due to its narrow mitigation perspective.

Since it did not concern itself in the beginning with the wise national management of natural resources, it found no need to develop the data base to support it. Although many Western governments emphasized information gathering on pollutants, they and most developing nations also feared the political implications of this knowledge and have been reluctant to press international agencies in that direction. Lack of data has, however, been identified as a primary impediment to sound environmental action.[109] Urged to incorporate environmental considerations early in development planning, the Bank announced in 1985 a cooperative program with NASA and UNEP's Global Resource Information and Data System aimed at evaluating better national resource-bases and environmental systems. Such knowledge would later be incorporated in country economic and sector work and would support both the identification of exploitable resources and the environmental framework of modernization programs.

INGOs, therefore, provide the Bank with a very useful link to the scientific community and with information which its own resources cannot generate. They supply a pool of external assistance and consultants and are less likely than international agencies to put demands on the organization's policies as a condition for cooperation. INGOs do not have to share the Bank's information or be associated with the details of the Bank's projects and programs.

In its attempts to disseminate its value among other units of the Bank and among governments, the OESA relied heavily on scientific organizations to educate other parties, and increasingly on broader environmental conservation organizations, such as Sierra Club International, the National Wildlife Federation, or the Natural Resources Defense Council to mobilize external suppport.

After the domestic arena and the challenge of AID's activities, these organizations turned their attention to the Multilateral Development Banks in the early 1980s. They have been quite successful at setting the agenda—for example, the protection of native populations—at generating information on project implementation and, above all, at mobilizing political support in the United States for a condemnation of the Bank policies and a specific set of reforms.[110] However, the OESA has let an ambiguous genie out of the bottle. These organizations have been extremely critical of the Bank's environmental record although they have spared the OESA. Their excellent access to Congress and their capacity to use dramatic examples to generate public protest were clearly evidenced in numerous hearings between 1983 and 1987 and during the 1986 annual meetings of the World Bank and IMF in Washington. There they organized a demonstration against the Bank's support for tropical deforestation projects.

The Bank has had difficulties responding to this challenge. These organizations are likely to hold both a reformist political perspective—which focuses on income and land distribution and citizen participation—and a narrower environmental perspective that emphasizes preservation and conservation, or unchallenged scientific criteria in the formulation of policy. They pay minimal attention to the political and economic dimensions of the solutions they advance or to the contradictions they may contain—for example, between citizen participation and the protection of natural resources. Although they have claimed that their goal has only been to force the Bank to fulfill its environmental pledge, the protectionist and political overtones of their arguments and their ability to form transnational coalitions,[111] have also unsettled many Third World governments. Their aim is to gain better access to information internally generated by the Bank and to be associated early in the decision-making process by claiming that they can be either "allies or enemies" in Congress. This also threatens the autonomy of the organization.

Closer links with INGOs are bound to cause problems for the Bank in its relations with its Third World clientele and the financial community. Closer attention to ecological arguments also threatens the achievement of other goals, such as capital transfer, that the Bank is pressed both by its creditors and borrowers to undertake. But their political success in a period of funding uncertainty for IDA and IBRD has forced it to pay greater attention to their actions. Congress threatened to hold IDA replenishments hostage to an improvement of the Bank's environmental commitment.[112] In a December 1987 draft report, the Bank acknowledged the influence of INGOs, on some of its environmental activities and on its joint reflection on this issue with the International Monetary Fund. Chapter 6 details INGOs' actions regarding tropical deforestation and the protection of indigenous populations and their impact on the policy of the organization.

The Bilateral Agencies

Like Multilateral Development Banks (MDBs), bilateral aid agencies compete with the Bank for good projects. Compared to the Bank, their autonomy is very slim, and the political character of the allocation of their aid provides a clear indication of the priorities of their governments. Bilateral aid agencies also differ widely in their attention to environmental questions. With the exception of AID, bilateral agencies have not been as concerned with the environmental consequences of their projects as the Bank has been. This neglect reflects national variations in the evaluation of the importance of these activities; the lower volume of aid given; and, above all, the political nature of their activities, which entails refraining from imposing measures to which the recipient is strongly opposed. Because aid is also a means to boost the donors' exports, the latter are not likely to promote standards that would make it so much more expensive for the recipient to borrow that it would turn elsewhere.

On the other hand, they could play a significant role in promoting environmentally sound development policies. Because the technical and financial standards of these agencies are looser than the Bank's, they have the opportunity to venture into experimental projects as well as backing them with extensive technical support. Several national aid agencies—such as the British Overseas Economic Cooperation Fund or the French Ministry of Cooperation—also enjoy special access to many countries' policy-making apparatus, which helps them promote specific policies and improve institution-building.

National aid agencies, therefore, are both potential competitors and potential partners of the Bank. They can undermine the Bank's programs, but they can also help it achieve its objectives and cooperate with it on national development goals. One example of cooperation is the increasing joint financing of Bank projects. About one-third of all projects approved in FY 1986 were to be co-financed, with bilateral agencies contributing 52 percent of the amount of co-financing.[113] But the advantages of co-financing, greater financial capacity to influence more projects and risk-taking, has not been translated into widespread action in favor of the environment. Few have had an environmental component. With the exception of French agencies that participated in a couple of reforestation and soil conservation projects, bilateral agencies have not used their participation in Bank projects as a conduit for improving the Bank's environmental performance.[114] Moreover, the most important bilateral agencies tend to concentrate on specific areas for political and historical reasons (the French agencies on Africa, the British on Commonwealth countries). Projects implemented by richer borrowers are rarely co-financed (e.g., in Latin America), even though environmental degradation may be acute in these regions. Finally, many of the same agencies whose work often rests on extensive technical familiarity with certain regions are reluctant to share their knowledge with outsiders.[115]

Although co-financing with the USAID has been minimal—$9.4 million for six projects in FY 1986—much collaboration has taken place at headquarters and in the field. The Bank rapidly moved to take the lead in poverty alleviation projects after Congress mandated in 1973 that U.S. foreign assistance concentrate on the needs of the poor.[116] Although it would be difficult to demonstrate a causal relationship, the informal ties between the two agencies, the resources of AID, and the importance of the U.S. government, easily led to a parallel evolution.

USAID's environmental mandate is broader and more demanding than that of the Bank.[117] In 1977, Congress gave USAID its first explicit mandate to help developing countries protect and manage their environment and national resources. In 1983, it was the first development agency to receive a direct conservation mandate. Appropriate projects concerned watershed protection and reforestation, soil conservation, the protection of wildlife habitat, water pollution control, resource surveys and training.[118] Although not equally active in all these areas (wildlife protection projects are minimal), USAID has made a definite effort to achieve "a leadership position within the international donor community on environmental protection."[119] Congress mandated USAID to conduct environmental assessments and impact studies for *each* project it finances. It singled out deforestation and soil erosion in 1978 and 1979 as most pressing problems. Furthermore, it funds data collection, national environmental assessments, or technical projects which the Bank finds harder to justify. Perhaps more than the Bank, USAID has been conscious of the political and institutional obstacles to the success of its program in developing countries,[120] and pledged to support environmental and natural resource institution-building and strengthen existing agencies.

Relations between the Bank and USAID, on the one hand, and the Bank and other bilateral donor agencies, on the other, are therefore likely to differ markedly. The Bank's problem with other agencies is promoting either its environmental perspective so as to avoid being undercut, or selective implementation of environmental concerns since these agencies often favor a specific class of recipients. But it finds in the USAID a useful complement to its own activities as USAID funding is more flexible: it can supplement that of the Bank (by conducting technical studies, for example) or help environmental projects succeed by building up environmental institutions, providing basic data and outside experts, or making available to the Bank their country environmental profiles.

Thus, even though USAID and the Bank can have strong disagreements and harbor deep suspicions toward one another—USAID viewed the Bank as a potential threat to its own population program—close collaboration with USAID's Environmental coordinator can effectively promote an environmental perspective within these organizations, as well as among developing countries, bilateral, and multilateral development institutions. Although growing, collaboration has been limited so far. Because USAID has been forced to pay closer attention to the environmental impact of the projects it funds, its experience has given proponents of these requirements stronger incentives and arguments in support of an extension of USAID's approach to the Multilateral Development Banks. The two organizations, however, have different organization-sets; face different constraints; and, therefore, hold different priorities and conceptions of their role.

The Policy Context: The Causal Texture

The Bank implements its environmental policy first by altering directly its relations with the actors that compose its organization-set. Favorable outcomes also depend on the extent to which it can change or control the context of the policy in which these relations take place.[121] This contextual variable refers to what Emery and Trist have called "causal texture." The causal texture of an organization's milieu is the pattern of interactions among the actors in the organization-set which create an area of uncertainty around the outcomes of its policies.[122]

The first dramatic example of the Bank's vulnerability to contextual change arose from the decision to finance European reconstruction through the Marshall Plan. Thus, it was later forced to change its primary goals from reconstruction to development and focus on the developing countries.[123] The subsequent involvement of the Bank as a mediator in certain political disputes—between India and Pakistan, for example—indicated its desire to preserve its leadership position among lenders and recipients.

The specific context of the Bank's environmental policy is the evolving relations between developing and developed countries, and the state of the international economy. Two of the demands formulated under the call for a New International Economic Order (NIEO) directly concerned the Bank: increased aid, and greater participation in the decision-making of international financial institutions. The recurrent call for an NIEO provided the Third World with a tremendous asset: unity. Despite marked differences among them, developing countries achieved a diplomatic cohesiveness in various forums that enabled them to articulate and press their demands forcefully.

This cohesiveness was apparent at Stockholm; and UNEP later provided another forum where international economic inequalities could be denounced and financial support for development sought. Indeed, Third World countries in the 1970s linked most environmental problems to the existence of North-South economic inequalities and to their state of economic dependence. The 1974 Cocoyoc Declaration blamed richer countries for the wasteful destruction and exploitation of the natural resources of Third World countries. Control of international markets allows them to obtain cheap raw materials and "indulge in careless and extravagant use" of them, preempt a disproportionate share of key resources, and affect resource use and depletion by virtue of their high consumption per capita.[125] Cocoyoc attempted to redefine development around the satisfaction of basic needs "to ensure the quality of life for all with a productive base compatible with the needs of future generations."[126] But only each individual country could define and pursue this quality of life as it best thought. It was therefore impossible to divorce environmental issues from larger questions of international political economy.

The Cocoyoc Declaration also reaffirmed national sovereignty over natural resources. This principle figured prominently in the "Charter of Economic Rights and Duties of States" adopted later that year, and its extreme enunciation triggered strong opposition from Western countries because it gave Third World countries the right of nationalization, a symbol of domestic power against which the Bank has long battled. Article 2 bore directly on international efforts to remedy environmental ills: "Every State has and shall freely exercise full permanent sovereignty, including possession, use and disposal, over all its wealth, natural resources and economic activities." [127] The World Bank was thus denied any legitimacy for enforcing environmental criteria or promoting its concerns through conditional funding. Rather, Article 30 urged all States to establish their own environmental and developmental policies in conformity with the responsibility of protecting, preserving, and enhancing the environment for the present and future generations.

Turbulence took three forms in the 1970s and 1980s: a more unstable international economy, the advent of a conservative and critical U.S. administration, and growing international initiatives in favor of global and Third World environmental protection.

The international economic woes of the 1970s and 1980s increased the unpredictability of the policy context. The developing countries suffered two shocks in the 1970s. One was the rise in oil prices which dearly hurt their balance of payments and put more pressure on wood and animal sources of energy, in part worsening deforestation and fertilizer problems. The other was the rise in grain prices at a time when many developing countries had become net importers of grain. Food shortages also tended to put more pressure on agricultural ecosystems, while population growth continued practically unabated. These factors also influenced Bank lending, which increasingly emphasized agriculture and energy production. This, in turn, provided new opportunities for, and impediments to, the promotion of an environmental awareness.

In the 1970s, the availability of petrodollars and the growing needs of developing countries for foreign exchange led to a sharp increase in lending from private banks, which threatened to diminish the relative importance of the Bank as a supplier of capital. But the recession of the late 1970s and early 1980s placed many developing countries in precarious financial positions. Demand for their goods diminished. Commodity prices kept falling, while interest rates increased along with the burden of servicing their debt. After an extremely dazzling sequence of "shocks"—oil shock (1979), increasing value of the dollar (1981 to 1986), and oil counter-shock (1986)—production growth rates diminished, per capita income fell, and indebtedness reached new highs. Protectionist tendencies threatened the exports of the more dynamic among them, while private capital transfers virtually dried up.

Although awareness of the urgency of the environmental dimension of development grew during that period, especially among the top political class, it became more difficult to act on it. The development bureaucracies had few incentives to implement the rhetoric of their political leadership. Rather, the problem was to maintain the economic gains of the previous decade, prevent a political explosion, and fulfill the immediate needs of the population. Not only the scarcity of funds, but a worsening economic situation implied a growing reluctance to institute regulations which would impede growth. A short-term economic and political perspective was emphasized at the expense of long-term ecological planning, precisely at a time when many developing countries were becoming conscious of the needs for such actions. New issues had emerged prominently: loss of land due to salinity from irrigation systems, erosion and overgrazing, deforestation, extinction of species, overfishing, dangers associated with the use of pesticides and declining availability of potable water. But only environmental activities which could be shown to be positively linked directly to economic growth could be contemplated. Even UNEP had difficulty obtaining from developed countries the minimal funds it was awarded at Stockholm.[128]

The election of Ronald Reagan ushered in a period of extreme turbulence for the organization. Not only was the international economy causing havoc with its clients' development prospects, but an ideologically conservative United States was questioning the World Bank's approach to development and its record of the 1970s.[129] These criticisms paralleled a general reassessment of the philosophy and activities of the United Nations system. The Bank had grown too quickly. According to its conservative critics, its new concern for the poor and redistribution gave it a political role that it should not play and led to financially unsound projects. The Bank favored "socialist" models, "utopian" and "harebrained" schemes that were incompatible with American values and interests. In particular, reliance on the state as an agent of change, environmental or economic, was inefficient. The role of the private sector had to be expanded. Finally, the United States needed to control the organization better to ensure that it fulfilled U.S. interests.

This new attitude was important for several reasons. First, it came from the most important actor in the Bank's milieu. Second, it was pressed forward through the budget process. The Administration openly sought to pressure the World Bank and other international organizations such as UNEP to reform their activities: tighten their operations, which meant freezing the growth of the bureaucracies; concentrate on fewer activities; be more responsive to the needs of business and rely on market approaches; and avoid undue "politicization" or the intrusion of issues which the United States deemed extraneous to the debate. The selection of Alden Clausen as President of the Bank in 1981 was meant to facilitate this change of direction.

OMB wanted to halve the U.S. pledged contribution to IDA-VI and cease the provision of paid-in capital to the IBRD. The American contribution to IDA-VI—covering FY 1981 to FY 1983—was eventually diminished by 25 percent and stretched out unequally over three years, with actual disbursements falling short of these new pledges. The goal of IDA-VIII (1987 to 1989) was the same as the original amount pledged for IDA-VI ($12 billion) in 1980 and did not represent a real growth in relation to IDA-VII and supplementary financing programs. Since 1986, the passage of the Gramm-Rudman Deficit Reduction Act has constrained American contributions to IDA and IFC as well as the increase of IBRD's paid-in capital. The Bank consequently spent much time trying to secure stable sources of financing. Although it attempted to make up for the shortfalls of IDA credits through special mechanisms, it experienced great difficulties adapting to a period of austerity at a time of increasing demand arising from the admission of China, the needs of the most indebted borrowers, and the deteriorating position of sub-Saharan Africa. The "Special Facility for sub-Saharan Africa" was created in 1985 and financed by a few developed countries to support structural and sectoral adjustment programs, emergency reconstruction, and rehabilitation.[130]

To respond to the debt crisis, the United States also sought to give the Bank a more prominent role as a capital transfer agency under the Baker plan. Developing countries also tried to redefine the Bank's role in this manner but criticized the conditionality of the structural adjustment loans on macroeconomic reforms. Coordination between the Bank and IMF was also seen as a form of cross-conditionality rather than as a means of channeling more funds to heavily indebted countries. These new demands in turn threatened the organization's specificity, autonomy, and effectiveness, and prompted efforts by President Barber Conable, as soon as he took office in 1986, to emphasize what the focus of the Bank should be: "We are a force for development, not primarily an agency for debt management."[131] Although it would help reduce the relative burden of Third World debt, increase adjustment lending, and try to shield the development process from the volatility of international financial markets and aid flows, the Bank also intends to continue stressing the importance of agricultural development, limit the amount of adjustment lending relative to investment, and take into account other objectives that had been assigned to the organization: reduction of population growth, integration of women into development programs, alleviation of absolute poverty, and protection of the environment.[132]

The Reagan administration, therefore, sent the Bank and developing countries several signals regarding the Bank's environmental policy. First, having played a crucial role in putting environmental issues on the international agenda and pressing for action, the U.S. was abandoning its traditional leadership in this area. Many American initiatives were abandoned: the United States refused to ratify the Law of the Sea treaty; requested major cuts for UNEP, only to be partially reinstated by the Congress; withdrew its support from the implementation of the U.S. strategy on tropical deforestation; opposed environmental regulations in general (on fluorocarbons and toxic chemicals), and took other damaging actions. After many years of U.S. support in the 1960s and 1970s, the Reagan administration consistently requested no funding for the World Food Program, the World Heritage Foundation, the Trust Fund to Combat Poverty and Hunger in Africa, the Center on Human Settlements, and other programs. Given the inertia of the Bank bureaucracy and the opposition of many developing countries, lack of U.S. leadership meant that the organization could limit itself to continuing the activities of the 1970s. There would not be major pressures to improve its record or expand lending for that purpose. The absence of American leadership would make it more difficult to press forward for those within the Bank committed to an active policy.

The higher importance attached to the Bank as a capital transfer agency also implied that the American executive director and other donors would put a higher priority on this function in cases of conflict between moving money and preventing the unsustainable exploitation of natural resources, except when lending threatened American domestic economic interests. Those environmental problems that bear directly on U.S. economic interests, such as tropical deforestation, would be more likely to be supported.

Further, heavily indebted countries needed to increase their export earnings rapidly to service their debts and were pressured accordingly by the IMF and official development agencies. The temptation to exploit natural resources quickly and minimize the costs of environmental mitigation measures was therefore difficult to control. Marginal lands were brought under cultivation for a few years until the soil and water tables were exhausted. Mexico was alleged to have constructed the Nacozari copper smelter primarily because—although copper prices are low—it will still earn some foreign exchange. This project has a serious transborder pollution impact on the United States, but it became clear that the Mexican debt situation would preclude installation of pollution abatement devices agreed upon with the United States.[133] A rapid increase in the exportation of precious tropical woods and wood-pulp would also alleviate these problems temporarily, and new settlements defuse domestic political unrest. Some of the most environmentally disruptive projects have been undertaken precisely in the most heavily indebted countries (Brazil, Mexico, Indonesia).

The preparation and supervision of environmental projects and components tend to place a high demand on staff time and move a limited amount of money. Given pressures on the Bank to limit the size of its bureaucracy, there are strong incentives to neglect complex or time-consuming projects—or neglect their close supervision—in favor of large capital-intensive ones. Poverty-oriented rural development projects, which have often included fuelwood and reforestation components, will have a lower priority. Finally, the reluctance to use the state as an instrument of change considerably limited the scope of the environmental policies that could be adopted and pursued in developing countries. It also favored specific solutions to environmental problems, such as changes in property rights. The Bank, for example, has attempted to tackle desertification and overgrazing problems through this means in Mali.

Continuing deterioration of the natural resources of the Third World, weakening of the governments' capacities or willingness to tackle this situation, the apparent shift away from environmental concerns, and renewed importance attached to agricultural ecosystems because of the continuing food shortages prompted new efforts to emphasize the importance of environmentally sound development. In 1980, the IUCN released its "World Conservation Strategy," while the U.S. government was promoting its *Global 2000* report. Both studies emphasized the natural constraints to development, which recurrent African droughts and continuing desertification made painfully clear.

The "World Conservation Strategy" was drafted in consultation with UNEP, FAO, UNESCO, and WWF, and launched with much fanfare by IUCN in March 1980.[134] It was an attempt by a conservation-oriented organization to redefine clearly the environmental "problematique" of the developing countries and form an international consensus behind it. The aim of the strategy was to "help advance the achievement of sustainable development through the conservation of living resources." According to its authors, it arose from the needs to arrest the destruction of natural resources which was proceeding at an increasing pace, present guidelines that could be implemented immediately, coordinate fragmented and poorly organized national and international programs, and reconcile conservation with economic development.

Global 2000,[135] took up the U.N. reflections on the interrelations between environment, population, and resources,[136] and attempted to make long-term projections of world population growth, resources, and environment through the end of the century. Although it suffered from inconsistencies among data and models and explained environmental destruction largely in terms of demographic pressures, it also helped put those issues back on the international agenda and underlined how much was not known about the magnitude and impact of a continuing resource impoverishment, environmental degradation, and population growth. Like the "World Conservation Strategy," *Global 2000* redefined the environmental problem as one of management: how to maintain the productivity of the earth's systems—air, water, forests, land—along national interest lines. Therefore, it seemed to provide a clear direction for the multilateral development banks. Lending for food, population, and health projects, as well as for the identification and institutional management of national resources should be promoted. Thus, as concern for meeting basic needs widens and the concept of sustainable development spreads, the nature of the environmental problems that the Bank should emphasize also changes. New issues have surfaced for which the Bank has little expertise, few organizational incentives to tackle, and poor access to available expertise, which is lacking in the developed countries whose environmental problems were of a different nature.

The organization, therefore, finds itself in a very unstable environment where its policy is constrained by broad questions of international political economy and diplomacy (what A. W. Clausen called a "ganglion of interdependent relationships"[137]), by evolving development concepts, by growing scientific knowledge, and by sudden emerging priorities which redefine and restrict the scope of its policy. The mission of the organization has considerably broadened since the late 1960s. It is expected to promote the economic development of Third World countries, alleviate poverty, and transfer capital. It must take account of the environment, integrate women into development, and promote appropriate technologies. These objectives will often conflict. For example, environmentalists will often press for high enough user charges so that anti–water-pollution systems can be maintained. Higher charges, however, also hurt the poor. Land settlements may help the landless into raising their standard of living at the cost of deforestation, as happened in Malaysia.

The Bank discovered the importance of international and national political variables the hard way, through the failure of its population policy. Its agricultural development policy has enmeshed it in political controversies and it found that it could not publicly denounce domestic political considerations in its efforts to fulfill the objectives of these projects.[138] As mentioned earlier, the promotion of an environmentally sound development strategy also suffers from domestic institutional weaknesses, a parameter that the Bank will have to manipulate.

The Bank's organization-set and task-environment create a zone of uncertainty around the outcomes of its actions. The characteristics of the Bank's milieu clearly constrain the implementation and help define the content of the policy. The Bank has used both adaptive and transforming strategies which result from its priorities and goals: adaptation so as to ensure an orderly flow of resource, transformation so as to achieve its mandate. The following chapter will identify the strategies that the organization has used in general to control its milieu and will discuss their use or potentialities with respect to the formulation and implementation of its environmental policy.

4

Controlling the Milieu

Chapter 4 takes up the specific strategies that the organization has used to cope with environmental issues and legitimize its environmental concern among external actors. These strategies have been used by the Bank generally, *as an organization*, to reduce the uncertainty of its milieu. They have also been used to cope with the new environmental value. Thus, this chapter discusses these strategies in general terms as well as the extent to which they have been used in the environmental context by the OESA, either through the Bank, or independently from the rest of the organization.

The World Bank and its Office of Environmental and Scientific Affairs (OESA) confronted a dual implementation objective. First, they had to convince other actors (governments, international organizations, aid agencies, the financial community) to adopt the necessity of incorporating environmental safeguards into development projects, while protecting access to key resources, money and projects. To that end, OESA tried to devise a definition that would gather the support of the Bank's clientele and used the Bank's resources to influence the behavior of states and international organizations.

The second objective was to integrate the Bank's environmental perspective into the preparation and implementation of its development projects. Rather than legitimizing the object of the policy, attention focused on legitimizing the means of the policy.[1] Ideally, environmental action should not stop at the immediate ecological constraints which could affect the viability of a project; it should also take into account long-term impact. For example, not only would siltation problems be considered during the planning of a dam, but so would problems associated with the displacement of populations, deforestation, loss of species, or reductions in downstream fish yield. At the level of the project, not only must environmental considerations be taken into account at the planning stage, but excessive damage during the implementation phase should also be prevented. Thus, the Bank had to identify the ecologically and politically appropriate means of carrying out this new value.

The selection, definition, and use of various strategies are primarily related to the power of the organization to control its milieu. Some consideration of the notion of power and of the characteristics of power relationships will therefore prove useful in understanding the uses and results of adaptive and transforming strategies.

Dahl's classic definition,"A has power over B to the extent that he can get B to do something B would not otherwise do,"[2] mainly points to relational power: the "ability *to change the outcomes* or affect the behavior of others in the course of explicit political decision-making processes."[3] But another form of power is also relevant here: the "capacity *to structure the environment* within which decisions are made."[4] This aspect clearly refers to the organization's ability to change what organization theorists have called the "causal texture" of the milieu by altering the capabilities of external actors or by changing the types of relations that govern their interactions.

Relational power, which forms the basis of most of the Bank's strategies, does not entail a unidirectional relationship: one actor can benefit more than the other, but each always has the means to influence the other. Developing countries are far from powerless vis-a-vis the Bank. Their degree of power depends on their ability to control the degree of uncertainty attached to their own actions, particularly regarding the Bank's access to two key resources, money and projects.[5] The Bank's overall strategy, therefore, will be to enhance the predictability of the behavior of the other actors that constitute its organization-set; that is, to decrease their margin of liberty while increasing its own. What resources can the organization use to that end?

The two basic sources of power of the World Bank Group are its financial capabilities and information, including expertise. The caliber of its economists is unsurpassed in the UN system, and their studies have been theoretically and practically influential. The organization also possesses information on its members which it controls closely, and it can use its analyses of governmental policies to its advantage. Money and information have also enhanced its access to key decision-makers within developing countries and international organizations. Secondary sources of power include weighted voting; internal ideological homogeneity (few staff members come from communist countries), which makes it easier to reach internal consensus; the existence of concrete problems to solve that requires taking specific actions rather than merely adopting recommendations; and the Bank's adherence to traditional banking practices.[6]

The Bank used these resources to build legitimacy. President Black's close adherence to traditional banking practices and cautious investment policies were designed to gain the support of the financial community. His achievements of the highest Wall Street ratings for the Bank's bonds demonstrated his success. Building legitimacy with respect to developing countries was also important. The World Bank has presented itself as the defender of Southern interests, appealed for more aid, acted as a mediator, and harnessed its intellectual and financial resources to alleviate the burden of underdevelopment. Despite periodic criticisms of the Bank's antidemocratic decision-making structure, or of its attempts to impose economically sound but socially adverse policies on certain borrowers, the organization has enjoyed and cultivated the basic support of its clients.[7] The "development credentials" of the Bank are unsurpassed and provide an obvious vehicle for its promotion of ecological values. In the 1980s, the Bank faced two challenges to the legitimacy of its activities: the United States and others have insisted on its playing a greater role in stabilizing the international economic system, and International Non-Governmental Organizations have taken it to task regarding the definition and achievement of poverty alleviation and the impact of its activities on the environment and on human rights.

Adaptive Strategies

"Coping" for Thompson and Perrow is the essence of survival.[8] The record of international environmental protection seems to support the contention that the most successful strategies are adaptive ones, for environmental issues are not perceived as being strong enough in themselves to justify transforming the international system of power relations. Because environmental protection is only a peripheral concern of nation-states, its promotion must itself fit into their prevailing economic and political concerns.[9] This is what adaptive strategies aim to do: they involve an adaptation to the "realities" of the international system. The problem for the organization is to cope with environmental uncertainty, not as in the case of transforming strategies principally by reducing the degree of liberty of other organizations, but by increasing the degree of liberty (i.e., the zone of uncertainty) attached to *its own behavior*. Accordingly, adaptive strategies involve both competitive strategies (boundary-spanning, diversification, secrecy, expansion, and the maintenance of alternatives), and strategies which rely more on cooperation (compromise, mediation, co-financing, and rationalization).[10]

Boundary-Spanning

Boundary-spanners are the individuals in the organization who are in direct contact with the actors in the organization-set. They perform three main types of activities: they represent the organization, protect it from external threats, and monitor events that are potentially relevant to the organization.[11] These activities involve learning about the environment accurately and quickly enough to permit organizational adjustments and evaluate the amount of resources which can be mobilized toward the organizational goal.[12]

The primary boundary-spanners of the Bank are the senior staff, the external relations office, and the regional offices. One important function of the president and the senior staff is discussing the work of the Bank with government officials. McNamara, for example, functioned as a boundary-spanner in the environmental area when he discussed policy items with the French Minister of the Environment. The most developed boundary-spanning activities involve the U. S. government and Congress with which the Bank has many channels of communication. Executive directors also function as boundary-spanners since they are in constant contact both with the Bank and their home offices, articulate the Bank's position to their governments, and report their government's position to the Bank president.

The public relations office of the Bank monitors the perception of the organization by other actors. Its tasks involve the dissemination of information on the activities of the organization, relations with other international organizations (the Bank has a permanent representative at the U.N. in New York and Geneva), and some training through the Economic Development Institute (EDI). Finally, the regional offices which identify and supervise the projects are in constant contact with the organization's clients, either at the Bank headquarters or through the field offices they supervise.

As an organization attempts to minimize external disturbances, it will increase its boundary-spanning activities.[13] The World Bank expanded its public relations activities during the 1970s and 1980s. The *Operational Summary of Proposed Projects* began in 1978, while the Bank also made a greater use of *UN Development Forum* and started publishing sectoral policy papers and comprehensive country studies. The number of field offices also increased from eighteen in 1972 to forty-five in 1987.

The 1971 administrative reorganization that separated policy-oriented from operational activities symbolized this expansion of the Bank's boundary-spanning activities. This reform resulted from the recognition that the more diverse and complex demands of its clients demanded greater internal differentiation. But, as boundary-spanning units seek to fulfill their mandate, they often tend to identify themselves with the needs, problems, and even perspectives of the external sectors with which they must keep good relations. The problems that this situation engenders for the promotion of a strong environmental policy have been outlined in chapter 2. The regional offices often favor their relations with their clients over a smooth internal functioning of the organization.

How has the environmental unit of the Bank taken advantage of the existing boundary-spanning structure to monitor the activities of other actors and publicize its concerns? Isolated within the organization, the OESA largely bypassed the boundary-spanners who function as representatives of the interests of both the organization and of its clients (executive directors, regional offices), finding it more advantageous to monitor its task-environment itself. It also enabled it to reduce the risk of becoming too dependent on boundary-spanners who may later be in a position to force OESA to modify its objectives and approach.

OESA allocated considerable resources to relations with its milieu. The head of the office spent about 40 percent of his time outside the Bank: in contacts with the United Nations, in discussion with member countries, or in communication with a variety of groups and individuals. Other staff members have built a network of professional relations, either within the Bank with selected members of other units, or outside the organization with selected members of other agencies (such as USAID or EPA). This reliance on informal coordination by individuals proved most useful to the office, but rendered its communication and information-gathering capabilities fragile. Conscious of this need, the OESA soon created a staff position solely devoted to activities concerning relations with other organizations of the UN system, such as attending the annual meetings of UNEP, that complemented the work of other members of the unit. The early emphasis on informal networks derived from the young and precarious bureaucratic position of OESA. With the expansion of its legitimacy and work, it found it easier and more necessary to enter into formal agreements with other organizations. These rapidly growing coordinating activities will be discussed in detail later since they involve not only monitoring, but also controlling, the milieu.

Two other factors explain the importance of informal boundary-spanning activities. Several staff members are scientists whose general boundary-making role in IGOs has been stressed.[14] They maintain close contacts with environmental and scientific professional organizations, publish, and may be active in networks external to the organization. These activities allow them to keep abreast of knowledge of ecological consequences of development as well as monitor the attitudes of other actors regarding the work of the Bank. Finally, high turbulence and poor receptivity to the unit's work—the very complexity of the organization's milieu—demanded extensive, flexible, and autonomous boundary-spanning activities. Chapter 5 will discuss also how these contacts have been used to force changes within and outside the organization in the 1980s.

Compromise

One way for the organization to reduce uncertainty is to develop stable relations with other organizations. To do so, the organization can compromise on its goals, the scope of its objectives, and the means it will use to achieve them. Compromise is more than the outcome or anticipation of coercion; it is an outgrowth of the "dialogue" the Bank claims governs its relations with other international actors, and it embodies the mutual dependency characteristics of power relations. It is the stuff of what the Bank calls "development diplomacy," that is, hard negotiations over the terms of the loans and the goals of the project or policy. Its control over the terms and contents of the loan, associated with its expertise and influence over other creditors, gives it a good bargaining position vis-a-vis the developing countries. On the other hand, the importance of the Bank's internal requirements, concern for the success of newly established programs, the sunken costs of years of project preparation, dependence on major borrowers, competition with other sources of international funding, a desire to keep the support of its clientele, and its position on the international scene can favor the borrower, especially one that has good administrative capabilities.

The first area over which the Bank compromised was the definition of the problem. In the early 1970s, the problem was defined as reconciling what many supporters of the environment perceived as two antithetical goals: avoiding damage to the environment without slowing down the rate of growth. Based on the debate about the economic costs of environmental protection and the questioning of the very concept of economic growth, many assumed with the Bank that a trade-off existed between the two goals. Primarily concerned with economic performance, the Bank and OESA had to justify both goals. While the developing countries tended at first to solve this dilemma by denying the necessity for environmental protection, the Bank tried to show that they actually were complementary. This reasoning served to gather the support of its constituency without alienating its creditors. Thus, the Bank helped articulate, and fully adopted, the Founex rationale which identified both poverty and modernization as the prime causes of environmental deterioration in the developing world. OESA concurred with Founex in identifying urban and rural poverty, rather than habitat destruction or a reduction in species diversity, as the major environmental problems that these countries faced. The first Bank publication on "Environment and Development" in 1971 echoed the main Southern objections to environmental protection, and implicitly endorsed their arguments. Eager to gain the support of its suspicious clients, the Bank made it a point to castigate those environmentalists who argued that a trade-off existed between development and environment:

The issue . . . cannot, must not, be viewed as one of economic and social development versus the environment. It is rather how this development can proceed in ways minimally disruptive to the environment, and in ways maximally promising of more equitable distribution of the fruits of such development, individual self-fulfillment, and social harmony.[15]

The adoption of the Founex rationale is easy to understand. The business of the Bank is development. To challenge the goals of development was to challenge both the expertise of the Bank and its very existence. Moreover, the Bank could not alienate its constituency by advancing unclear ecological arguments which, as the developing countries perceived it, seemed primarily to benefit the developed countries. Furthermore, a more comprehensive policy would have met with strong opposition from the financial community which tended to regard anti-pollution measures as the maximum scope of the policy, and protection measures as economic opportunity costs. Thus, instead of challenging the goals of development policy or the paths towards modernization, the Bank responded incrementally and focused on the methodology of projects preparation and implementation, adding one variable to an accepted development project analysis without questioning its core activities.

Following this approach, the Bank initially defined its scope as one primarily of mitigation of ecologically adverse effects, rather than protection or enhancement of the environment. Its goal was "to assure that projects financed by it do not have seriously adverse environmental and health consequences or, if they are likely to have such consequences, that measures are taken to avoid or mitigate them."[16] The key word here is "seriously." How serious is serious? And according to whose criteria and values is the degree of seriousness to be assessed? These questions raise the dual questions of expertise and standards.

In the absence of a centralized international policy-making body which could set uniform standards, the OESA first relied upon the U.S. Environmental Protection Agency's expertise and consultants. Thus, the narrow scope of the Bank's policy corresponded to the developed countries' experience with their own national problems and was ill-adapted to the specific environmental problems that the Third World faced. The growing concern for vanishing biological resources, although shared and often promoted by developed countries, was only minimally embodied in the available expertise. Hence, developing countries could argue for less stringent standards on the grounds that their economies could not afford them, and that the small number of industries and high absorptive capacity of the ecosystems allowed relaxed standards.

Consequently, the general approach the Bank takes is "tailored to local circumstances."[17] Environmental protection measures and standards are adapted to each project and each country. With respect to industrial projects, a lack of monitoring capabilities and a greater assimilative capacity of the ecosystem can warrant the inclusion of standards below those the Bank or developed countries favor. Flexibility is given to engineers and consultants. Furthermore, the scope of environmental components and mitigation measures can also be discussed during the negotiation stage of the project cycle to take the specific economic situation of the recipient into account. The latter may even press for a relaxation of the standard guidelines to gain a competitive edge for a particular plant.[18] Thus, the standards finally accepted are the result of compromises between the requirements of the environmental unit, the Bank's perception of the costs and benefits of its projects, and the borrower's desires. This presumably ensures greater compliance and avoids setting unrealistic standards which have only a symbolic function. Even negotiated standards, however, have often been ignored.

Although flexible, standards and other environmental protection measures involved additional expenses which developing countries claimed should be indirectly or directly met by richer countries, as discussed in Chapter 3. The emphasis upon "appropriate" standards reflected, in part, cost concerns which proved a determinant factor in the decision to implement them. In practice, additional expenses were kept low, around an informal target of 2 to 3 percent of the total cost of the project.[19] In the case of more costly environmental protection components which the Bank judged to be indispensable, the organization resolved the problem of the additionality principle essentially by acceding to it.[20] In effect, the organization agreed to lend or grant money to finance these extra costs. If, for some reason, the Bank were unable to do so, the OESA could help the borrower locate other sources—such as USAID—willing to cover those expenses. This underscores the importance of the boundary-spanning activities of the OESA staff since these arrangements were arrived at informally. It also ensured that additional funds were transferred to the recipient to accomodate ecological demands. However, they were added to the total liability of the borrower and thus remained relatively unattractive.

The absence of a formal requirement of an environmental impact statement (EIS) on the American model also kept costs low. This has enabled the organization to accommodate objections from the staff as well as from borrowers. Not even simple environmental analyses are conducted for each project. EISs are required only if major ecological damages are suspected. As long as it is Bank policy to require that the financing of environmental studies be charged to the borrowing entity,[21] few environmental impact studies will be undertaken. In exceptional cases involving very poor countries, however, the Bank may finance such studies.

Though it reduced conflict, this general approach, centered around mitigation and flexible standards, had drawbacks. Rather than holistic and long-term concerns, the environmental analysis of the project was limited to the immediate and visible consequences of the project. Reliance on an economic rationale which favored an environmental perspective limited to the costs which can be directly identified and calculated compounded this tendency. The very rationale for the project goes unquestioned: the environmental analysis starts with the assumption that the project is needed. If efforts to include mitigating measures are unsuccessful because they were too expensive or undercut the rationale of the project, the Bank will nevertheless go ahead with the project, assuming that its economic and development benefits outweigh its environmental costs. Thus Mahbub ul Haq could justify the destruction of a national park by an irrigation project as "a cost that society has to cheerfully bear if there are no other economical alternatives."[22] In fact, both the economic and humanistic rationales demand it. The Bank's policy was therefore reduced to being *mindful* of the ecological impact of development and to *efforts* at minimizing them. The relative compromises that the Bank has reached over the scope of its involvement in favor of the environment underline the greater weight that economic or political motivations carry in its relation with its borrowers and creditors. The World Bank's role as an agent of social or environmental improvement will always be subordinated to its role as an investment agency.

Playing Off

The diversity of the Bank's milieu generates conflicting external demands. In this situation, full compliance with any set of pressures can be dysfunctional because it restricts the range of the organization's subsequent options.[23] For example, denying any value to the environmental problem would have alienated several developed countries, mobilized public opinion and several international organizations, and led to poor project performance in some cases.

Organizations can employ three strategies to solve the problem of conflicting demands: they can deny the legitimacy of the latter; ration their own effort, that is, give sequential attention to these demands; or play one group off against another.[24] For example, a prime barrier to influence is a lack of capacity to comply with the demand, and the Bank has repeatedly contended that article V, section 10 of the *Articles of Agreement*, prohibiting political conditions on lending, prevented it from injecting human rights or similar provisions into its decisions. As earlier chapters have indicated, the Bank often used the second strategy. It emphasized social sectors of interest to the developing countries in the 1960s, later responded to developed countries' pressures in the energy and environmental sectors, and emphasized its concern for the poor. In the 1980s, it sought to develop private sector financing and lending for structural adjustment.

The Bank uses the third strategy perhaps more widely. To reject overt U.S. pressures, it usually argues that imposing blatantly political conditions would alienate most of its members and hamper the work of the organization. The typical Bank attitude has been to play the developing countries off against the developed countries, arguing for more development aid, on the one hand, and for deeper changes in its recipients' policies, on the other. In the late 1970s, it handled U.S. political pressures by appealing to other donors. West European opposition to the American ban on loans to Vietnam, for example, allowed the organization to show some autonomy by proceeding with the proposed loan in 1979.[25] The absence of any subsequent loans to that country in the 1980s, however, indicates the limits of this strategy.

The capacity to pit one group against another has been enhanced by the Bank's diversification strategy, which gives it much more flexibility in coping with external demands. The argument that sound lending practices are necessary if the organization is to preserve the trust of the financial community, has often been advanced to justify the strict conditions it attaches to its loans. Thus, the very complexity and diversity of its task-environment, a source of turbulence and great uncertainty, also provides opportunities for some autonomy that the organization would lack were it faced with a simpler organization-set.

Environmental policy embodies the results of this approach. By pre-empting forceful demands and expressing the worst fears of the developing countries, it was able to impose a definition of the problem that left its primary function unquestioned and minimized the scope of the policy. At the same time, raising the issue enabled it to raise awareness among developing countries and strengthen its oversight of all aspects of a country's social and economic choices. Facing harsh criticisms of its environmental record in the 1980s, the Bank again relied on the apprehensions of the developing countries as well as on the concern of the financial communities for larger transfers of resources to these countries and for a rapid mobilization of their economic resources.

This position creates opportunities when the organization's leadership is dynamic enough to take the initiative. But if it waits and relies on building various coalitions to avoid doing anything about these demands, it may eventually find itself forced to comply partially with them and antagonize all parties in the process. By delaying the involvement of INGOs into the implementation of its environmental guidelines and giving preference to capital transfer at the request of donors and borrowers, the Bank saw heavy opposition to its environmental policy grow quickly. Its image was tarnished, and it faced congressional pressures that fueled opposition to increases in its operating capital, forcing changes that were more extensive than it would have perferred. These are discussed in chapter 5.

Linkage

Tying the promotion of environmental goals to more widely shared values has long been urged as an effective strategy. As Boulding simply put it: ". . . conservationist policies almost have to be sold under some other excuse which seems more urgent. . . ."[26] Both developed and developing countries accept more readily those environmental issues that are linked to public health concerns. Only public health, for example, can justify the large expenditures on air and water pollution control in the developed world. Likewise, if environmental issues are to be taken into account at all by poor countries, it is often because they are linked to public health matters, rather than to conservation.

The Bank has closely linked health and economic benefits to the promotion of environmental concerns. The first environmental loans went for urban water pollution in Brazil (São Paulo), Yugoslavia (Sarajevo), and Finland. The development of the Water Supply and Sewerage sector was wholly linked to the maintenance or promotion of public health. The Bank also emphasized measures destined to minimize the higher risks of schistosomiasis and onchocerciasis resulting from irrigation projects. The development of the tourism sector provided a handy argument in favor of more conservation-oriented policies. As early as 1963, a World Bank mission to Kenya urged greater wildlife protection if the middle-income tourist trade were to be developed. The development of the park system figured prominently in the report of a subsequent mission in 1975.[27] The rationale for this measure was ostensibly economic. Protection was seen as a means to immediate economic ends, not as an end in itself. President Nyerere expressed the contingent aspects of a conservation policy dramatically: "Personally, I have no wish ever to see a wild animal, but if they bring in money which can be used in development, then they must be looked after."[28] When interest in related values wanes, however, so does the successful promotion of environmental objectives. The reduction of support for these two sectors in the late 1970s and early 1980s (tourism disappeared altogether as a separate sector and health funding was cut substantially) generated fewer avenues for the justification and implementation of environmental concerns.

Utilitarian arguments are the only politically acceptable ones for the leaders and citizens of the developing world. The emphasis upon energy development that arose in the late 1970s, proved beneficial in furthering environmental concerns. It provided the best vehicle for justifying environmental programs. Many forest protection or reforestation schemes were justified, not so much because of their ecological benefits, but because they provided a renewable, traditional, and much-needed source of energy for the poor. These project components were even more attractive since they could also be tied to the need to meet the basic needs of poor farmers for fuelwood or building poles.[29]

Of course, an emphasis on forest production is not necessarily synonymous with ecologically sound policies. An increase in forested acreage may hide poorer ecosystems. Non-indigenous species can be introduced in single stands because they are more productive, thus completely modifying the ecosystem.[30] The Bank has, in fact, supported deforestation projects designed to introduce faster-growing species in the same area to maximize wood production. Yet, the emphasis on energy production and conservation allowed for a more pronounced promotion of renewable energies.

The OESA developed its economic rationale steadily from the early 1970s. The acceptance of the concept of "sustainable development" by the international community and the Bank has strengthened the Bank's rationale for injecting environmental criteria more forcefully into individual projects as well as into development programs, as discussed in chapter 2. In the words of President Clausen: ". . . in order to be sustainable, development must include vigorous and studied attention to resource management. . . . For sustainable development and wise conservation are, in the end, mutually reinforcing—and absolutely inseparable—goals."[31] The program of action that the Bank developed for sub-Sahara Africa gave significant attention to the ecological limits and determinants of development. With the development of the health and forestry lending sectors, the Bank needed to rely less on these justifications and enlarged its vision by adopting UNEP's international security theme. In 1985, for example, the Bank maintained that peace itself was at stake: "If the environment and national resources that underpin and support national economies collapse, the social and political consequences of such dislocations are likely to assume wider dimensions, thereby posing a threat to regional security and international peace."[32] Domestic tranquillity and international stability demand that greater attention be paid to the environment; the ultimate argument, but also the most difficult to support.

Secrecy

Restricting access to information regarding their behavior is a common strategy organizations use to ward off external threats. Having ensured the allegiance of its employees, the organization can project its ideology and a certain image only to the extent that it can adequately control the flow of information it generates.

Secrecy is an effort to assure power through the control of critical information. This control is directed against IGOs, governments, or individual outsiders, and the staff of the Bank uses it widely to preserve its autonomy vis-a-vis its clients, creditors, and peers. Secrecy applies to the details of negotiations between lender and recipient, to country data and policy assessments, and to in-house reports. Even much of the Bank's standard operating procedures in project analysis are not made available to outsiders. The U.S. Congress, for example, has often complained about the lack of access of the U.S. executive director to information on which Bank lending decisions were based, although he enjoys more than do his counterparts.[33]

The Bank defends secrecy on the grounds that much of the information it gathers is confidential. This confidentiality, the Bank argues, is necessary to ensure a sound dialogue between the lending agency and the recipient. It also helps build the image of an organization which enjoys some autonomy vis-a-vis its creditors, thus promoting its influence among its clients.

Secrecy also affects the implementation of the project. The organization shields itself from criticism over its policies largely by avoiding scrutiny of the implementation of its projects. Failures are seldom publicized, and the causes of shortcomings rarely studied by outsiders. This can lead to inertia or lack of innovation. To be sure, political considerations often prevent the organization from agreeing to external review of its projects. No recipient wants to see the political benefits which accrue from the implementation of a loan dashed by a critical evaluation of the project. Nevertheless, this attitude makes learning from experience more difficult. Only under American pressure did the World Bank set up an Operations Evaluation Department in 1971, which it reluctantly agreed should be hierarchically independent of the president and report directly to the directors. Secrecy has prevented assessing the environmental limits to the success of many projects, as well as their ultimate consequences. It has enabled the organization to ignore disturbing elements which would bring its appraisal methods into question.

Secrecy is the epitome of passive adaptation. But it also constitutes a prerequisite for the success of other strategies. It is essential when the World Bank Group plays parties off against one another. It also forms the basis for leaking information as a sanction. Compromises can largely be achieved because the parties are assured of some secrecy over the process and even over the terms of agreement. Secrecy also gives the organization more flexibility in establishing and using constituencies and in using various negative sanctions. But secrecy again points up the ambiguous effects of many strategies. They may be favorable to the organization in the short term, unfavorable in the long term. Or they may protect the organization effectively but endanger particular policies (such as environmental policy).

Coalition

Coalition is a strategy for gaining support from the organization's milieu and enables the Bank to control both its clients (by preventing them from using a competitive strategy), and other donors (by defining mutually agreed upon goals), thus managing competition over domain and clients.

Coalition also evolved as a response to an increasingly turbulent international environment. Whereas in its first fifteen years, the Bank sought to build and reinforce its autonomy in order to gain the confidence of the financial community, it has been forced in the last two decades to cooperate with other organizations as its own activities expanded and uncertainties increased. Four aspects of cooperation will be considered here: (1) coalition building with donors through the development of aid consortia, (2) agreements reached with other international organizations on policy domains and objectives, (3) the co-financing of projects, and (4) coalition with non-governmental organizations.

CONSORTIA

One of the Bank's earliest attempts to control its task-environment has been to establish aid consortia. The Bank has organized groups of donors to coordinate aid policies to a particular country, starting with India in 1958. They were specifically designed to secure aid pledges to meet the specified targets of the recipients' development plans, and helped minimize the uncertainty attached to fluctuating bilateral contributions to national development plans the Bank had helped set up. Strictly speaking, only India and Pakistan have consortia. The idea subsequently evolved into creating consultative groups which have all the features of consortia, except that they are not specific fund-raising sessions: members can restrict themselves to general statements of good intentions. The main aim of these groups remains harmonizing donors' policies toward a particular country in light of the Bank's identification of the problems it faces.

As the convener, head and secretariat of the consortium, the Bank evaluates the recipients' policies for the donors while helping the recipient mobilize funds for its programs. Since it is highly valued by donors, the Bank can use these groups to gather leverage over a country whose economic policies it would like to influence. This added leverage is compounded by reliance, on the part of several donors, on the Bank's judgment for the allocation of their foreign aid (Sweden, Canada, the Netherlands).[34] And although the Bank's leverage may be undermined if a powerful donor differs with the Bank on major issues, it can turn to the recipient and to other donors for support.

As a mediator, the Bank influences both parties: "Bank's influence has been exercized not only on India . . . but also on the Consortium members to increase their aid, to improve the terms, and to reduce the debt service.[35] When the recipient is not devoid of resources, influence can be mutual: "India has influenced the Bank into accepting public sector financing and non-project aid, while the Bank influenced India's agricultural policies."[36] Thus, from an organizational viewpoint, consortia help increase environmental certainty regarding donor contributions, the recipients' acceptance of Bank's policy suggestions, and the success of the Bank's programs in that country. This function may be interpreted differently: the Bank regards it as a means of promoting international aid efficiency, whereas critics tend to view it as taking advantage of the temporary weakness of a country to impose questionable policies and permanent relations of dependency.[37]

COOPERATION WITH INTERNATIONAL ORGANIZATIONS (IGOS)
The expansion of its domain in the early sixties forced the Bank to come out of its relative isolation from other international organizations. After some initial squabbling, it signed cooperative agreements with FAO and UNESCO in 1964, which defined their respective domains. This trend toward cooperation with other agencies with greater experience in functional areas grew in the 1960s and 1970s, as the Bank modified its development policy to emphasize basic needs and new sectors (agriculture, tourism, education, and health, for example).

The typical institutional response to formal cooperation with UN agencies has been to set up a separate unit within these organizations charged with conducting the cooperative program.[38] Cooperation was seen as a mutually beneficial exchange of information and money. WHO, for example, has put its experts and experience at the disposal of the Bank while the latter helped that organization analyze, develop, and finance projects. The Bank ostensibly saw these efforts as attempts to "educate" the other organizations on its own approach; that is, as a way of developing greater rigor in project evaluation. The separate units were also designed to shield the Bank from what it considered the pernicious influence of the UN specialized agencies.

The purpose of formal cooperative agreements with FAO, UNESCO, UNDP, or WHO is ostensibly to secure access to a key organizational resource by facilitating a smooth flow of projects to be financed by the organization (WHO and water supply and wastes treatment projects, for example). The agencies are to cooperate with the Bank group "in assisting member countries to identify and prepare projects for Bank consideration and in appraising; supervising; and, when requested by a country, providing the technical assistance component of such projects. Under the agreement . . . the agency "has 'primary responsibility' for assisting countries in project identification and preparation."[39] The investment center within

FAO that grew out of the cooperative FAO/IBRD program has employed a staff of about seventy agricultural economic experts who ensured that FAO programs follow the Bank approach.

Like any other international organization, the Bank has tended to see itself as the centerpiece of the UN development assistance system. Being self-centered, it sees UNDP as providing a small supplementary source of funds and other agencies as sources of technical assistance, while it conducts the development process. Collaboration with other agencies has not always been successful, primarily because of the Bank's commitment to its independence. In the population field, for example, discord followed cooperative attempts when the Bank insisted on collaboration only on its own terms to which many agencies in the population field were not as ready to accede as they were in other sectors.[40] In sectors in which the Bank has no expertise, such discord can easily doom a policy.

Four factors encouraged cooperation with other agencies on environmental protection issues: (1) the invasion of the domain of other organizations caused by the promotion of environmental issues; (2) the interdependent, synergistic, and systemic nature of environmental problems; (3) the need for knowledge; and (4) the need to control other competitors. Cooperation could follow the model already established with other organizations where these agencies act as technical partners, providing assistance to governments and staff support for Bank missions. Its broad definition of the environmental issue involved the Bank further in the turf of other organizations. For example, the Bank co-sponsors the Onchocerciasis Control Programme in West Africa and research programs on tropical and diarrheal diseases with WHO and UNDP.[41] This agreement limited the Bank primarily to financing basic health care and vector control activities, while WHO mostly focused on research and technical assistance and recognized the Bank's financial resources and its greater experience in the identification, appraisal, or supervision of health care programs.

FAO is one of the most important international agencies concerned with environmental issues. Collaboration with FAO followed the Bank's growing involvement in the forestry sector. The Bank also houses and co-sponsors with FAO and UNDP the Consultative Group on International Agricultural Research (CGIAR), set up in 1971, which supports research in developing countries. In the industrial field, where the Bank started its environmental action and where it has remained very active, OESA had a close working relationship with UNIDO, ILO, OECD, and the UN Economic Commission for Europe. In other instances, the Bank's absence was conspicuous. The Bank did not participate in the elaboration of the IUCN's World Conservation Strategy, which aimed to represent a consensus of policy on conservation efforts in the context of world development.[42] Neither does it belong to the Ecosystem Conservation Group, which includes UNESCO, FAO, IUCN, and UNEP. Conservation as an environmental policy objective has very slowly been accepted by the Bank.

Informally, OESA had good relations with UNEP, although it did not cooperate with the latter as much as it could have. In effect, the activities of the two organizations complement each other. UNEP is primarily concerned with assessment and management. Its mandate is to develop awareness of the environmental dimensions of their activities within international organizations and states. Consequently, it primarily identifies problems and suggests means to solve them, though it has a minimal operational role. The two organizations basically exchange information and seem to have little influence on one another. The aim of collaboration is more the coordination of activities than the development of joint programs.

The foremost and most concrete example of World Bank/UNEP cooperation was the February 1980 Declaration of Environmental Policies and Procedures Relating to Economic Development designed to encourage development-finance institutions to adopt sound environmental guidelines in their lending. The idea originated within both UNEP and the Bank, and OESA promoted it actively. UNEP's aim was to reaffirm a sense of commitment to the Principles and Recommendations for Action developed eight years earlier at Stockholm relating to environmentally sound development and environmental management. The Bank's active role in its adoption stems from two considerations. First was its desire not to see its programs jeopardized by the policies of other development institutions. The non-observance of environmental guidelines by other MDBs could render the Bank's own added expenditures futile, since damages from nearby development projects could nullify its efforts to protect an ecosystem or a population. Thus a single project loan would yield less influence on a particular program if other donors, who also account for a significant portion of the financing of the program, did not follow the same policy guidelines. In that case, the government has fewer incentives to accept the Bank guidelines. This problem, which also arose in the population context, often impeded its actions in favor of natural systems or indigenous populations, as it did in Brazil, Indonesia, and the Philippines.

It was also an attempt to reduce the Bank's competitive disadvantage.[43] Additional expenditures (even though the Bank may directly finance them or identify sources of financing), stricter project assessment and evaluation, and potential delays in the adoption of projects, could incite recipients to turn away from the Bank to other development banks over which they have greater control. This concern is similar to that of businesses that support some regulation because it increases their knowledge of their competitors' behavior.

The Committee of International Development Institutions on the Environment (CIDIE) was created in 1980 to supervise the implementation of the Declaration.[44] Progress has been slow, however. The Bank has charged that the management of other institutions has been reluctant to support and lend resources for the fulfillment of its objectives, and that much of the work of the CIDIE consisted of the Bank assisting other institutions in implementing the declaration. Mostafa Tolba, UNEP's executive director has condemned pro-forma endorsements of the declaration that led to little changes in actual behavior. The Bank itself was criticized years later for still offering no course on the integration of environmental criteria into development planning in the curriculum of the Economic Development Institute, despite a pledge to that end at the second CIDIE meeting in 1981. Dr. Tolba's strong words applied to all members:

The main failing seems to be that members of CIDIE have gone along with the Declaration in principle more than in major shifts in action. . . . It was intended that CIDIE would provide a mechanism for the critical review and appraisal of member's efforts to integrate the environmental dimension into their development co-operation policies and programmes. After five years it did not yet reach that stage. All of us, members of CIDIE, I presume, are insisting that CIDIE should be doing something more than just talk.[45]

The next logical step is drawing in bilateral aid agencies. Building on the signing of the Declaration by the Commission of the European Communities, the Council of Ministers of the European Community passed a resolution in 1984 expressing their desire to adhere to similar principles. Cooperation with USAID has been extensive, as discussed in chapter 3, both at the environmental level and at the broader level of development funding. Tropical forestry, for example, has been discussed regularly by staff from the two organizations. Cooperation often results in a rough division of labor between the Bank and USAID. The Bank tends to take on projects that have a large price tag—such as infrastructure—whereas USAID is more willing to fund training and institution-building. Cooperation, therefore, regulates the flow of projects, enables the organization to stretch its financial resources farther, and allows units within the Bank to overcome internal constraints to their activities.

Cooperation between UNEP and the Bank, however, could be much more extensive. They both aim at institution-building in the field but do not join forces. Although they collaborated on the Habitat and Water and Desertification conferences, the Bank has largely ignored the conservation component of UNEP's work. Furthermore, there is generally very little staff exchange between the Bank and the specialized agencies. The Bank's units are staffed by Bank officers, while few of them are on secondment in the agencies' units devoted to the cooperative programs.[46] In UNEP's case, the absence of an institutionalized cooperative program with UNEP has compounded this situation. There is no UNEP officer in the Bank, nor is there any Bank officer at UNEP. Arrangements for seconding UNEP officers to the Bank could prove useful in fostering further awareness of the environmental perspective among the Bank staff. Moreover, increased collaboration with other agencies manifested itself prominently in their active participation in Bank missions. These missions often include FAO, UNESCO, WHO and ILO staff. It seems conceivable, therefore, that they could include representatives of UNEP who would assist the Bank in drawing country environmental assessments. No such field collaboration has, however, taken place (which is due as much to UNEP's lack of manpower as to the Bank's unwillingness to expand the scope of its missions).

Yet, the lack of extensive cooperation between the two organizations stems more from the particular character of UNEP's mission—which stresses fostering awareness, information-gathering, and the provision of modest incentives—than from any rigidity on the part of the Bank. The latter is a development agency and not an environmental one. Since the Bank pays attention to the environmental dimensions of its projects and is a leader among its peers in that area, UNEP's role was limited throughout the 1970s to exchanging information (on desertification, for example). Conflict is further reduced because both share a similar definition of the problem and adhere to the concept of "sustainable development" which approaches ecological problems in a management perspective of multiple use and resource conservation. Although the declared environmental policy of the Bank fulfills much of UNEP's objectives, its reluctance to implement the CIDIE declaration forcefully has caused some frustration.

A logical follow-up to these attempts is to control the activities of consulting firms whose general lack of environmental awareness has often impeded an effective environmental policy. The consulting firms which the Bank and the UN system use can provide a conduit for the acceptance of environmental regulations by other organizations and by developing countries (to a much lower degree) that rely on their expertise. In that respect, OESA's dynamic role was welcome. For example, in cooperation with USAID and the World Environment Center (an association supported by the Bank, and public and private group), it sponsored in March 1981 a conference on "Environmental Practices of Consulting Firms Working on International Development Projects," designed primarily to exchange information and identify shortcomings.

CO-FINANCING

Since 1975, the Bank has pursued a cooperative program to increase public and private financial participation it its operations. In December 1975, for example, it led a consortium of sixteen banks in the financing of an expansion program of a major steel company in Brazil. The co-financing of Bank projects has since become a regular and important feature of the Bank's work. The operational staff is encouraged to consider co-financing possibilities at an early stage of project preparation.[47] This strategy has had several purposes:

First, it acts as a vehicle for recycling the tremendous surpluses that befell OPEC after 1973, in accordance with the urgings of the developed countries. The Bank encouraged OPEC members to set up their own funds and bilateral assistance programs, which then, instead of competing with the Bank, provided additional financial resources. The Bank helped establish these institutions, staffed and organized them, and set up their information systems.[48] Such was the case of the Abu Dhabi Fund for Arab Economic Development, the Arab Fund for Economic and Social Development, the Venezuelan Development Fund, the Saudi Fund for Development and the Islamic Development Bank.

The strategy increases the flow of capital to developing countries. In fact, rather than increasing the absolute amount of bilateral aid transfers, only their allocation through the Bank was modified. This enabled the Bank to further consolidate its leadership position in development financing.

Next, it promotes more effective use of assistance to developing countries through policy coordination in accordance with the Bank's preferences.

It influences other co-lenders by demonstrating to them the thoroughness of the Bank's analyses of national economies and of its projects appraisal and supervision methods. The Bank argues that co-lenders have been "socialized" into the ways of the Bank. This is presumably an attempt to gather support from its creditors by demonstrating its expertise and its requisite role as an intermediary between donors and recipients.

Finally, the strategy increases the Bank's "presence" in developing countries. Co-financing allows the Bank to spread itself thinner over a larger number of projects.

There are three sources of co-financing: bilateral aid agencies, export credits, and private banks. The role of the Bank varies with each of them. Whereas private sources rely on the Bank for the preparation, appraisal, implementation and supervision of the project; bilateral agencies, which are also associated in the preparation and appraisal, rely mostly on the Bank for supervision.

With respect to "official" sources of aid, the Bank distinguishes between "joint" and "parallel" financing. The latter is becoming more common as other donors oppose the former, which involves agreement by agencies to provide financing for goods to be procured under international competitive bidding. Parallel financing corresponds to a situation where each lender administers its *own* part of a project. Hence, international competitive bidding is restricted to that part of the project financed by the Bank. Since the Bank and the borrower agree to divide the project into separate packages (one for the Bank, one for the export credit agencies), parallel financing provides the Bank and the recipient with a way of circumventing the international competitive bidding requirement of the *Articles of Agreement*.

With the growth of parallel financing, export credits have recently become more important, expecially for larger projects. Although, in theory, the agencies can have some input into the preparation and appraisal of the project, in practice, they participate because the Bank is already involved and only after it has appraised the project. Thus, they "rely heavily on the Bank's judgement in supporting a project."[49]

The Bank makes co-financing very attractive to private institutions. It provides them with information on the country and the project and incorporates a "cross-default" clause into the contract whereby the World Bank reserves the right to suspend disbursements or accelerate repayments if the private banks do so for a good reason. Another attractive provision provides physical and price contingency allowances into the agreements. They are designed to avoid cost overruns and enhance investment security.[50] The terms for each project component are different, however. That is, the Bank enters into a separate loan contract with the borrower. The latter, in turn, often benefits from better terms from the banks when the loan is linked to one from the World Bank.

This strategy has allowed the World Bank to reduce major sources of uncertainty. It needed to do so for, having become the largest provider of aid by promoting the advantage of "apolitical" multilateral financing, the Bank faced a backlash in the 1980s in favor of bilateral agencies. The U.S. Congress showed much greater reluctance to finance multilateral development banks (MDBs) over which it felt it had little control. Congress was more willing to rely on USAID, whose activities can apparently lead to clearer and faster political pay-offs. The Reagan administration's emphasis on the role of the private sector in economic development accentuated this phenomenon, giving prominence to export-credits and bilateral military aid. The World Bank found in co-financing a convenient way of assuaging that administration's discomfort with the lending activities of multilateral institutions.

Co-financing also provides the Bank with a way of controlling or influencing the lending criteria of other organizations. In this regard, it could prove useful to environmental concerns since the Bank—being more enlightened than most agencies (except USAID and perhaps the Swedish International Development Agency [SIDA]) can demonstrate and implement greater awareness of these issues throughout the project cycle. Furthermore, co-financing helps mitigate the restrictions on Bank lending. Chapter 2 discussed the impact of the charter requirement that the organization's funds be used to finance only the foreign-exchange costs of pre-identified goods and services. Co-financing can palliate this shortcoming and support the local cost of projects as well as unforeseen side effects during implementation. Finally, parallel financing increases the capability of studying the results of Bank projects when an aid agency (such as SIDA) provides more information on its evaluation than does the Bank.

The attractiveness of co-financing for all parties involved has led to quite a successful program. Total co-financing increased from a total of $496 million in 37 projects in FY 1973 to 7.4 billion in 99 projects in 1982, to $5.6 billion in 111 projects in FY 1987. This level corresponds to a certain stabilization around 30 percent of the Bank's total lending and about 50 percent of its projects.[51] Private lending accounted for much of the fluctuation in co-financing. Whereas in FY 1982 private lenders alone committed $3.3 billion, their contributions amounted to 579.5 million in FY 1986.[52]

As the Bank acknowledges:

> By making use of these other sources of funds, the Bank has been able to expand its programs for developing countries in spite of resource constraints, and the strategy of encouraging development of the productive sectors has not resulted in it being forced to forgo its important institution-building role in the more traditional infrastructure sectors.[53]

Thus, co-financing has enabled the Bank to increase lending in social and agricultural sectors, while preserving its hold over more traditional (and financially rewarding) infrastructural projects where most of its expertise lay. It enabled the organization to influence the lending criteria and development policies of its competitors without relinquishing any independence since the World Bank Group is still in charge of the preparation, approval, implementation, and supervision of the projects. The only cost to the organization has been a slight diminution in the secrecy that surrounds its activities.

COOPERATION WITH NON-GOVERNMENTAL ORGANIZATIONS (INGOS)

Chapter 3 indicated the extent to which the Bank's activities were increasingly scrutinized by non-governmental organizations. Following the evolution of many other international agencies, the Bank has pledged in principle to cooperate with them, although its record has not lived up to the INGOs' expectations. In practice, however, cooperation is increasing. Faced with stable or even declining resources, the Bank has turned to non-governmental organizations for support within donor countries. During the negotiations and ratification of the seventh IDA replenishment (IDA-VII), many of them—ranging from the U.S. Catholic Conference and the Chamber of Commerce of the United States to the International Food Policy

Institute and various environmental groups—testified before Congress in favor of a higher replenishment level than the one negotiated by the Reagan administration.

The Office of Environmental and Scientific Affairs followed the example of UNEP in trying to develop support among environmental groups against the opposition of the rest of the organization. Increased congressional scrutiny of the Bank's environmental record in the 1980s (see chapter 5) was encouraged by the activism of these groups. Their various testimonies blamed the organization, while exonerating the OESA, for what they considered a poor record, using much information provided by the environmental unit itself and voicing the latter's complaints about staffing, financial resources, and organizational inertia.

OESA also turned to non-governmental environmental organizations for scientific information and, perhaps more importantly, used them in some cases as vehicles for gaining information regarding the nature of proposed projects and the implementation of approved projects. For example, environmental and anthropological organizations successfully mobilized public and official opinion against the Bank-funded POLONOR-OESTE project in Brazil, discussed in chapter 5. In Chiapas state, Mexico, only after the Natural Resources Defense Council pointed out the potential negative impact on watersheds and endangered species of a regional development program, did the Bank include environmental safeguards.[54] Other organizations in India and the Philippines also alerted the Bank and their American counterparts to the potential dangers of proposed projects or to failures to comply with the agreed-upon environmental guidelines.

Coalition with non-governmental organizations helped the Bank build political support for its growth and enabled OESA to overcome its limited means. Such support, however, has a price. These organizations have made demands with respect to Bank lending. Some asked for an expansion of private sector financing, others that greater attention be paid to the poor. Environmental groups pressed for a reorganization and expansion of the Bank's environmental policy. They publicly denounced its record and, in the process, gave ammunition to congressmen desirous of limiting the American contribution. Discouraged by the evolution of the Bank's environmental record and by the divorce they perceived between rhetoric and practice, they have even threatened to withdraw support of replenishment levels and other financial initiatives of the organization.

Coalition has proven a useful strategy for controlling the organization's environment. The Bank's intermediary function helped it control the demands of both donors and recipients. Agreements with other organizations acknowledged the right of the Bank to move into their domains while remaining operationally insulated from them. Rather than leading to mutual dependence, joint programs have amounted to a dispersion of the Bank's approach within other agencies. The organization gained expertise without compromising its methodology. Co-financing has enabled the Bank to expand its lending policies without sacrificing existing programs. It also enabled it to socialize other donors in its thinking and influence their development policies at the micro-level, while reducing the autonomy of the recipients and building itself as a necessary partner in many development projects. Finally, through cooperation with non-governmental organizations, it has gained political support and stretched its resources. The usefulness of this strategy obviously depends on the presence and strength of like-minded constituencies within the donor and borrower countries, a development the Bank has actively pursued.

Rationalization

Although it is constantly involved in negotiations with its borrowers, the World Bank does not like to bargain. Engineers and economists tend to feel that they alone have mastered their fields. Decision-makers, therefore, strive to reduce uncertainty and limit the incidence of bargaining by routinizing decision-making along rational-analytic lines. Formal programming and budgeting techniques spring up from these views. Cost-benefit analyses, quinquennial country programming (one will recall that McNamara introduced PPBS in the Department of Defense), and sectoral lending plans are a few examples of this technique.

Economic rationality has provided the main basis for decision-making. The Bank defined the environmental problem in economic terms, a language and rationale with which both the staff and its clients were familiar. While the Bank in the early 1970s was affirming the primacy of development, it was also attempting to show how environmental protection and economic growth could actually complement each other. Economic rationalization attempted to circumvent the central dilemma of international environmental protection, namely the perception that conservation and human welfare are mutually exclusive goals.[55]

One line of argument maintains that the benefits of environmental protection are so pervasive that they make themselves felt in the economic system, even though most are intangible. For example, the Bank has justified health components on productivity grounds: sick people cannot use their tools efficiently and are often absent, thus accounting for a lower productivity.[56] Because many irrigation projects have increased the incidence of waterborne diseases, their ultimate social costs justify an early involvement in the control of these diseases at the project design stage. Diarrheal diseases are also a prime cause of infant mortality and negatively affect tourism.

Another line of argument refers to the familiar prevention-is-better-than-cure reasoning: ". . . a relatively small investment in prevention is usually far less expensive, as well as more effective, than subsequent remedial actions that are certain to become necessary later on."[57] This reasoning applies best to pollution problems. As we have seen in previous chapters, its effectiveness is restricted to those projects whose consequences are clearly perceived and affect people, and is more likely to be accepted by national policy-makers who can afford a longer timeframe, a rare situation in the developing world. Irrigation projects have also benefited from this approach as their negative side-effects—salinity, diseases—were increasingly felt and as rehabilitation work constituted the bulk of lending in this sector. Conservation, however, is more difficult to justify in economic terms, which explains in part its neglect by the Bank. The prevalent attitude is to approach conservation in utilitarian terms as the management of untapped and renewable resources, which the concept of sustainable development illustrates.[58] Emphasis is placed on the long-term diseconomies of short-term benefits (a welcome dimension of project analysis) and on rational multiple-use management of natural resources (an extension of the technocentric approach to environmental problems).[59]

The reliance upon an economic rationale implies that efforts be made to modify traditional cost-benefit analyses and develop measures of environmental welfare, discussed in chapter 2. If primary importance is to be given to economic criteria, one would expect the organization to devote much of its considerable research capabilities to devising a new economic doctrine or new economic instruments that would allow it to incorporate environmental considerations into its project and policy appraisals. A few attempts to extend welfare economics theory have, however, been unfruitful, and the Bank failed to direct efforts toward the development of non-monetary methods of social costs evaluation. Rather, it left it to other centers to propose innovative methods and applications.[60]

With the preeminence of economic rationality, the staff can use technical standards to limit the range of issues it should consider and the diversity of criteria that can be used to evaluate their decisions. Economic rationality, then, is an indispensable protection against external political and technological threats, as stated by President Black:

. . . We must, to borrow a phrase from President de Gaulle, "encase ourselves in ice," when we talk about economic aid. We must remove the taint of ideology from the language of economics—render it as antiseptic as the language a Hamburg exporter uses when he makes out a bill of lading—and then stick to our standards. I know of no other way in which it can serve to gain agreement from others on the necessary minimum requirements for sound economic growth.[61]

To Black, the economic yardstick guaranteed the Bank's independence and impartiality. As Fatouros pointed out, "the claim of freedom to act as if politics did not matter, or did not exist, is an important component of the Bank's official ideology."[62] Technicity becomes a means of ignoring the political origins and impact of the Bank's lending decisions and rejects external pressures. Thus, the political consequences of bringing women into development, of promoting agricultural settlements, of facilitating the multinational corporations' involvement in the development of mineral resources are ignored. Instead, objective and well-established economic criteria are invoked. From an environmental viewpoint, when the merits of a loan and of environment components are phrased in general economic terms, what cannot easily be cast in micro or macroeconomic terms is likely to be disregarded. And if the basis for standards is not public health or welfare or the environment, but the size of the economic trade-off; not what is best, but what is economical, will be preferred. For example, the Bank insisted that the added environmental and health costs do not exceed about 3 percent of the total project cost. Higher ratios may diminish the overall rate of return of the project and be opposed by the borrower. The Bank has claimed since the early 1970s that higher expenses were, in fact, unnecessary.

On the other hand, if economic criteria are not used to reach a decision, but to justify those made on other grounds; then economic rationality only shields the organization from pressures coming from actors which do not control key resources. However, as the organization succumbs to various pressures while trying to maintain some sense of rationality by invoking economic arguments, it also tends to lose credibility in proportion to the flexibility of the economic reasoning it can demonstrate. This situation has indeed plagued the definition of its environmental action. While economic arguments enabled it in the beginning to defuse opposition to this new issue while limiting its involvement, the economic reasoning it used to justify attention to health, women, and the poor made it more difficult to maintain a restricted scope for its environmental policy or justify its poor implementation record.

Rationality applies to objectives as well as methods. The Bank defined its goals—from rapid growth to "redistribution with growth" to sustainable development—so as to gather the support of its clientele without alienating its creditors. These efforts reflect a strategy of disjointed incrementalism which helps the organization cope with uncertainty by allowing decision-makers to modify their behavior according to changing situations. This strategy implies variable tactics but constant objectives. Thus, if rationalization is to succeed as a strategy, it must involve a clear sense of direction, a "development philosophy." The Bank has to lead the way. Bureaucratic inertia and increasing pressures on the organization to redefine its goals in accordance with the interests of segments of its constituencies, however, have impeded such efforts. Scrambling to secure resources by adopting the rationalizations of external actors haphazardly and inconsistently had produced, by the mid-1980s, external dissatisfaction and internal chaos. Planning was de-emphasized and the private sector re-emphasized under American pressures. Western banks and the largest Third World debtors demanded that the organization become more of a short-term provider of capital to countries experiencing debt servicing difficulties at the risk of neglecting its traditional long-term development mission and jeopardizing other activities. Its commitment to the poor was increasingly questioned. The addition of a volatile international economic environment and the increasing pressures that transnational organizations put upon it, make it indispensable for the Bank to define a vision that would serve to coordinate its activities, galvanize the staff, and increase control over its milieu. Failure to do so will condemn the organization to a complete loss of its autonomy and to reduced relevance and effectiveness.

Diversification

One of Thompson's coping strategies is adding to the organization's domain. As he emphasized, "an organization is dependent on some element of its task-environment (1) in proportion to the organization's need for resources or performance which that element can provide and (2) in inverse proportion to the ability of other elements to provide the same resources or performance."[63] Diversification reduces dependence on a single resource: "Under norms of rationality, organizations seek to minimize the power of task-environment elements over them by maintaining alternatives."[64] The Bank's two main resources are money and projects. By extending vertically and through other strategies, the Bank has been able to control the number of projects submitted to it. On the financial side, the Bank's charter seemed to ensure that the organization would not become dependent on erratic annual appropriations governed by political considerations external to the work of the organization. After their initial subscription, governments pledged a certain amount of callable capital to the Bank and could not withdraw their funds unless they withdrew from the organization. The Bank would then use private capital and its profits to finance development projects.

The creation of IDA and the expansion of the organization, however, have increased the Bank's dependence on its creditors. Through periodic IDA replenishments and capital increases, they can influence Bank policies, or even threaten its survival to a greater extent than expected. Congressional delaying of IDA IV and V, American reduction of pledged commitments for IDA VI, and opposition to significant increases in IDA VII have made the vulnerability of the organization painfully clear.

A diversification of capital sources would thus enable the organization to dampen the influence of its main contributors, expecially the United States. As McNamara emphasized: "It is our job in the World Bank to look at the world money markets as a whole and where there are surpluses and reserves that can be tapped."[65] Many at the Bank acknowledged this need after IDA-V: ". . . an institution such as IDA cannot in the long run be too dependent on any single creditor."[66] Encouraged by its principal members, the Bank undertook a multifaceted diversification policy which affected the place of borrowing, the currencies in which its outstanding capital is held, and the origins of co-financing capital (see "Co-financing" above).

The European and Japanese economic recoveries enabled the Bank to develop the German, Swiss and Japanese capital markets in which to sell its bonds. After 1973, the Bank turned to OPEC and promoted an increase in Saudi Arabia's capital commitment, "quite a revolution in our access to capital markets" according to Burke Knapp, the number-two man under McNamara.[67] In 1974, out of a net borrowing of $2.8 billion, $2.2 billion came from OPEC. The importance of these markets subsequently subsided with the reduction of their capital surplus.

Its record regarding capital diversification is impressive. In 1963, 44 percent of the Bank's outstanding securities was held in the United States. By June 1972, despite an enormous increase in Bank borrowing, 35 percent of its outstanding securities was held by U.S. investors (with 26 percent in Germany, 10 percent in Japan, and 6 percent in Switzerland).[68] The Bank now borrows in more than 100 countries. This diversification also affected the currency of issue. By 30 June 1986, about 26 percent of Bank securities was in U.S. dollars as against about 32 percent in 1980 and 75 percent in 1963. At the same time, 25 percent were in Japanese Yens, 18 percent in Deutsche Marks, and 17 percent in Swiss Francs.[69]

Whether diversification really increases autonomy is unclear. It has been suggested that an opening toward OPEC increased the organization's vulnerability to political demands, as shown by the Bank's failure to criticize OPEC for the oil-price hikes that put many developing countries in a very difficult position or by the political support McNamara provided that organization by acknowledging "the slow, long-term decline in petroleum prices which called for correction."[70] On the other hand, the availability of capital gave the Bank good arguments for demanding greater financial contributions and for increasing its presence in the most seriously affected countries.

Oppenheim further claims that this diversification strategy has cost the organization support in U.S. financial markets. Diversification would make the organization dependent on even less reliable financial sources. But this reasoning ignores the central reason for diversification: by avoiding so great a concentration of resources; access, use, and possession of the resources cannot be made dependent on the organization's compliance with their holder's policies. As the number of sources of funds expands, the ability of any one of them to yield overwhelming influence over the organization diminishes.

Yet, this strategy has its limits, and its theoretical benefits overlook political considerations and assume too readily a high level of competition among the organization's external actors. The large reduction in the U.S. share of IDA-VI was indeed offset by increases from Japan and Germany. The Bank also started drawing the newly industrializing countries (NICs) into the process: Mexico, Argentina, and Brazil contributed to IDA-VI for the first time. It was able to create the special fund for African development against U.S. opposition. Yet, since other donors had set their contributions as a percentage of the American share, expected resources which individual increases could not offset fell significantly and constrained subsequent IDA replenishments.

The consequences of diversification for environmental policy are unclear. They are likely to be minimal as far as environmental criteria are concerned, for business shares very similar environmental perspectives, as well as economic, financial, and banking criteria the world over. It is doubtful that Japanese bankers will be less concerned about rates of return on investment, labor intensive projects, or local costs financing than American bankers.

Indirectly, though, when money is in short supply, the added environmental components of many projects are less likely to be funded by the Bank, and environmental rehabilitation or conservation projects are postponed. IDA's financial woes of the 1980s indeed negatively affected the environment. Thus, a geographically and institutionally diverse source of funds, by ensuring a more constant supply of scarce resources, actually helps dampen pressure on environmental components.

Expansion

Between 1962 and 1984, World Bank lending increased by nearly five-fold in real terms (see figure 4.1). As the international economic environment became more and more turbulent, the Bank felt a greater need to assert its relevance and preeminence in international developmental lending. Changing developmental doctrines, the growing competition of private and regional banks, and the growing needs of its recipients forced the Bank to expand its domain. Thompson hypothesizes that organizations facing many constraints will seek to enlarge their task-environment, especially if they are unable to achieve power in other sectors. The history of the evolution of the Bank's goals, structure and lending, illustrates this strategy.

It has been suggested that the creation of IDA was a device to gain the support of the developing countries against its main creditors.[71] It alleviated the possibility that big borrowers would default on Bank loans, and created a pressure group in favor of the maintainance and growth of the size of its lending. Similarly, the expansion of Bank lending into social and agricultural sectors was a response to pressures from developing countries as well as an attempt to avoid being bypassed by other lending institutions. In an attempt to control all the determinants of the success of its policies, the Bank developed its health sector. To maintain its international standing among lending institutions and to pursue simultaneous development objectives, McNamara chose to expand lending rapidly at a time when commercial banks were increasing their lending volume and were threatening its relative importance as a supplier of capital.[72] Energy provides a clear example of this strategy. As the developed countries became more concerned with energy supplies, the price of oil, and the prospects of Third World competition, the Bank increased its energy lending dramatically and promoted the idea of a separate energy affiliate which would manage a $25 billion fund for energy development. One problem, however, is that often the same reasons (such as the price of oil or balance of payments difficulties) that justify an expansion of lending also constrain the ability of donors to expand their contributions. The Bank faced this contradiction throughout the 1980s which diversification and other strategies could not effectively remedy.

Figure 4.1. Growth of IBRD/IDA Lending in Real Terms, 1962–1984

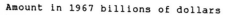

Amount in 1967 billions of dollars

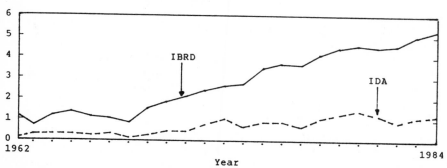

Year

SOURCES: World Bank, Annual Reports; Datadisk, February 1985 (Cambridge Planning and Analytics, Inc.)

Expansion strengthens the Bank's international position, helps defuse contradictory pressures, and increases the Bank's resources and flexibility. Yet it has serious disadvantages. There is a risk that the growing bureaucracy will stultify the organization. Communication within the organization grew more difficult with the tripling of the professional staff within fifteen years, from 1,348 in 1971 to more than 3,806 in 1986. In-fighting increased with a diversification of ideology; between the partisans of centralization and planning and those wishing to emphasize private enterprise, between the supporters and opponents of an emphasis on social lending or an increase of structural adjustment lending. In-fighting also became more acute when expansion of the Bank's resources slowed dramatically in the 1980s. "Uneconomical" sectors that were added in the 1970s and the new "social" criteria for project appraisal that were developed came under attack. Indeed, although growing resources allowed for the adoption and implementation of environmental concerns in the 1970s, their development became dependent on the ability of the organization to keep expanding, shield itself from the opposition of external actors, and modify its internal ideology toward greater receptivity to these concerns. When the milieu changed, pressure increased to limit the environmental activities of the Bank, which progress in its institutionalization and routinization could not overcome.

As external links increase, internal links weaken. This affects the organization's innovativeness. The Bank was criticized in the 1980s for its conservatism and its failure to foresee and adapt to the international economic crisis, and to understand how the latter would affect its operations. Its inability to devise a new development strategy in the face of the failures of even well-designed projects and its lack of intellectual leadership were faulted.[73]

Another drawback is more political. Expansion means that the question who controls or influences the organization becomes more important. As the Bank's activities and visibility increase, so do the demands put on it. The controversy over seating the Palestinian Liberation Organization and the growing scrutiny of its operations by the U.S. Congress are symptomatic of the dangers of expansion.[74] The size of the staff prompted the United States to pressure for its reduction along lines that would "streamline" the organization in accordance with its preferred mode of operation. The increased attention paid to it by INGOs, and the subsequent criticisms of its environmental record that followed also stemmed from this new prominence, and created new pressures at a time when the organization was less capable of meeting new demands.

Finally, expansion creates new vulnerabilities. As it took the form of ever-increasing amounts of lending, quantity not quality became a criterion for judging staff performance, which in turn worked against the thorough consideration and implementation of environmental components (see chapter 2). Growth also implies that a greater number of projects need be identified routinely. The need to lend in order to justify further capital increases can thus lead to a dilution of the Bank's ideology and weaken the organization's future negotiating posture. For example, as it strove to assure its dominant lending position in India, it yielded on financing for local cost and public entities.

The tragedy of the Bank's situation is that expansion is inevitable. The organization must control its milieu. Had it not expanded, its position as a leading intellectual and financial development institution would have vanished, and the purpose of the institution with it. The dilemma lies in the possibility that through expansion, the organization might make itself more vulnerable to external influences and lose adaptive flexibility, thereby endangering its goals.

Transforming Strategies

The World Bank's mandate is the transformation of its recipients' economies. It creates and diffuses knowledge, formulates and helps implement policies, and develops investment programs designed to fulfill specific development goals. Adaptive strategies will not suffice to protect the organization from its milieu. Their chief drawback arises from their dilution of the content of the policy. They are not pro-active. In an adaptive context, the organization changes its structure and behavior to fit a given milieu. The ultimate aim of the Bank's environmental policy, however, is to have developing countries adopt environmental criteria to maximize the short-term success of its projects and the long-term prospects of the borrowers' economies. Ultimate control and certainty rest on the organization's transformation of its milieu to its advantage. This chapter addresses five major transforming strategies that the Bank has used to implement its environmental objectives: education, standard operating procedures, sanctions, control of demand formation, and action on the causal texture of the milieu. Rather than directly protecting the organization, these strategies attempt to create a milieu more conducive to the achievement of its goals.

Education: The Cultivation of Understanding and Attitudes

Education is the strategy of the weak. Exhortation was the specific mandate of many new environmental institutions, from national ministries to the United Nations Environment Programme. Although OESA was given some leverage in its ability to assess projects, its limited staff and poor bureaucratic position forced it to rely on education.

Probably the major obstacle that the Bank's environmental units faced in implementing this policy was the wide disbelief of the staff, clients, peers, and financial community in the magnitude and relevance of environmental problems in developing countries. As Caldwell noted: "The first step toward the transformation of behavior and institutions required for a defense of the Earth is to convince enough people that the change is necessary."[75] Few were convinced that it was a problem which concerned the developing countries or which deserved being highly placed on their development agenda. Faced with a hostile milieu, education became one of the pillars of OESA's strategy to implement its concerns. Among the various methods it used to this end, two stand out: training at headquarters or in the field, and the dissemination of specific guidelines.

Soon after its creation, OESA first directed its sight internally. It sought to educate the staff of economists and engineers in the importance of the environmental dimension of their work, not only as an adjunct to development projects, but as a distinct approach to answering the dual problem of economic growth and poverty. Much of this internal education, which today remains essential, has been performed after project evaluations had pointed to the consequences of neglecting ecological variables, and to the role that past development schemes played in the rise of new environmental problems, such as desertification and flooding.[76]

OESA sought to diffuse knowledge in several ways. It conducted informal seminars to interested staff members of the Bank. More promising was the publication of basic guidelines to evaluate the potentially disruptive effects of development projects in an attempt to facilitate the adoption of an environmental perspective into the project cycle and educate the staff in asking the relevant questions. The first environmental handbook appeared in 1973 and constituted "[t]he first major effort of a lending institution to establish criteria for evaluating the environmental impact of its investment projects."[77] It was later followed by a few other detailed checklists.[78] Together they constitute the most comprehensive set of guidelines of any development assistance agency.

These handbooks were widely adopted by national bureaucracies; international organizations, especially other development banks which preferred them to developing their own; and, irregularly, by Bank staff. But mere adoption does not imply that these guidelines will be observed. The staff of the Bank was under no obligation to do so: no systematic procedures were devised to incorporate them into project identification and appraisal. Several were also vague or incomplete.

The development of sectoral guidelines was slow and limited to the industrial sector. None concerned agriculture, the single largest lending sector. Their publication fulfilled the immediate objectives of the Bank's policy. Eager to ration its work, it turned its attention first to the avoidance of major environmental disasters, while pointing to the environmental determinants of project success. It refined its approach later to include multi-purpose resources management and a greater ecological perspective in its recommendations.

Several attempts were made to give sector policy papers an environmental dimension. It was only in 1976, however, when several sectoral papers written in the late sixties and early seventies were revised, that policy directives began being built around sounder environmental practices. Both the Forestry and the Village Water Supply papers insisted on the primary importance of the environmental aspects of these activities and justified environmental rehabilitation schemes. The 1980 *Health Sector Policy Paper* identified those environmental conditions that may cause or exacerbate health problems in developing countries. In the case of onchocerciasis (river blindness), for example, the Bank acknowledged that ". . . the development of water resources may help the prevalence of the simulium fly (which breeds in swift waters near the gates of artificial lakes) and the incidence of the disease."[79]

Yet, further revisions of sector policies did not reflect any dramatic improvement in the environmental thinking of the staff (and of the Executive Directors who approved them) or a deeper understanding of the place that an environmental perspective should have in their work. Admittedly, mere awareness does not ensure that environmental protection will be given great consideration in the field. Nevertheless, it would have the merit of providing a different, more sophisticated (if less measurable) and ecologically sounder definition of development problems. This was accomplished in few papers. *The Forestry Sector Policy Paper* stands out in its presentation of the multi-purpose management perspective inspired by the practice of the U.S. Forest Service. Forests are viewed as resources which should be made to fulfill different functions: ecological, anthropological (food, fuel, habitat), industrial (timber), scientific, and recreational (tourism). The Bank proceeded to define the problem as one of reconciling these five objectives.

While acknowledging the ecological importance of forests and the need to secure a sustainable exploitation of its resources, the Bank still saw a "divergence of economic and social interests" in the case of the exploitation of the Philippines forests, rather than a problem of economic analysis. The aim of the Bank forestry policy remained "the promotion of forest development,"[80] not conservation. Thus, the Bank could support clearcutting a virgin forest followed by reforestation using fastgrowing non-native species such as eucalyptus, which provide fuel, lumber, and stabilization of the watershed, but also impoverish the ecosystem. Yet, this paper was unique in its appreciation and treatment of the ecological dimensions of forest exploitation, even though the realization and articulation of these issues came only in 1978, eight years after the creation of the position of environmental adviser, and long after they had been raised elsewhere.

At the same time, the *Fishery Sector Policy Paper*, issued in 1982, was

criticized for reflecting poorly on the Bank's Agriculture and Rural Development Division's awareness of sound environmental management
principles. Widely accepted principles of fisheries management, such as
maximum sustainable yield (to avert overexploitation) or habitat protection, were ignored. No commitment was made to implement measures to
ensure sustainable fishery production. The paper was thus faulted for
ignoring the principles of the World Conservation Strategy, the pledges of
the 1980 Declaration on Environmental Policies and Procedures Relating
to Development, and the rhetoric of the Bank's own president.[81]

OESA also tried to incorporate environment values into the in-house
Economic Development Institute (EDI) which trains nationals in the
appraisal of development projects. As a training institute for future
decision-makers in developing countries, the EDI is ideally placed for con-
veying the Bank's ideology. OESA's attempts to change the EDI curriculum have met with little success. Although the institute offers one seminar
on population and development, and one on water supply and sewerage, it
does not offer any general course on either ecology or environmental sciences. OESA, in collaboration with UNEP, did develop a course on environment and development but failed to have it adopted. As one staff
member put it, EDI has been "environmentally hopeless," and seemed at
best to be content with last minute ad-hoc talks on a particular topic as
an adjunct rather than as an integral part of the training it dispenses. The
most effective use of the curriculum of EDI, however, would not lie in the
addition of an extra course or two, but in the incorporation of an environmental perspective into each course. Its neglect led to sharp criticisms by
UNEP, the U.S. Congress, and INGOs.

The Bank has directly promoted environmental awareness within countries by financing training components in some projects. In Indonesia, it
has contributed to the strengthening of existing urban programs in environmental education and in the establishment of two additional ones in
provincial universities. But these initiatives remain rare for they depend
both upon the recipients' request and upon the organization's willingness
to lend for educational components.

The Bank refrained from technical assistance for a long time (the position of training adviser was created in 1970), although the IDA charter
specifically authorized it to give such assistance.[82] Fear of being identified
with the activities of the rest of the UN agencies may explain this early
reluctance.[83] Its change of attitude followed the new type of projects it
supported. Projects became more complex and their success depended on
sound operation and implementation over a long time. Lending for technical assistance climbed from $39.5 million in 1969 to $218 million in 1976.
Van de Laar, acknowledging a "worsened research climate in the Bank as
a consequence of its evolving operational style," suspected this increase to

be in part an attempt to economize on the Bank's administrative expenses, especially research, as it transferred such costs to the borrower.[84] But it was more a reflection of the complexity of the new projects and of the need for continuous adequate supervision. It also served another purpose discussed below, namely the creation of domestic constituencies.

Typically, training constituted the second leg of OESA's approach to the cultivation of understanding and attitudes: "The most important practical result of the Occupational Safety and Health guidelines is to convince the local sponsor that the problem exists and is serious. If he is convinced and if the project provides money for it, the next major step is training and technical assistance."[85]

Although training can also take place through the education sector, OESA included it mostly as a component of agricultural projects to prevent soil erosion. Training can take place at three levels. It can be directed to (1) managers who become assistants to expatriate officers for a couple of years, (2) to experts and extension workers in specially built training centers, and (3) to farmers in regional centers.[86]

The training components of a project provide an opportunity to educate the staff and officials of developing countries at the very important level of the project. It is imperative to train local staff not only in the operations of environmental techniques, but also in ways to minimize unnecessary environmental damages during implementation. Along with institution-building and research, technical assistance is viewed as a major means to change policies in the forestry sector.[87]

Education has had a rather mixed record. Although awareness has indeed grown within and outside the Bank, actual behavior has not reflected these improvements. being "environmentally aware" does not ensure adoption of proper environmental practices or say anything about the quality of this awareness. It may mean thinking of environmental impacts and dismissing them without detailed studies. Or it may mean meeting existing national standards and Bank procedures passively, without promoting the larger purposes of the Bank's policy. Thus, other means of implementation are necessary. Through environmental education directed at the Bank's recipients, however, the OESA also sought to improve its own internal influence within the project cycle. Education eventually led to the development of new rules and procedures and to the creation of a specific constituency in developing countries, two strategies described below.

Creation of New Rules and Procedures

Routineness formalizes and programs the organization's relations to its milieu. In particular, it reflects the institutionalization of attempts to reduce uncertainty. The creation of new standard operating procedures ensures that the minimal goals of the policy will be met since similar criteria are incorporated into all projects. For example, the Bank insists on detailed contracts for each project to minimize future conflicts. As Katz and Kahn point out, "Rules change the basis of power away from threat and coercion toward legitimacy."[88] In that sense, rule creation is a form of conflict management.

Not only does it help build legitimacy, it also fosters autonomy when the organization has some discretion over the enforcement of the rules. Routineness can be the outcome of successful strategies, when it results from an agreement between the principal actors on the legitimacy of such rules and procedures. It can also be a pro-active strategy designed to enhance the stability of the organization's milieu since the Bank can unilaterally (or with the support of the developed countries) adopt lending rules that will ensure that its minimal policy goals will be implemented. In that sense, it corresponds to the promotion of norms and constitutes an alternative to education and bargaining.

The function of OESA was to review each project for its environmental impact. Thus, environmental review became an integral part of the project cycle. As chapter 2 explained, ecological guidelines could be incorporated into the projects at each stage of the project cycle. The earlier the OESA's input, the greater its influence on the design of the project. It could integrate its concern at such an early stage that it would become impossible to assess the additional costs incurred.

But the incorporation of rules into the operations of the Bank has been remarkably slow. Until 1985, the OESA was unable to systematize its enforcement of environmental guidelines in the Bank's *Operations Manual*, a confidential document which describes the procedures that must be followed throughout the project cycle. This delay reflected the degree of opposition that existed to adding environmental criteria to the performance and evaluation of the Bank's operations. Rather than systematic procedures, the Regional offices preferred a case-by-case approach until the failure of this approach became too apparent.

Other attempts have largely met with failure. The Bank sought to internalize the calculation of environmental costs and benefits by modifying its appraisal methodology, but it has proven difficult to develop a suitable approach that could be readily adopted by the staff.

The potential of this strategy was well perceived by many developing countries who opposed the Bank's new environmental policy in the early 1970s. Through the project cycle, the Bank influences national decision-making by influencing the choice of criteria for decision-making. It decides whether a development project will lead to environmental disruptions or defines the policy-making framework derived from the choice of economic standards in the definition of the values to be served. For example, the forestry sector policy paper required that all appraisal documents for all forestry-related projects in the future include an evaluation of the perceivable environmental effects of the projects.[89] The requirement that impact studies be conducted when strong environmental disruptions are suspected (as in steel production or irrigation projects) provides a certainty that environmental constraints have at least been considered in the design and appraisal of the project. Unlike USAID, however, the Bank does not require a systematic environmental document for each project. This absence, noted earlier, stems from economic, bureaucratic, and political factors.

Sanctions

An obvious attribute of the Bank that distinguishes it from most other IGOs is its ability to enforce its policies. Increased capitalization and expanded lending strengthened its relative position vis-a-vis other bilateral agencies and heightened its importance to developing countries. Despite the stagnation of its resources in the 1980s, the balance-of-payment difficulties of many Third World countries and the reduction in private capital transfers enhance the relative position of the Bank.

The use of positive and negative sanctions is the first means of control that comes to mind when analyzing the Bank's relationship to its milieu. Indeed, leverage is not a dirty word for the Bank. The organization uses it openly and relies upon it.[90] McNamara advocated the use of leverage to secure the necessary changes in borrowers' policies that would encourage income redistribution.[91] Influences can be gained by either bestowing rewards after an event or trying to induce the event by setting the conditions for the granting of the loan.

Positive sanctions take the form of loans and political support for the organization's clients. The Bank rewards countries which adopt its suggested development approach by giving them the means of implementing their policies. This role was further expanded through the development of structural adjustment loans in the 1980s which are expressly conditioned to macroeconomic changes. Positive sanctions, however, are not limited to the provision of funds. They also include the organization's flexibility in interpreting its mandate, and in setting conditions to its loans, as discussed in chapter 2. Instead of rigidly following criteria which call for IDA funds to go to countries with a per capita GNP below a certain level, the Bank decides above this threshold. "Blending" loans and credits enables it to adjust the terms to the country's situation and to the requirements of the project or in accordance with the Bank's interest in the promotion of certain policies. Blending is also a means of counteracting the attractiveness of the terms of the Bank's competitors—given their weaker analytical probes—when it is forced to raise its interest rates. Other positive sanctions include the identification of co-financing sources, the provision of technical assistance and lending for projects with no rate of return (such as natural resources inventories). This panoply of positive sanctions enables the organization to implement its controversial policies and, with education, has constituted the main instrument for the promotion of environmental values. For example, when Kenya saw its tourist industry decline in the late 1970s and asked for help, the Bank conditioned a loan on demonstrable efforts to curb poaching.[92]

Conditioning assistance to the fulfillment of specific environmental stipulations was a very dramatic and symbolic gesture. Despite implementation difficulties, it undeniably contributed to heightened awareness of these problems, especially in Latin America.[93] Whether supported or actively resisted, these measures became part of the agenda of development. Moreover, the Bank's imposition of conditions on its loans often allows governments to implement unpopular measures and avoid direct blame. These standards may also "become internationally infectious: politicians in one country find it easier to push through reforms if they can show that the same thing is being done elsewhere."[94]

Coercion constitutes a very powerful and well-publicized strategy. Formal negative sanctions include the suspension of a loan, its cancellation, or the acceleration of maturity. Every project agreement contains a provision which authorizes the Bank to declare its principal and outstanding bonds due immediately in the event of a borrower's default or violation of the agreement. The "cross-default" and "non-effectiveness" clauses included in co-financing agreements also provide tighter enforcement capabilities. In January 1981, the Bank suspended a $250 million loan to India for a fertilizer plant because of a decision by the Indian cabinet to replace an American consulting company that engineering experts selected by the Bank had chosen. The decision seemed to be a shift away from the Bank's requirement of international competitive bidding.[95] This episode was remarkable because of India's importance to the organization as a major debtor whose interests the Bank has widely defended. There are fewer inhibitions to using this leverage toward smaller countries.

Outright loan cancellations and suspensions are rare, however. From a political perspective, coercion is very costly, and the Bank resorts to it only reluctantly. It values a continuous good relationship with each borrower, especially with its largest debtors. Moreover, very large projects are often parts of larger development programs supported by several multilateral and bilateral organizations (such as the environmentally infamous Namrida and POLONOROESTE projects of India and Brazil). These projects will not stop just because the Bank is pulling out. Thus, the Bank often faces the classic dilemma of either staying and hoping to exert some positive influence or getting out and witnessing worse ecological damage as well as difficulties in its future position in the country.

No loan was canceled on environmental grounds until 1986, despite numerous instances of failures to respect negotiated guidelines. Instead of formal sanctions, the Bank prefers using informal ones, such as slowing down the rate of disbursements or refusing to lend for future projects of this type. These threats are much more common and have been made at various times to enforce environmental agreements especially in the context of industrial development projects.

A more indirect coercive method is linked to the Bank's prestige within the financial community. The Bank's assessment of a country's creditworthiness, for example, determines in large part the attitude of major lending banks. Similarly, the failure of a borrower to implement agreed-upon guidelines may have repercussions on that country's borrowing prospects in international markets.

Finally, it is worth mentioning lesser-known coercive strategies which the Bank has used. One is to leak confidential information that it has gathered during its economic evaluation—the government's openness to the Bank's missions is a condition for lending—to pressure a government into taking specific measures. Hayter mentioned the case of Costa Rica where the Bank leaked its evaluation of the government's education policy and created a "furor" in Parliament and in the media.[96]

As a method of ensuring the project administrator's compliance with Bank policies, it can choose to dissociate itself publicly from him, bypass him, or have him removed. Tunisia's second most powerful official was condemned to ten years of hard labor after the Bank issued a document critical of his management: "Ben Salah was tried for high treason for willfully misleading Bourguiba by suppressing World Bank reports which accused Ben Salah of mismanagement."[97] The mere threat of circulating highly critical reports may be enough to ensure compliance.

Various factors hinder the effective use of negative sanctions, however. First, the organization must maintain the support of its clients to secure IDA replenishments and capital increases, as well as to guard against competitors and promote its ideology. It has therefore been reluctant to oversee closely the implementation of its projects. This problem affected the environmental sector considerably. The Bank has often been unable to monitor the recipient's compliance with negotiated ambient standards, monitoring being equated with interfering with a nation's sovereignty. It has been unwilling to take the political risks associated with pursuing environmental demand, which the lack of personnel often precluded in the first place.

Second, the effectiveness of sanctions is obviously a function of the organization's degree of unity in pressing for the specific behavior. A controversial policy like the environment will have a hard time marshaling the arsenal of sanctions of the Bank in its favor. The case of the POLONOR-OESTE project described in chapter 5 provides a good example of the reluctance of the organization to apply sanction despite gross violations of the negotiated agreements. Only after strong external pressure, and following repeated assertions that all was well, were disbursements first halted, then Bank participation canceled. Whether this helped effect a change of behavior in the recipient's policy remained doubtful given the political and economic reasons that justify these projects and the willingness of other donor agencies to finance environmentally or socially destructive projects.[98] This case also showed the limits of assigning environmental conditions to a specific project. Brazil can proceed with a controversial project by using capital destined to the financing of other projects.

Third, the effectiveness of these sanctions will depend on the size of the recipient and on the degree of Bank penetration into the country. Whereas it tends to be more drastic with the least developed countries for which the Bank Group is the predominant source of capital—the case with many IDA recipients—the Bank finds it harder to control effectively the use or allocation of the funds it lend to NICs (Brazil, Mexico, Argentina, Yugoslavia) or to countries with powerful institutions and expertise, like India. Moreover, this type of leverage depends on the ability of the organization "to deliver." In a well-publicized case, the Bank was unable to follow through on its commitments of larger amounts of aid to India after it forced certain policy changes on the reluctant government.[99] Its failure to secure more funds from the members of the consortium and delays in IDA-II replenishment showed that, in this particular case, it lacked the leverage it claimed. According to Escott Reid, this failure subsequently weakened the Group's bargaining position. The NICs also have had access to the eurodollar market, which, until the debt problem became acute in the 1980s, "reduced the significance of the Bank in their external financial flows, . . . and thereby its leverage in pressing for new distributional objectives."[100]

The debt crisis of the 1980s strengthened the Bank's arsenal of sanctions. Yet, the very turbulence of the international system that makes its clients more dependent on the organization also inhibits the effective exercize of positive sanctions. With the dramatic decrease in private capital flows and a growing need to service their debts, governments have become more dependent on two international institutions which were given a prominent role in managing this problem, the World Bank and the IMF. Although a significant shortfall in financial resources hampered the organization's capacity to use its leverage effectively, the Bank nevertheless found itself in a new position to influence macroeconomic policies to an unprecedented extent. The expansion of sectoral and structural adjustment lending has also helped remove a limitation to the Bank's ability to use its leverage: the existence of projects. At the same time, however, the urgency that led to this new role also brought new pressures on the Bank to disregard other standard operating procedures and "move money" to the most indebted nations.

When one leaves the realm of macroeconomics to consider the environmental components of development projects, the limitation remains that actual disbursements are not linked to the observance of conditions on general environmental policy performance; rather they are tied only to the observance of conditions attached to a specific project. Thus, the Bank will not hold disbursements or even condition a loan based on its evaluation of the borrower's national policy regarding the exploitation of natural resources, but will look at its performance on a particular project. Only an extension of the scope of sectoral adjustment lending could remedy this situation.

Nevertheless, sanctions are very powerful instruments of policy implementation. It is precisely the Bank's potential to use this strategy effectively that makes its environmental policy so important not only to its own development policy, but also to the success of other international organizations devoted to the promotion of environmental values.

The Control of Demand Formation

> Inevitably, the movement to protect the biosphere and defend the Earth is concerned with institutions as well as with behavior, because through institutions human effort is guided and social goals attained. The transformation of institutional structures is in fact the transformation of society.[101]

Caldwell's 1972 call for the institutionalization of environmental objectives was primarily achieved through cooptation and the creation of new constituencies.

Selznick's pioneering study of the Tennessee Valley Authority (TVA) focused on the process of co-optation as a means of securing a stable milieu. He defined co-optation as "the process of absorbing new elements into the leadership or policy-determining structure of an organization as a means of averting threats to its stability or existence."[102] Co-optation is a substitute for coercion. As a means of adjusting to a hostile environment, the TVA co-opted representatives of its opposition into its management. This process, however, also entailed some loss of the organization's autonomy as the new elements helped shape the organization's policies in accordance with their own interests.

Now, for Selznick, co-optation was an *adaptive* response of the organization to its environment. We shall here approach it as *transforming* strategy because the nature of the Bank's co-optative process is slightly different. The Bank creates constituencies and builds support where none existed, not by allowing external actors to exert some influence over the organization's decision-making—albeit indirectly—but by making the personal success of external groups or individuals intrinsically linked to the promotion of the Bank's objectives.

Co-optation of the development administrations of developing countries followed aspects of the TVA pattern. To minimize political threats or the effects of economic instability, each project is a legally independent entity, and the Bank favors autonomous management in a new institution independent of the rest of the national bureaucracy. As Caiden and Wildavsky have observed, "[T]he general effect is that of an 'enclave' an oasis of certainty in an environment of uncertainty."[103] Managers also tend to link their careers to the success of the projects and to their ties with the Bank. Pakistan's Planning Commission, for example, used the Bank to expand its own domain.[104] Certainty is also enhanced because the new management substitutes its own methods for the traditional rules. Thus, these managers usually "speak" a language similar to that of the Bank and share identical values.

The graduates of the Economic Development Institute (EDI) form the basis of the Bank's constituency. EDI primarily "educates" influential and promising officials as to the Bank's priorities and methodology: "[EDI] . . . is earning for us an even wider circle of friends and stimulating critics in those countries which are our primary concern. These men are the men who will be making the key development decisions in the underdeveloped world of tomorrow."[105] The fellows of EDI return to influential positions in national planning bodies or Bank project administrations. The Bank also circulates a monthly newsletter to a list of graduates, and even sets up libraries for them in client countries.[106] This explains why the OESA, nongovernmental organizations, and UNEP, all considered the incorporation of an environmental course and perspective into the EDI curriculum to be so important. Only when these graduates are convinced of its value is environmental protection likely to be accepted within developing countries. In the meantime, proposals from the local environmental ministry can be ignored by planners or officials who closely follow the training they received at the Bank.

Under President Black, administrative constituencies were only alternate channels of communication. Under McNamara, the Bank emphasized the importance of creating a technocratic vanguard in an "advanced sector" which would integrate the "backward sector" of the country. The emphasis on five-year country programming, and on devising national development strategies also underlined the importance of national planning agencies which the Bank has actively promoted throughout the developing world. Noteworthy examples include the Damodar Valley Corporation in India, or Thailand's Royal Irrigation Department, "a kingdom within a kingdom." These agencies secure the dynamic entrepreneurship of growth-oriented groups of public officials in what Hirschman called a "miasmic bureaucratic environment," performing "in marking contrast with the fumbling or 'milking' approach of some official Thai ventures in manufacturing".[107] These agencies can grow rapidly and become totally autonomous from the government itself, as illustrated by the expansion of the Thai Royal Irrigation Department into other sectors.

The creation of these autonomous agencies has been the prime means of institutionalization of the Bank's concerns. In effect, they "transform . . . the Bank's project administration into cohesive development constituencies with power in their governments."[108] Thus, the Bank can use these agencies to further its own objectives in the country, or to convince government members of a consortium to accept the Bank's recommendation for that country.

In addition to national planning institutions and sectoral agencies, development finance companies (DFCs)—publicly funded banks often established with the help of, and linked to, the Bank—"represent . . . one of the most successful efforts in institution building."[109] Although primarily set up to fund industrial projects, DFCs have been very useful in "new style" projects. Effective environmental protection, however, is subordinated to their awareness of its importance since the Bank's scrutiny of the projects they fund is relatively low.

Although these agencies could be very effective instruments for implementing the Bank's environmental objectives, their nature complicates the achievement of this goal. Given the technocratic approach that the Bank has promoted in developing countries and institutionalized in these agencies, their influence over policy-making and policy implementation actually impedes the development and promotion of environmental values. They became many more obstacles for OESA and other environmental units to surmount.

The OESA also tried to create its own constituency within developing countries and it has benefited from the efforts of UNEP to that end. Just as an objective alliance exists between finance ministries and World Bank organizational interests, another existed between OESA and national environmental ministries. OESA has supported their bureaucratic battles, and these agencies have supported OESA's. For example, it is only after the Indonesian environment minister visited the Bank headquarters that the national park component of a project was finally approved.[110] OESA has also made itself available for advice on the establishment of national environmental institutions and policies. In many countries, however, OESA's influence was also limited by the mandates of these agencies:

many ministries have been assigned the dual function of regulating as well as promoting resource development.

The Bank units involved in environmental issues have been more successful with non-governmental organizations. Two of UNEP's more successful strategies have been to develop close working relationships with transnational environmental groups and build indigenous scientific lobbies. UNEP's Mediterranean protection plan, for example, received a boost when reluctant governments were convinced by *their own* national scientists that the problems identified by the organization and developed countries deserved remedial action.[111] The more projects that include environmental components and training, the greater the national constituency in favor of such a perspective. One of the few remarkable developments of the early 1980s in developing countries was the emergence of active and successful environmental groups. In some cases, these groups have managed to define the national policy agenda; as in India, the Philippines, and Malaysia. Undertaking studies on the national state of the environment, they have defined problems and provided another means of support for the environmental units of the Bank. Their usefulness has been felt less at the policy level than at the preparation and implementation stages of the project cycle: they have identified likely problems associated with particular project proposals and alerted OESA to shortcomings in implementation.

OESA therefore benefited from the activities of other international organizations that reinforced indigenous scientific communities and grassroots organizations. UNEP, FAO, UNESCO, WHO, and ICSU helped countries develop their national scientific capabilities and disseminated scientific information, while the World Wildlife Fund (WWF), supported by USAID, helped build the capacities of environmental organizations (as in Panama). Yet the institutionalization by the Bank of the influence of environmental organizations first depended on the existence of projects or lending programs in that sector, which the dearth of major environmental projects made difficult (except perhaps in the Forestry sector). Thus, its environmental lobby remained weak. The inconsistence of official support for environmental problems on the part of the Bank is therefore important. By not actively and constantly pressing for greater environmental measures on a scale similar to population issues, the Bank removed bureaucratic ammunition from the national agencies in charge of environmental matters.

Alteration of the Causal Texture

One of the remarkable features of the World Bank's relationship with its milieu is that the organization does not limit its control to the direct relationship with its task-environment; it also wishes to influence the relations among external actors which impinge on its success: "The organization, through political mechanisms, attempts to create for itself an environment that is better for its interests."[112]

The Bank has indeed assumed a distinct political role in the past as a mediator between countries: between India and Pakistan over the Indus River waters; between Iran and Britain over oil nationalization; and between Egypt, Britain, and the United States over financing for the Aswan Dam.[113] With McNamara, the focus on the causal texture became even more dramatic. The president of the World Bank, for example, denounced arms spending, and asked for the removal of trade barriers. Amid a new protectionist wave, Alden Clausen followed in McNamara's footsteps:

> We ourselves must understand and we must persuade our compatriots at home to understand that to increase protectionism would be to impose an exhorbitant cost on the developed and developing countries alike—whatever the current domestic economic difficulties may be—it is within our power to resist the enormous protectionist pressures that now exist—and we must do so.[114]

In the 1970s, the Bank presented itself as a bridge between the North and the South, as an institution which could promote a "real" dialogue, away from the "noise" of political rhetoric. The creation of the Pearson Commission and the promotion of some of its findings, and the Bank's role in the establishment and promotion of the Brandt Commission testified to its profound desire to dampen the turbulence of its task-environment. The growth in Bank lending and the expansion of its domain forced it to become more involved in international matters previously external to its concerns, and provided it with the very capability of bringing the two sides together. This bridge-building strategy stemmed from the very stake that the Bank has in its clients. To broaden its basis of support, it was "to make the Third World feel the World Bank is their Bank, and they full partners in it, receiving help as a right."[115] The organization made it clear that its primary constituency was its clients.

The creation of the Development Committee by the Bank and the Fund in 1974 illustrated this "matrix" function. This committee was established at the ministerial level "to provide a focal point in the structure of economic cooperation for the formation of a comprehensive overview of the development process and to consider all aspects of the transfer of real resources to developing countries."[116] It provided another forum for the North-South dialogue, albeit one limited to considering only development issues while an Interim Committee in the Fund dealt with monetary reform. After the acrimonious conclusions of the 1977 Conference on International Economic Cooperation and of the 1980 UNIDO meeting, the

Bank emphasized the committee's potential usefulness as a forum "in which to promote international consensus . . . and to facilitate decisions in appropriate bodies" over issues and recommendations put forth by the Brandt Commission.[117] Developed countries which appreciated the freedom from power politics and political rhetoric praised "[t]he constructive role of the development banks as a forum in the North-South dialogue, . . . particularly by contrast with many less constructive approaches which have been proposed in other fora."[118]

In the 1980s, the Bank turned its efforts to debt issues. It was already active in trying to find an international solution to the debt problems of several developing nations (while formally opposing any rescheduling of its own), and in attempting to harmonize the lending policies of bilateral aid agencies and IGOs. But it was unable to foresee the extent of the crisis that it would become thanks to the general decline in the price of primary commodities. The 1985 "Baker initiative" enhanced its role as a capital transfer organization and increased its ability to engineer domestic economic changes it considers necessary. This new emphasis, however, also threatened its traditional focus on development projects.

With the growing dependence of industrial nations on the non-fuel mineral resources of developing countries, conflicts between them and Western mineral companies have sharpened. The Bank believes that it can play the role of an "active catalyst" and bring the various parties together.[119] The creation of the International Center for the Settlement of Investment Disputes (ICSID) within the Bank in the 1950s provided such a forum for the resolution of investment disputes between multinational corporations and developing nations. As Schneider has suggested, ICSID could also be used for the settlement of environmental disputes.[120] Problems associated with the exploitation of tropical forests, for example, lend itself to this kind of resolution process as they involve powerful lumber companies whose activities either can damage the forestry policy of these countries or, conversely, can be more enlightened than these countries would wish.

The debt crisis was aggravated by significant reductions in private capital flows. The Reagan Administration's desire to reduce the role of national governments in the economy and enhance the development of private enterprise as a motor of development led to the establishment of a mechanism designed to complement the work of the Center for Investment Disputes and protect foreign investments in developing countries. In 1985, the Board of Governors approved the Multilateral Investment Guarantee Agency (MIGA), designed to promote private investments in developing countries through coverage against the risks of adverse currency fluctuations, political violence, and expropriations. It was hoped that its remarkable voting structure, where capital importing and capital exporting countries will have equal power, will reduce future investment conflicts. MIGA came into being in 1988.

Conclusion

Saddled with new objectives, the Bank has used a vast array of strategies to promote them. It is precisely the availability of many effective strategies that makes the Bank so important for the promotion of international environmental concerns. Three questions remain: (1) How effective have they been? (2) Can we rank them according to their effectiveness? (3) How do they relate to one another?

The question of the general effectiveness of these strategies will be considered in the following chapter. With respect to *individual* strategies, a precise assessment of their contributions to the adoption and implementation of the policy would be difficult in the absence of extensive surveys. Moreover, most strategies do not lend themselves to computation or scientific inquiry. How is one to assess the effectiveness of the pedagogical role of the Bank, compared to that of other organizations? The effectiveness of a strategy, for example, cannot be objectively deduced from the frequency of its use: rare instances may point, as Libby argues, to the power of this strategy;[121] but the opposite conclusion would also hold: the organization may never have intended to use this strategy in the first place.

Are certain strategies more important than others? From a rational viewpoint, the organization should first turn to adaptive strategies: in the short run, coping is more important than transforming. Second, the Bank will tend to favor strategies which draw on resources it can independently muster (money and expertise, as opposed to projects). And third, strategies which can be implemented independently of the target's actions will be preferred. Thus, Thompson's adaptive strategies, rule-making and sanctions, would be favored over others. Two problems arise at this point, however. First, some strategies entail greater political costs than others. Second, what is good for the organization as a whole may not be good for its particular policies. Two other criteria must therefore be added. Strategies which rely on independent resources, entail no or few political costs, and can lead to progress in the particular policy area should be emphasized—hence the importance of education, linkage, and compromises in the Bank's environmental policy.

Of course, strategies do not exist in a vacuum. As the case of the World Bank demonstrates, an organization typically uses several adaptive and transforming strategies concurrently. But what is their synergistic effect? How do they relate to one another? Is the success of one affected by the success or failure of another? We have seen, for example, that some strategies, such as secrecy, are prerequisite for the success of others (e.g., playing off, compromise). Are others mutually contradictory? Part of the problem vanishes if we dissociate the strategies used by the Bank Group from those used by OESA or other environmental units. There may be contradictions because Bank units have their own links with the organization's task-environment. Thus, the diversity of strategies used and the character of conflicts that occur within the organization-set often directly echo internal strategies. Opposition between Indonesia's development and environment agencies, for example, mirrored the Bank's internal bureaucratic disagreements.

5

The Art of the Possible

I cannot say the Bank is no longer financing projects that are environmentally destructive.—James Lee, Environmental Adviser to the World Bank

The effectiveness of the Bank's environmental policy can be approached from three complementary viewpoints. First, one can assess the degree to which the goals are effectively implemented. Second, one can compare the policy outcomes to desirable outcomes. And third, effectiveness can be understood from an organizational viewpoint: the institutionalization of awareness and the success of the strategies used in controlling the organization's task-environment. Those strategies important for the organization's attempts to reduce uncertainty may not be those which would effectively promote a specific policy.

The Bank's Environmental Policy Revisited

After a long period of relative immunity from scrutiny, the Bank's environmental policy faced sharp criticisms in the 1980s. UNEP deplored its lack of progress in carrying out its commitments within the Committee of International Development on the Environment (CIDIE). The organization itself became more divided: some units reflected the negative position of their clients' development agencies that the international financial crisis had exacerbated, while the OESA and other units reflected the growing awareness, acquired by other agencies within recipient countries, of the adverse impact of past projects. Donors moved away from the activism of McNamara out of indifference or outright hostility to these goals, and because an adverse international situation exacerbated the economic difficulties of the borrowers and precluded major political or economic commitments behind these objectives. Finally, having concentrated on domestic issues and a few dramatic international causes during the 1970s (e.g., whaling and ocean pollution), environmental organizations, especially American ones, took advantage of the growth of environmental movements in developing countries and turned their international activism toward the World Bank. At the same time, the U.S. Congress found in environmental issues pretexts for adopting protectionist measures of various kinds or oppose multilateral lending.

Nearly fifteen years after the nomination of an environmental adviser, the environmental record of the Bank appeared ambiguous. The forestry sector can help guide a reexamination of the Bank's environmental policy, since it addresses the critical environmental problem that most developing countries face: the degradation of their natural resources. The *Forestry Sector Policy Paper* has also been repeatedly presented as a model paper while the record of the Bank in the moist tropics has generated strong criticisms.

The Forestry Sector

The depletion of forest resources has been recognized as one of the major threats to the global ecosystem. The richness of the tropical forest in plants and animals; its importance in the water cycle; its use as a source of energy in many developed countries; its potential as a renewable material for industry; and, above all, its fragility make it urgent to limit its reckless destruction and develop sound policies for its management. The *Global 2000* report dramatized this urgency in 1980: "If present trends continue, both forest cover and growing stocks of commercial-size wood in the less developed regions . . . will decline 40 percent by 2000. . . . By 2020, all the physically accessible forests in the LDCs is expected to have been cut." [1]

A 1985 report co-sponsored by the Bank indicated that eleven million hectares of tropical forests were cleared every year. While 70 percent of the people in the developing countries depend mainly on wood for fuel, supplies are inadequate in sixty-five out of ninety-five developing countries. In India, the cost attributable to flood damage and destruction of reservoirs and irrigation systems by sedimentation from misused slopes has averaged $1 billion each year since 1978. By 2000, the thirty-three wood exporters of the developing world will be fewer than ten. [2]

The major causes of deforestation vary with geographical regions, and so does its intensity. Some countries may need to conserve this resource while others can afford to exploit it. [3] In the dry tropics, fuelwood gathering and overgrazing are major causes of the disappearance of wooded areas. In the humid tropics upon which we shall focus, several activities have contributed to the problem: The first is highway construction through tropical forest areas that facilitate both planned and unplanned colonization (Brazil).

Next is massive resettlement programs to low-density regions (Brazil, Indonesia) where governments seek to promote economic and political objectives. These "armies" of poor peasants are largely insensitive to the need to conserve natural resources and to economic arguments centering upon calculations of rate of return: they want to feed their family immediately. They have neither an economic nor an ecological approach to the exploitation of the forest. In Brazil, many are pushed there not only by population growth as the Bank insists, but also by skewed land distributions: the availability of a "frontier" avoids changing land tenures and property rights (the Brazilian government has abandoned its projected land reform). By contrast, the distribution of Somoza land to the Nicaraguan landless peasants in 1979 relieved the pressure on the Atlantic coastal forest.[4] The labor-saving modernization of industry and agriculture in the south and south-east of Brazil and in Honduras has also pushed peasants toward the frontiers.[5]

Spontaneous colonization at the margins of inhabited territories by poor peasants also contributes to deforestation in the humid tropics. The problem here is not so much the slash-and-burn techniques they use, but the frequency with which they do so in the same area. This phenomenon provides the main argument for linking deforestation to poverty and population issues. Although the 1985 Tropical deforestation report identified the poor as "the primary agents of destruction," whether they are the main "culprit" is less clear.

Another cause is industrial exploitation by lumber companies that open up tracts, remove precious woods, thus destroying much of the cover in the process and facilitating immigration (as in Indonesia). Multinational corporations have been criticized, but they probably constitute better potential instruments for promoting and implementing conservation standards than local governments and enterprises, although they are reluctant to engage in long-term programs. Industrial exploitation also takes the form of removing the climactic vegetation to fulfill the demand for pulp wood and replanting with rapid growth species. Even alternatives to clear-cutting have proven disappointing, the forest failing to regenerate as expected.

In 1984 and 1985, three countries (Malaysia, the Philippines, and Indonesia) accounted for 83 percent of the world trade in tropical woods (Indonesia alone had a 55 percent share). Brazil has not really started the systematic exploitation of its forests.[6] These exports provide significant foreign exchange for these states, as well as important resources for the local peasants. Thus, progress in convincing governments that they should stop deforestation and protect their remaining forests depends on willingness on the part of donor countries to underwrite many of these efforts through compensatory foreign exchange income that would be lost as the result of the non-exploitation of those resources. It is neither the Bank's nor the developing countries' problem alone. According to figures from the Office of Technology Assessment, the value of tropical hardwood exports increased about *seventeen* times (from $270 million to $4.7 billion) between 1954 and 1979, which made them one of the five most important revenue earning commodities produced by the developing world, earning about as much foreign exchange as sugar, cotton, or copper.[7] In an international economic environment where many of these countries face higher debts and interest payments, falling commodity prices, import restrictions on the part of the developed countries, and domestic pressures; incentives to exploit one's natural capital are almost irresistible. Relying on falling export prices would not be a sound strategy for there is much evidence that falling prices, rather than stemming production, encourage further exploitation on the part of marginal producers.

 Tree-crop plantations of rubber, palm oil, and cocoa that the Bank has financed in several countries, can be successful; but the Bank has often supported sites in tropical forest areas cleared specifically for this purpose.[8] According to the FAO, clearing for export-oriented agro-industry (e.g., peanuts) has accounted for 70 percent of African deforestation.

Cattle-ranching activities, especially in Central and South America, and to a lesser extent in Africa, are an additional cause of deforestation in humid tropics. A third livestock project for Botswana approved in 1986 drew wide criticisms as a financially and ecologically unsound project. The Bank has been involved in supporting cattle-ranching in Latin America since 1963 with grave deforestation consequences.[9] With the aim of increasing export earnings, the World Bank— with IDB and UNDP— provided over $1 billion to these countries between 1971 and 1977 for livestock production and meat processing. As part of its beef-oriented export policy, Brazil's Amazonian Development Agency encouraged the establishment of ranches and used defoliants to clear areas of at least 25,000 hectares per ranch.[10] This frenzy has since slowed down considerably. Myers and Tucker claim that since 1960, cattle ranches have constituted the largest source of forest clearing in Central America.[11] These immense private estates are owned by the political, bureaucratic, and professional elite who have few incentives to stop these practices. In the Brazilian Amazon, it has been estimated that 60 percent of deforestation was due to highway construction and cattle-ranching, and only 17.6 percent was done by peasants.[12]

Hydroelectric dam projects that flood large tracts of tropical forests can lead to watershed deforestation, often to a loss of water quality and an increased incidence of water-borne diseases. They can force the resettlements of populations (Brazil, Zaire, Colombia, Thailand, Malaysia).

In addition, government policies may either encourage deforestation or impede its prevention. Many of these policies have broad political implications and are not easily changed. A major obstacle is tied to property rights which can hurt conservation efforts in four ways:

First, in some countries, property rights are acquired through land development, that is, the removal of forests for agriculture. This is true of the Phillippines, Thailand, and of the Brazilian Amazon (a practice reminiscent of the U.S. Homestead Act).[13]

Second, in most countries forests are state property, and communities residing within the forest or at its perimeter enjoy only usufructuary rights if any. Since the state does not reach everywhere, and the training and reliability of the bureaucracy are often limited, effective protection becomes problematic. It proves difficult to prevent corruption between timber contractors and Forestry Department officials who encourage illegal felling to take advantage of high timber prices.[14] In Nepal, when the government nationalized large tracts of village communal forests in 1955, villagers had fewer incentives to protect and reforest what were now government lands. They continued cutting the wood (often legally) which resulted in large hillside deforestation and flooding as far as India.[15]

Third, generous tax and credit subsidies have made cattle-ranching an attractive tax shelter in Brazil, even when the operations make little economic or ecological sense.[16]

Finally, concessions terms are often short (20 years in the Amazon), which gives loggers strong incentives to take advantage of the high timber prices as quickly as possible and few incentives to worry about the long-term sustainability of the forest, as in Indonesia.[17]

The involvement of the Bank in the forestry sector is in many ways emblematic of its general approach to environmental problems and of the obstacles that it faces. Until about 1976, the Bank was mostly concerned with lending for industrial forestry projects, such as pulp and paper industries. But the growing awareness of the economic and ecological role of forests, and active support by such countries as France and Canada, led the Bank to undertake what it called social forestry projects. These involved the protection of watersheds, the stabilization of sand dunes in arid areas, soil productivity, fuel production, and water control. In the face of growing energy shortages, the production of fuelwood as components of rural development projects was emphasized. Accordingly, lending increased from an average of about $10 million from 1968 to 1977 to more than $100 million from 1978 to 1982.[18]

This new focus was embodied in a remarkable policy paper that acknowledged the threats to forests, identified their ecological and economic role, and proposed a balanced management strategy toward "broadening" the scope of lending to include projects with a wider emphasis on environmental and protective forestry, the establishment of fuelwood plantations in rural areas, and support for on-going national forest programs.[19] It pointed up the problem of uncontrolled agricultural settlements and the need for technical assistance, information, training, inventories, and institution-building. This did not mean that traditional industrial concerns were abandoned; rather, more resources would be channeled to conservation projects.

In practice, however, *direct* funding of this sort emerged slowly. Thirty-eight projects totalling $1.1017 billion were funded from FY 1980 to FY 1986. Of those, $567.7 million or 51.5 percent were exclusively for industrial development (e.g., pulp and paper, sawwood); the other half $534 million or 48.4 percent of the forestry loans addressed social concerns (e.g., fuelwood, building poles), amounting to 2 percent of total agricultural lending for that period.[20] Five projects in Nepal, Burkina Faso, Haiti, India, and Mauritania were in areas which were suffering heavily from deforestation.

Typically, the forestry activities of the Bank (like all its environmental activities in general) were not limited to direct funding. Forestry components formed an increasing part of rural development projects in order to prevent soil erosion or modifications of the hydrological cycle. The Bank experimentally funded such a component in the 1975 Caqueta settlement project in Colombia. In 1980, five agricultural projects had a forestry component. However, they mostly involved plantations for industry and energy. Clearly, conservation and rehabilitation lending did not materialize dramatically.

At the same time, the Bank continued funding projects that were highly destructive of forested areas, especially in Indonesia and in the Amazonian basin. Thus, although there was some progress as measured by the number and type of projects, internal consistency was elusive. In 1986, besides a $16.7 million loan to Malawi for fuelwood supply and the development of policy instruments to encourage tree planting, a $50 million loan to Malaysia was also approved that will reportedly lead to the clearing of 20,000 hectares of tropical forests.[21] Although the specific situations of various countries differ, the number and extent of apparent inconsistencies reflect contradictions that exist in the Bank's task-environment which the organization is unable to overcome.

This sector witnessed the typical pattern of environmental policy-making. Policy impetus and crucial receptivity came from the developed and the developing countries respectively, not from the Bank itself. Nongovernmental organizations in alliance with international governmental organizations dramatized these issues and advocated drastic measures. This activity helped catalyze an in-house questioning of past practices before evolving into new policy guidelines. Catastrophes (the Sahelian droughts and Southeast Asian floods) propelled the problems of desertification and soil erosion to the frontpages of newspapers and generated more calls for action. Canada and France, the latter stimulated by its experience and political interest in West Africa, supported demands from developing countries for Bank action, an action made more urgent by the worsening energy situation. American executive and congressional actions spurred in part by non-governmental scientific organizations subsequently helped maintain pressure and give impetus to this area.

Although some of its units can often show imagination, the Bank, as an institution, has rarely initiated new policies or sweeping changes. As in the case of industrial pollution, the Bank relied on the experience of others, in this case that of the Canadian foresters and French agronomists. Agencies like USAID have often been more imaginative, pioneering involvement in the so-called social sectors. As Asher pointed out: "For most of its life the Bank . . . has been a follower rather than a leader in thinking about the nature of the development process and how to expedite and enrich that process."[22] But once it has adopted a new perspective, its real contribution, it is argued, lies in the development of a methodological construction and economic rationale for tackling these concerns. The methodological construction of its environment policy, however, remains elusive.

Furthermore, although the new policy appeared to break with tradition; it, in fact, amounted to an addition to the type of projects funded, not a substitution for them. Industrial forestry projects (like traditional infra- structural projects) were not abandoned. The Bank expanded its activities, rather than restructured itself to address ecological scarcity.

Despite growing international mobilization and internal recognition of the extent of the problem, economic constraints are likely to prevent spec- tacular increases in lending for rehabilitation projects. For example, clear- cutting in the tropics demands replanting and planned land management. Although the Bank requires restorative measures, it does not always do it because it tends to be expensive. The estimated cost of the soil conserva- tion and rehabilitation components of five selected projects, for example, ranged from 9 to 25 percent of the total cost of the project. These figures were much higher than the politically acceptable 3 to 5 percent range quoted by the Bank's Office of Environmental and Scientific Affairs for all environmental projects. This prompted the Bank Forestry adviser to sug- gest that such measures not be implemented automatically, so that it would be up to the recipient country to agree to them.[23]

Furthermore, many reafforestation loans are hard to justify economical- ly, for their economic benefits are distant and their social benefits diffuse. Ecological benefits also tend to be long-term and are easily overlooked in cost-benefit analyses, which use high discount rates that stress short-term economic costs. Moreover, such projects involve mostly local currency, rather than foreign exchange, which does not make the loans attractive to the World Bank, or even to many developing countries in need of hard currencies, as discussed in chapter 2.

The Bank sought to demonstrate its concern, gather support, and in- fluence its borrowers by sponsoring a task force in 1985 which addressed

Third World forestry problems in collaboration with FAO, UNDP, and the World Resources Institute. The resulting report assessed the problem and developed a five-part program that included the rehabilitation of 150 million hectares of seriously degraded tropical watersheds; the preservation of 100 million hectares of threatened forests; a five-fold increase in fuelwood planting rates by 2000; the improvement and expansion of industrial forestry; and the strengthening of research, education, and training.[24] It also called for greater efforts on the part of development agencies, and urged national leadership and local participation. The amount of private investment needed to make an impact over the next five years was estimated at about $8 billion (although this figure refers to deforestation in developing countries in general, not to tropical deforestation per se).

John Spears, the Bank's Forestry adviser, has recommended that governmental and multilateral aid agencies (1) increase assistance to countries to set up biotic reserves, (2) increase financing for sustainable farming, (3) encourage more reforestation with fast-growing species for fuelwood and industry, (4) adopt policy measures aimed at discouraging further settlements, (5) withhold loans for extensive cattle-ranching, (6) restrict logging, and (7) increase financial and technical assistance to further research in agro-forestry.[25]

The sector policy paper and subsequent actions attest to a significant evolution in the Bank's thinking. Yet, despite a sophisticated understanding of these problems in the Agriculture Department and OESA and despite requests from borrowers, lending failed to match the rhetoric. In 1975, there were only five projects totalling $34.5 million devoted to social forestry; in 1985, twelve for a total of $332 million. Much more should have been done to meet the demand or elicit it when much of the misery of sub-sahara Africa or East Asia was attributed to erosion or deforestation.[26]

Organized opposition to the Bank's activities revolved around two major lending programs in the 1980s: Indonesia's transmigration program and Brazil's POLONOROESTE colonization plans. Their detailed examination will cast some light on the problems that the Bank has faced and on the limits of its environmental commitment.

Indonesia's Transmigration Program

With a total of 143 million hectares, over 70 percent of its territory, Indonesia has the second largest tropical forest area in the world. But its rate of destruction has been high. Since 1950, 49 million hectares have been lost, not all to planned deforestation. In 1983, 3.6 million hectares were lost to a large fire in Kalimantan (Borneo) that was aggravated by previous careless exploitation.

Indonesian governments have demonstrated an increasing awareness of the problem. A Ministry of Forestry was established, environmental legislation enacted, forest land use plans developed and adopted, conservation areas established, and reforestation planned.[27] Three-quarters of all donor funding for forestry went for watershed rehabilitation. The Minister for the Environment has been active in seeking support from the Bank for these projects against development-oriented agencies. In addition to increasing its support for forestry, the Bank helped finance the Demoga-Bane National Park as part of an irrigation project. This receptivity reflected not only a growing awareness within the government of the seriousness of these issues, but also a rapid development of indigenous environmental protection organizations which testified before the U.S. Congress about the transmigration program.

This enterprise, the largest resettlement program ever attempted, was designed ultimately to transfer, over a period of twenty years, 65 million of the nation's 165 million inhabitants from the overcrowded islands of Java, Bali, Madura, and Lombok—7 percent of its territory—to less crowded areas in Borneo, Sumatra, and Western New Guinea.

Its purposes were to relieve the economic and social problems of the inner islands caused by extreme demographic pressures, reduce unemployment on Java and provide needed manpower to the outer islands, strengthen national unity through ethnic integration, and improve the living standard of the poor. Significantly reducing population pressure appeared problematic, so that political concerns seemed to lie at the heart of the program. Costs to the tropical forests were obviously enormous. Under the latest five-year plan, for example, no less than 560,000 hectares of tropical forests were to be destroyed. Spillovers from farmers abandoning existing and new sites—for every hectare of usable land created by the program, four additional hectares were adversely affected—were expected to bring the total to 2.8 million hectares.[28]

World Bank involvement started in 1974. Along with other international organizations and major western donors, the Bank made five transmigration loans (totaling $433.5 million) and two swamp reclamation loans (totaling $87 million) in support of this program. By 1986, 4 million people had been resettled.[29] Budgetary constraints forced the government to reduce the number of families relocated in 1986 and 1987, although all settlements were to be in forested areas.[30]

Problems encountered followed a typical pattern. Poorly conceived and hastily implemented settlements led to indiscriminate deforestation on soils of various quality. Ill-adapted agricultural practices degraded the soil, thus making the use of fertilizers less effective. Invasions of forested areas outside the settlements were uncontrolled and the support system for settlers deficient. Some settlements were established in inhospitable sites, and failures were common. These problems were recognized by the Bank's environmental unit whose recommendations and analyses were ignored.[31] In many cases, the amount of ecological destruction (an estimated 270,000 hectares per year[32]) and the weak economic benefits derived from such schemes did not seem to warrant continued support.

These problems did not stem from poor implementation alone, but were rooted in the very conception of the projects. While the Bank's environmental guidelines called for detailed studies designed to mitigate environmental destruction and species extinction, preparatory studies were rarely conducted. Thus, the basis for initial decision-making proved slim. The cost-benefit analysis of the staff appraisal report for "Transmigration V" ignored the economic and environmental costs of deforestation, focusing instead on the social value of providing land to the landless, increasing food security, and improving regional development.[33] That is, the analysis privileged the poverty alleviation objective of the organization.

Aside from the usual problems associated with unsuitable agricultural practices, a major issue concerned the treatment of tribal peoples. Faced with the loss of their crops, buildings, and traditional hunting, gathering, and fishing grounds (for which they must theoretically be compensated), these groups often faced no alternative but to integrate into transmigration settlements where they were ostracized and despised by outsiders.

Conflicts between settlers and local tribes increased. The populations in West Papua (Irian Jaya) that resisted the takeover of their lands were accused of supporting secessionist movements and were subjected to security operations. Confrontations between Papuans and the Indonesian army—with their concomitant human rights abuses—have led thousands of Papuans to seek refuge in Papua New Guinea.[34]

The Bank had been at the forefront of other agencies in paying attention to the fate of indigenous populations. The farsighted guidelines it published in 1982 stipulated how these groups should be treated, especially regarding their land rights and cultural integrity. The draft appraisal report of the fifth transmigration project in 1985 raised those issues in reference to Bank guidelines and suggested appropriate measures, although its final version was much less explicit and referred primarily to the policy of the Indonesian government.[35] Under Indonesian law, the exercize of traditional land rights was subordinated to state interests. It was further weakened through special legislation pertaining to the transmigration program. The Bank was unable to impose its own guidelines.

Given these faults, how could the Bank assert that the project had "the potential to provide enormous environmental benefits in both the sending and receiving areas"?[36] Some improvements indeed took place. Environmental impact assessments were required, and the Bank helped support studies to improve the methodology of site selection. The Bank also argued that these projects would help relieve overcultivation of environmentally vulnerable Java and Bali. It also assumed that the sites would be chosen carefully, that appropriate farming technology would be used, and that adverse ecological impacts would remain limited. Although in practice, many sites were rejected on social and environmental grounds (almost half of those proposed, according to the U.S. executive director[37]), many others were retained. The Bank also contended that Java's few remaining unspoiled forests would be saved from population pressures, although this appeared unlikely to happen in the absence of other specific conservation measures.

This program generated national concern in Indonesia and fierce opposition on the part of many ethnological and environmental groups in the United States, Great Britain and the Netherlands.[38] These organizations waged a worldwide campaign that denounced its impact on the forest and on the indigenous populations. In October 1986, they sent Barber Conable a detailed report condemning the Indonesian project and repeating previous requests to stop its funding.

But this opposition was not based solely on the Bank's failure to abide by its own guidelines. Rather than limiting themselves to identifying difficulties and proposing remedies, these groups challenged the political nature of the program itself and sought its cancellation. Their concern for the integrity of the tropical forests and of inhabitants hid opposition to what the government regarded as nation-building, to a reinforcement of the authority of the central government, to export-led agriculture, to social inequalities, and to a repressive regime—in short, to a mode of development and political institutions that they found inimical to their own political preferences. As in numerous other instances, environmental battles provided a domestic and international conduit for political opposition.

The INGOs' position required ignoring the contradictions that may exist between environmental protection, social justice, and poverty. Indeed, when faced with such trade-offs, the Bank privileged poverty alleviation. Yet, as in the Brazilian case to which we turn next, many opponents actually feared that such projects might succeed, thus postponing the social and political reforms they deemed indispensable. This has often complicated the development of broad coalitions of environmental and scientific groups united behind specific demands, and contributed to the Bank's inertia.

Brazil's POLONOROESTE Settlement Program

Involvement in Brazil's colonization of the northwestern state of Rondonia became emblematic of the multiple contradictions in the Bank's environmental policies and of the difficulties that the organization has faced in advancing this value. Perhaps even more than the Indonesian transmigration program, it became a *cause célèbre* behind which the opponents to the organization's environmental record rallied in the 1980s.

The first phase of Brazilian colonization of the Amazon took place in the 1960s. Many settlements ended in failure, and official attempts to resettle large numbers of people along the Transamazon Highway were abandoned only four years after road construction had started. Then cattle ranching moved in.

Both economic and political arguments induced the Brazilian government to start the Transamazon Highway and other colonization projects. The various official and non-official justifications for the successive plans centered around the social mobilization potential of the "frontier," promotion of national integration, relief of the overpopulated northeast (in the case of POLONOROESTE), national security arguments (to prevent the de facto colonization of ill-defined and mineral-rich border regions by Brazil's neighbors), and around prospects for the exploitation of valuable natural resources (iron ore, bauxite, tin, gold, timber, tree-crops), particularly in the northwest. Clearly, to argue against such projects on environmental or economic grounds alone (the standard strategy that the Bank and OESA have used to promote their environmental values) may not work with Amazonian countries.

The second phase occurred in the 1970s, spurred by the economic troubles that the country was starting to experience. The state of Rondonia was identified as a priority colonization region in the 1970s for various reasons in addition to the more general ones mentioned above: its location in the direction of the pioneer front movement toward the northwest (Mato Grosso), the presence of an unpaved road opening it up, the relative high percentage of public lands, and the existence of more fertile land than average in the Amazonian region.

The improvement of the main road leading to the northwest region in 1969 had led to large spontaneous immigration in the late 1970s, fueled by rumours of fertile soils, the government's policy of alloting large 100-hectare holdings (of which fifty were to be set aside as forest reserve, although similar attempts in the north have failed), and growing unemployment in the southeast. With a massive immigration of people with few resources and no employment, the region became dangerous and volatile. The Brazilian government invited the Bank in 1979 to survey the region, assess its development potential, and identify possible financing. In 1981, the Bank decided to help finance part of the POLONOROESTE project, which was set up in May 1981.[39] The project was expected to relieve unemployment and settle some of the 2.5 million landless emigrants, mostly from the south and south east. It illustrated the government's policy of encouraging the small farmer despite the existence of a larger capitalistic mode of agricultural development in other areas of Amazonia.

POLONOROESTE was a group of 39 settlement projects budgeted at

$1.55 billion for 1981 to 1985, of which the Bank lent $434.5 million. Forty-two percent of the project cost was for the surfacing of the penetration road completed in 1984, 24 percent for the settlement of 20,000 peasants in new areas, 23 percent for integrated rural development projects, 3 percent for the protection of the Indians, 2 percent for health components (mostly malaria control, and 1 percent for environmental components.[40] The affected area was estimated at 410,000 square kilometers, although the project area itself was 244,000 square kilometers (about the size of West Germany). By 1986, 500,000 settlers had moved in.

One of the remarkable features of the project was the inclusion of extensive environmental provisions. Soils were to be surveyed to ascertain their fertility and suitability, site colonies more appropriately, tailor land use to its carrying capacity, and decide on the proper size of each holding. A system of national forests for efficient sustained management would be promoted. It would include some institution-building (such as strengthening the national Brazilian institute for forest development); the identification of several sites for forestry development to be demarcated, protected, and inventoried; the creation of four new forest control posts; and the monitoring of deforestation. The program was to finance a conservation system of eight units (one national park, three biological reserves, and four ecological stations) totaling 2 million hectares with a five-year budget of $8.9 million. A $7 million research component was to finance baseline ecological studies, biotic inventories, and hydro-meteorological and biogeochemical studies to increase knowledge of the ecosystem and improve management strategies.

Already formally guaranteed in perpetuity by the Brazilian constitution, Indian lands were to be delimited on the map, then physically demarcated and accorded official reserve status. Demarcation would be sped up, border disputes resolved, and illegal settlers evicted (at a cost of $3.2 million). Health and education components were also included ($750,000) along with a tribal economic development program ($5.1 million).[41] In a compromise with the Bank, Brazil's Indian agency, FUNAI, was given authority to implement and monitor the program after Brazil had temporarily withdrawn from the loan negotiations over these issues.[42]

The decision to finance the highway project was conditioned on the inclusion of these measures. Yet the Bank also reasoned that Brazil would proceed with or without Bank participation; Bank financing might therefore help promote the inclusion of human and ecological concerns in the development of the region.[43] The Bank's involvement did lead to some benefits. Squatters were removed from some Indian lands; one reserve was demarcated. Agricultural research and extension services improved in some areas.[44]

Several internal Bank documents indicated that the project would fail, yet they were ignored. The all-weather surfacing of the main road (BR

364) was completed ahead of schedule in September 1984 whereas other components were hardly started. This facilitated uncontrolled migration (fueled by government propaganda) which outstripped the capacity of the Brazilian federal state to manage the development of the region. Growing social inequalities, urbanization, and land conflicts ensued. Contradictions between the interests of the peasants, the need to protect the environment, and the rights of the Indians became more acute. Projected reserves were invaded, a trend that Brazilian authorities were unable or unwilling to arrest. The construction of a transversal road presented additional problems. It threatened biological reserves, cut across traditional Indian lands, and opened an untouched valley in an area determined to have soils too poor for small farmer agriculture, a violation of the Bank's loan agreement. The Bank did not object to this road, although no adequate protective measures had been adopted or implemented.[45]

The region experienced large outbreaks of malaria. Two hundred thousand settlers reportedly contracted it, forming the basis of a critical review of Bank involvement by a well-known columnist.[46] The Bank staff warned that the fragile soils could not support the kind of agriculture that would be needed to feed half a million settlers; what had been a productive rain forest became eroded farm land. The turnover of settlers was extremely high, 80 percent in four years in some areas. Yet settlements on poor soils, steep hillsides, and along the banks of rivers continued in violation of the Brazilian forestry code. The Brazilian Forestry Development Institute lacked the capacity to enforce these provisions locally.[47]

Official colonization, squatting, and the sale of large areas to cattle ranchers outside the official settlement zones had a dramatic effect on the forest. Deforestation proceeded exponentially. According to Landsat data (which tend to underestimate the amount of destruction), by 1975 the area deforested was 1,216.5 square kilometers (0.5 percent of the forested area of Rondonia). By 1980, it was 7,579.3 square kilometers (3.12 percent), and 13,955.2 square kilometers (5.74 percent) in 1983.[48] This progression threatened to eliminate the forests of the state of Rondonia by 1995.

There was also a large gap between the measures negotiated with the Brazilian government and the realities of the protection of the indigenous populations. For example, some 165 mining, exploration, and research authorizations were granted to large firms within indigenous areas. Funds allocated to the agency responsible for indigenist policy were used to cover administrative expenses and equipment rather than field activities such as land demarcation or health protection. Illegal deforestation went unarrested.[49] In spite of financial support, FUNAI's performance improved little and its commitment to the welfare of Indians still remained to be demonstrated, according to critics. Three years after the start of the project, the roads were virtually completed while the majority of Indian lands was still awaiting demarcation. A 1984 evaluation team from the Bank reported that the "most serious issue identified by the mission relates to the growing imbalance within the program between infrastructure construction, which is proceeding at a fast pace, and farmer services and forestry and natural reserves development, which are almost not proceeding at all."[50] The team concluded that disbursements should be halted "unless serious measures are actually implemented by the Brazilian authorities to reverse this trend. . . ." Yet, they continued.

The original inclusion of extensive environmental and ethnological measures into the projects financed by the Bank provided non-governmental organizations with a useful basis for their denunciation of the project and their challenge of the Bank's environmental record. In alliance with their Brazilian counterparts, American groups wrote presidents Clausen and Conable to denounce the project. They organized hearings every year beginning in 1983 around the environmental and ethnological record of the development banks, and contacted congressional committees overseeing IDA replenishments and capital increases sought by the Bank. Protestations against the Bank's activities centered on deforestation and the fate of tribal populations. A coalition of environmental organizations tried to picket the 1986 annual meetings of the World Bank and IMF to denounce support for POLONOROESTE.

Despite critical internal documents, the Bank denied that the program was a failure and insisted that careful analysis and planning had been conducted prior to approval. But after three years of repeated public criticisms in Congress and by environmental groups, the Bank briefly suspended payments in 1985. At that time, discussions were apparently held between Sen. Robert Kasten, Jr., chairman of the Senate's Subcommittee on Foreign Operations of the Committee on Appropriations; the Bank; and American environmental groups. This led to the termination of financial support for the construction of the transversal penetration road and a redirection of financial resources to activities that would minimize the negative environmental impact of the project, many of which had been originally included in the project but had been ignored by the implementing agency.[51] Although massive projects were halted by the new government in 1985, unofficial (that is, unsupported) settlements continued. There are now several pressures on the Amazonian forests arising from road construction (with its spillovers); hydroelectric dams; large mineral, agro-industrial, and cattle projects; urban growth; and some lumbering.

The Bank's Environmental Record Revisited

The OESA had set itself five broad objectives in 1972: (1) to ensure that development projects did not "unduly" harm the environment and social well-being of a country, (2) to develop increased awareness of environmental problems associated with the development of developing countries, (3) to marshal the necessary resources and expertise to study the problem, (4) to encourage research and training in that area, and (5) to improve information and technical cooperation among countries.[52]

Although environmental and ethnological organizations have tended to regard the Bank's actions as representative of its environmental policy as a whole, this greatly underestimates the Bank's contribution to the protection of workers and to the avoidance of unnecessary destruction of natural resources. The thrust of the Bank's policy has been directed toward pollution control (internal and external to the factory, water pollution control) and the prevention of environmental side effects which would endanger the economic viability of the project.

Its record of avoiding inappropriate siting of industrial activities improved greatly. The problem of watershed deforestation was recognized very early and addressed in project planning. Watershed areas were set aside as parks and reserves (e.g., Guavio hydro project in Colombia, Pantabangan and Magat watersheds in the Philippines).[53] Aware of the experience of the Anchicaya Dam of Colombia, which lost four-fifths of its original 5-million-cubic-meter capacity to sedimentation, the Bank warned Colombia in the early 1970s about the fate of the El Penol project, predicting "catastrophic consequences" unless sweeping environmental measures were taken.[54] It has also assisted national forestry programs (Nepal).

Since 1971, the environmental impact of hundreds of projects has been mitigated. The scope of the policy has broadened. More reforestation projects were supported, wildlands management was given the attention due it in the early 1980s, and funding for water supply and sewerage increased. The rehabilitation of existing irrigation systems now comprises most of the new lending in that area.

To argue that there were problems or to fault the Bank for failing to impose its views on reluctant borrowers does not mean that its policy was a failure. Environmentalists and the Bank itself may have been far too ambitious given the interests of other international organizations, the priorities of the developing countries, the lukewarm support on the part of major donors, and the poor state of scientific knowledge. The Bank's business is development, which entails exploiting resources as efficiently as possible. Its problem, therefore, was to speed up development without endangering the resource base. It was a management problem. This implied remedying disruptions (e.g., replanting, reforesting), not conservation per se.

The Bank's concern for the environmental consequences of the projects it funds far exceeded the attention paid to them by commercial banks or most national and international development agencies. In 1983, the ADB had two environmental officers, IDB none. Neither had detailed procedures for examining the potential environmental impact of projects, such as separate environmental assessments. IDB has been particularly reluctant to acquire the means to improve its performance in the area. Nothing indicates that its "environmental checklist" must be reviewed during project preparation. IDB is very closely attuned to its Latin American clientele, suggesting the extent of national opposition to the promotion of environmental values.

The bulk of the Bank's work has clearly been directed toward meeting the first objective that OEA set itself in 1972: to ensure that the environmental impact of development projects are taken into consideration during project preparation. We have seen, however, what limitations existed to that approach. The Bank tried to mitigate harmful effects, not to suppress them. The short-term economic justifications of the project superseded its long-term environmental impacts. Environmental destruction was justified so long as it was balanced by economic benefits and did not endanger the project itself.

This situation was directly linked to a major shortcoming of the Bank's policy. Preoccupied with the early stages of the project cycle, the OESA did not pay enough attention to the direct implementation of the projects for which it had negotiated environmental guidelines. Implementation and the enforcement of regulations are crucial elements of an effective environmental policy. Busy with promoting the idea of environmental protection and lacking resources, OESA neglected the operational phases of the policy. Once environmental caveats were introduced into a project, it did not follow that they would translate into an improved situation in the field. Poor implementation, rather than design, often caused environmental damage.

Problems exist with the training of the work crews. Road-building may entail the unnecessary destruction of the valuable top soil of nearby fertile agricultural lands and accelerate deforestation and the destruction of wildlife. The OESA staff stressed these problems at length. Rather than the absence of air pollution control devices, the chief problem was often management failure to maintain and operate the equipment properly, associated with a lack of real concern for pollution problems.[55] Training should, therefore, be an automatic part of the environmental guidelines incorporated into the projects, but, as we have seen in chapter 5, this component is often lacking.

Implementation problems often result from poor supervision, so that the ignorance of environmental guidelines is often a mutual failure of the Bank and of the implementing institution. Thus, after compromises have been reached, there is actually little assurance that they will be observed. For example, the Bank does not ask the sponsor of the project to meet certain monitoring and analytical requirements to enforce agreed upon standards.

This stemmed from OESA's limited resources and from the greater difficulties of supervising implementation compared to the earlier stages which are completely controlled by the organization. Implementation is a politically sensitive area. The Bank is likely to avoid disturbing its relation with a particular country if the environmental problems are minor.[56]

The record of the Bank's involvement in the Indonesian and Brazilian colonization projects also illustrates the problem of coordinating all the components of a project. Governments complete those components they favor first and neglect the complementary ones that may later become moot or lack financial support altogether. These difficulties—associated with the lack of guarantees that any environmental provision implemented will continue to be observed when the project is completed and the loan fully disbursed—give extreme importance to the education of the borrowers' bureaucracies and of the Bank's regional units, the second objective of OESA.

Linkage to other values may have favored the adoption of environmental concerns, but it also explained a certain reluctance to expand its scope dramatically. Forestry projects were first intended to alleviate energy problems, not combat desertification or protect watersheds and climactic forests. But when the energy crisis receded, so did the perceived need for reforestation. When the sole justification for including conservation components was ecological, funding was unlikely, especially in periods of economic recession.

The funding of deforestation and then reforestation projects in the same area illustrated the limits of the best-intentioned environmental policy, the problems of coordination, and the dilemma the Bank still confronts. Its policy was defined in economic and social terms. Projects that fulfilled both objectives were therefore irresistible, especially if they could be couched in environmental rhetoric. Yet it was also apparent that those objectives often conflicted with ecological ones (such as the preservation of ecological diversity). Settlements in tropical forests are intended to alleviate poverty, a goal upon which both developing and donor countries have insisted in the 1970s, but at the cost of tropical deforestation.

Chapter 4 discussed at length the various strategies that the Bank has used to educate its clientele. There is no question that awareness of environmental issues has greatly improved within segments of the bureaucracies of developing countries. Interest groups have also developed and pressed for change. Although the extent of the Bank's contribution is unclear, it has played an important role in educating not only the developing countries but also the developed world and environmentalists about the need to recognize and meet the different priorities of developing countries. It helped them recognize that the environmental problems of the Third World may differ from those of rich countries, that the poor operate under different constraints, and that they also pursue distinct economic and political goals. The Bank was instrumental in getting the notion of sustainable development accepted as a compromise.

But increased awareness does not automatically result in different behavior. Apart from those regions whose tourist industry depends on some environmental protection (including from the tourists themselves), as in the Seychelles islands, Kenya, and Bali,[57] few countries are ready to take drastic actions in favor of the environment if the consequences of environmental degradation do not directly bear on their short-term economic prospects. Neither does increased awareness solve the problem of finding the means for remedies. Countries may be locked into a downward spiral of environmental degradation from which they cannot escape without outside support. Yet this support did not come from the Bank. It tried slowing down the spiral, not improving the situation by sponsoring extensive rehabilitation or environmental enhancement projects (the rehabilitation of irrigation schemes and social afforestation projects being few and isolated exceptions).

Developing awareness applies not only to developing countries, but to the Bank itself. In fact, as we saw, this internal constraint has been a major impediment to the Bank's policy. Internal coordination was erratic. The 1978 *Agricultural Land Settlements* sector policy paper, published one month before the *Forestry* paper, did not show that awareness of these problems had permeated the staff of other sectors. It briefly mentioned the importance of paying attention to ecological problems, but failed to identify them in detail. Its final chapter discussed future policy and adopted a very cautious position: "Support by the World Bank for the projects *may well depend* on assurances that longer-term environmental impacts have been appropriately considered, and that suitable safeguards are provided to protect the nonrenewable resources in the project area."[58] It was a laudable statement, but written seven years after OESA was given the mandate to do just that: review projects for their environmental consequences, provide safeguards for minimizing environmental disruptions, and condition disbursements to the observation of those safeguards. The agricultural projects department in 1978 still understood it as a goal to be realized at some future time. This shows how slowly the ideology of OESA spread within the Bank given the different priorities of its units. The priority of the Agricultural Unit was to get most of the potentially arable land into production. Thus, the environmental questions revolved around avoiding "the gravest socio-economic and ecological problems associated with spontaneous colonization."[59] In short, colonization was to be regulated, not questioned. Protecting the environment may take the form of establishing isolated natural preserves harboring remnant tribes while allowing indiscriminate "colonization" of the rest of the region.

For many engineers, environmental problems stem from man's failure to control nature, while economists approach them as components of poverty.[60] If poverty is the root of environmental problems, growth and technology should take care of the ecological problems of the developing world. When the former director of the Economic Development Institute complained in a booklet on the environmental problems of the tropics that environmental factors had been neglected, he was referring to the physical constraints to development (poor soil, climate, diseases) that must be overcome. Rather than reassessing the usefulness of a Western pattern of development ill-adapted to tropical situations, research should be directed toward facilitating it. For example, one must conquer local diseases (e.g., with insecticides, drainage), because they make cattle-raising of western breeds impossible, not develop a cattle-breeding program with domestic stocks. One must reassess the use of certain lands for that purpose, study the impact of this technology on the food chains and the ecosystem structure, or question the need for extensive irrigation projects.[61]

The Bank has played a positive role in the coordination and promotion of environmental concerns among multilateral development banks. Linkages between OESA and national environmental policy-making bodies were also developed. The Bank also contributed to institution-building: for example, a 1982 Indian forestry project included the establishment of a "social-forestry wing" in the West Bengal State Forestry Department and Brazilian forestry and Indian agencies were to be strengthened under POLONOROESTE. Environmental institution-building, however, did not involve creation of independent agencies such as those supervising infrastructural projects, although they are more likely to lead to the development of a successful constituency.

The preeminence given environmental values naturally varies among countries. It remains limited in Latin America. When it occurred, it was often at the central level of government and among the better-educated citizens of those countries. Scientific associations, for example, have taken a more active role in the promotion of conservation values (although Third World scientists are few), and public opinion is starting to influence policy (as in India and Brazil). Yet, although environmental concerns have been translated into new legislative instruments, implementation remained problematic.

Indeed, concern for the environment has gained no more than minimal acceptance in the countryside. Incentives to conserve rarely exist. Hunting may be prohibited in the settlements along the Transamazonian Highway, but settlers find it irresistible to supplement their poor diet with fresh meat.[62] The project manager is not rewarded on the basis of his care for the environment, but according to his profits and economic efficiency. The operation of anti-pollution devices is costly—the trained manpower that would operate them is needed elsewhere—and the victims of pollution are politically unorganized and lack means of redress. Thus, although, in principle, effluent standards using the best available technology may be preferable to emission fees, in practice, neither may work.

Furthermore, the underdevelopment of field administrations has been one of the great bottlenecks of development.[63] What is true for agricultural projects is even more true for environmental projects or environmental components. The case studies of colonization schemes illustrate these basic institutional problems identified in chapter 3. The local administration is unable or unwilling to prevent the poor from endangering the viability of new forest plantations or bar them and large firms from violating natural and indigenous reserves.

To be sure, some progress has been made in that area. The Bank has tried to fulfill its third and fourth objectives of encouraging training and research and improving information and technical cooperation. If training has been more often emphasized, particularly in the agricultural sector; research, on the other hand, has been neglected. The only significant research enterprise the Bank sponsors outside the institution is the Consultative Group on International Agricultural Research (CGIAR) which it jointly heads with FAO.[64] But the CGIAR is concerned with improving the technology of the Green Revolution, not with promoting environmental conservation or minimizing the environmental side effects of the same revolution. Internally, the OESA was unable to conduct much research on its own. Nor has it encouraged extensive studies by outside consultants as other offices have done. It largely failed to take advantage of the unique opportunities it had for evaluating the development activities of the Bank and disseminating the results. The guidebooks it published, useful as they were, did not break any new ground. We still know little about the environment of the developing countries and little support for research condemned the Bank to react to environmental problems as they came up. In short, it failed to marshal the necessary resources to study the environmental problems of the Third World.

Finally, the fifth objective of improving international cooperation among countries is also in its infancy. It has not contributed to bilateral cooperation on environmental matters, despite transborder pollution or shared natural resources. The Bank's potential in this area is significant because of three factors mentioned in chapter 4: (1) its national preeminence in many developing countries; (2) its training and promotion of common values leading to the establishment of a transnational network of like-minded development officials; and (3) the significant role it has often played in solving bilateral conflicts and the existence of an instrument for doing so in the future (the International Tribunal for the Settlement of Investment Disputes). Given the Bank's international presence, a particular environmental agency could use the Bank to collaborate with its counterpart in other countries.[65] The nucleus of transgovernmental coalitions would be formed. Thus, with the rise of environmental issues; with the internationalization of many problems once considered purely national affairs; and with a growing need for international scientific and technical cooperation in solving environmental problems of the developing countries; the World Bank could play a significant role in the establishment of an international environmental "regime" since it stands at the center of the forces which govern the resolution of these issues.

Before reviewing several reasons why the environmental policy of the World Bank did not evolve as expected by environmentalists, we must first consider the nature and consequences of the criticisms they expressed in the 1980s.

The Campaign against the Bank's Environmental Record

The Critique

In 1976, the International Institute for Environment and Development (IIED) launched a study of the environmental procedures and practices of nine multilateral development agencies that formed a basis for the 1980 CIDIE Declaration.[66] The World Conservation Strategy was adopted that same year, and the U.S. Congress passed the International Environmental Protection Act in 1983, emphasizing the preservation of diversity worldwide.[67] These provided bases on which various international and nongovernmental organizations could assess the Bank's performance and pressure it to improve it. After successful demands for change in USAID's environmental procedures, American environmentalists turned their attention to development Banks in 1983.

They found receptive ears in Congress and were also encouraged by OESA itself, which sought to use them in its internal battles and to further educate borrowers. Criticisms were therefore directed toward the organization as such, especially toward the regional offices and the leadership, while positive assessments accrued to OESA and scattered units (such as forestry). The first detailed hearings on this topic were held in 1983. There were indeed many causes for concern and these criticisms uncovered and addressed issues that were troublesome. Yet the certain parochialism of the approach, associated with a failure to place the issue in its economic and political context, hindered much progress until 1987. What were those criticisms?

Many concerned the reluctance of the Bank to press developing countries forcefully to address environmental issues. Critics also pointed out the

Bank's lack of commitment stemming from internal opposition on the part of some regional offices and segments of the leadership. Environmental guidelines were only suggested measures and often failed to cover important sectors or reflect the current state of scientific knowledge. Major policy papers, such as the Fisheries Sector Policy Paper, reflected a poor knowledge of ecological principles on the part of the staff of other units. Despite earlier pledges, the EDI curriculum still ignored environmental principles. Environmental review took place too late in the project cycle. Lack of staff and resources forced OESA to be involved only on a catch-as-catch-can basis and limited its ability to supervise the implementation of the projects and negotiated measures. Other organizational goals, such as the need to move money, conflicted with the promotion of environmental concerns.

The Bank has often been unable to monitor its borrowers' compliance with negotiated ambient standards, monitoring being equated with interference in a nation's internal affairs. As in the case of POLONOROESTE, the organization has been unwilling to take the risk of losing the support of its clientele by pursuing environmental demands forcefully, which lack of personnel has precluded in the first place. Although OESA's de facto coalition with INGOs enabled it to overcome some of its limitations and gain information on projects in preparation or under implementation (notably in Mexico, India, and the Philippines), projects were still allowed to proceed despite failures to follow negotiated guidelines. The Bank failed to confront borrowers who postponed the implementation of environmental components or abandoned them altogether. (This problem was not unique to the environment; it was even worse as far as economic policy agreements were concerned). Although the OESA recommended that some projects be rejected on environmental grounds, the Board of Directors often ignored or was unaware of these recommendations.[68] In several well-publicized cases, the Bank failed to follow its own principles.

Thus, projects which have an adverse environmental and ethnological impact are still promoted. In addition to the specific criticisms regarding support for Indonesia's and Brazil's colonization programs, hydroelectric projects are also heavily condemned. Rapid silt-up due to the deforestation of surrounding watersheds still occurs, although in attenuated form. Critics point to deliberate destructions of existing wildlife sanctuaries or portions of parks (Thailand, Malaysia, Brazil, Zaire). In one case in Thailand, the preparation report suggested that animals could move elsewhere, neglecting to examine the carrying capacity of surrounding areas.[69] In Malaysia, the Tembeling river project will flood 8 percent of the peninsula's sole national park. Shelved in 1976 after negative environmental studies and domestic opposition, it was revived in 1982 to increase electricity pro-

duction.[70] In other cases, scarce fertile agricultural land and tribal homelands are flooded.[71] Since most fertile land is already under cultivation,
these people must move to more marginal areas.[72]

The Solutions Advocated

The solutions advocated reflect the critics' definition of the problem as
rooted in organizational shortcomings and sought to apply to the Bank
measures that they had previously pressed USAID to adopt.

One obvious recommendation was to expand the staff of environmental
specialists. The negative effects of OESA's small size were acute because
of the limited support that existed for these issues within and outside the
organization. An internal Bank memorandum acknowledged that fourteen
years after the nomination of an environmental adviser, environmental
issues were not routinely considered, but were taken into account only
after the OESA or external actors had alerted the organization to potential
problems.[73] Thus, the organization relied on OESA's small staff to identify
potential problems and suggest corrective measures. New environmental
specialists should also be placed in each regional unit as well as in the
technical offices in Washington. This follows the U.S. experience with the
implementation of the National Environmental Policy Act. Specialists are
needed both at the project preparation and the review level. As Ortolano
suggested: ". . . perhaps the best strategy for locating environmental specialists is to place them in more than one organizational unit" to improve
communication.[74] Thus, environmental specialists engaged in the definition of objectives, the formulation of alternatives, and other basic planning
activities could be located within the planning unit. OESA staff could then
review plans and reports, and link engineers and outside environmental
activists.

According to its environmental critics, the Bank should perform more
evaluation studies, but, above all, integrate considerations of sustainable
use and environmental protection into both the economic appraisal of the
project and the economic planning of the country. INGOs should become
part of the regular consultation process before a loan is approved as well as
during implementation. The Bank should not hesitate to withhold disbursement or cancel a loan when negotiated protective measures are not
implemented. More environmental conservation and rehabilitation projects should be funded, and national environmental plans drawn up. They
should incorporate similar principles to those required of USAID, such as
respect for species diversity. Development schemes should first be aimed at
protecting the resource base of each country (although what is a resource
remains unclear, and, presumably, all natural resources are given equal
value). Finally, environmental critics asked that the Bank ensure that

projects comply with international law. This demand applied not only to countries which had ratified specific international conventions, but also to those that had not.

Finally, two other points are worth mentioning. The Bank itself, according to critics, has often lain at the root of the environmental problems of many countries. Not only was the way it appraised earlier projects without regard for their environmental impact to blame, but many features of its development policy were themselves harmful. The emphasis to this day on the technology of the Green Revolution and on the development of exports forces countries to exploit large areas carelessly and has often led to catastrophic environmental consequences.[75] It thus indirectly contributed to the Latin American distinction between "nature" and "natural resources" which these countries have used to justify their exploitation of the Amazon forests. In that regard, national parks may weigh little in the face of a promotion of mineral resources exploration and exploitation.[76]

An even more basic problem is linked to the desire of the organization to "integrate" all sectors into the national economy. Development policies based on Western models have often created poverty and environmental degradation where it did not exist. Where man was in an equilibrium relationship with his environment, the Bank and the process of "nation-building" have broken this relationship (as in Indonesia). When African governments sought to control nomadic peoples through forced settlement, the environment was no longer able to support their continuous pressure, and its degradation exacerbated the effects of droughts.[77] The ultimate environmental value of the few environmental projects and components that the Bank supports may therefore be of little consequence if the organization keeps promoting development policies that lead to grave environmental disruptions and social instability.

The Tactics Used and Their Results

There are basically two kinds of environmental organizations involved at the international level: networks of scientific or technical organizations and primarily political groups that present scientific studies (often second-hand accounts) to national legislatures and bureaucracies along with their own opinions and preferred solutions. Although both have lobbied national authorities and advocated specific solutions to environmental issues, the latter have been much more involved with the U.S. Congress and argued as much in political as in scientific terms. These environmental groups formed a powerful coalition with ethnological groups, which enabled them to tie environmental issues to issues of human rights, and which also explain their relatively limited focus on tropical deforestation and dam building.

In trying to force the Bank to change its policy, they primarily relied on public campaigns and key congressional committees. Their immediate task was to influence the behavior of the United States executive director and take advantage of his country's dominant role in the organization. Given the Reagan administration's initial reluctance to press the issue forcefully, they urged Congress to demand specific reforms and pressure the Department of the Treasury to instruct the U.S. representative accordingly. They also sought to influence the Bank more directly by threatening not to support IDA replenishments and IBRD capital increases in the absence of environmental progress, and by organizing public demonstrations.

They failed in their attempt to form a coalition of donors behind these reformist objectives, but were more successful in gaining support from NGOs in several developing countries. They organized hearings with sympathetic chairmen of technical subcommittees, in the process guaranteeing that their views would be represented before powerful appropriations committees. They helped draft recommendations and arranged for the testimonies of spokesmen of foreign environmental groups. The same witnesses appeared over and over again, representing the same coalition of environmental organizations and repeating similar arguments.

Congress has a long record of involvement in international environmental issues, starting with the Stockholm Conference. In the late 1970s, it strengthened USAID's environmental requirements. In the 1980s, it promoted the issue of tropical deforestation actively. An amendment to the 1981 Foreign Assistance Act called on the Executive Branch to accord priority to the problem of tropical deforestation. It included a section on biological diversity in the 1983 Foreign Assistance Act and called for a U.S. strategy to conserve endangered species.

Although congressional committees have no jurisdiction over international agencies, they have effectively pressured them through the U.S. government. The U.S. director must veto loans that threaten American agricultural interests. Given its dependence on the U.S. for IDA replenishments and IBRD capital increases, the Bank has listened closely to Congress, a role that President Conable, a former member of the House of representatives, was very much encouraged to fulfill. In 1984, the House adopted a set of nineteen INGO-sponsored recommendations to improve the environmental performance of multilateral development banks. They included provisions designed to strengthen the environmental review capabilities of the departments of Treasury and State, called for more staffing and training programs, identified ways to foster environmental actions by developing countries, and provided guidance for the U.S. executive directors. The World Bank was urged to expand the OESA, designate an environmental specialist in each of the six regional offices, add environmental courses to EDI's curriculum, involve INGOs in project and program formulation, involve national bureaucracies other than development agencies in the project planning process, and use the recommendations of the 1980 World Conservation Strategy as lending standards. The U.S. executive director was to work for those changes and oppose loans that were environmentally destructive (see appendix for text). In 1986, the House reiterated its recommendations and strengthened requirements concerning the need for trained staff in the banks, and it added directives to promote greater INGO participation. Management changes within the MDBs were are also urged to create institutional incentives for the staff to inject environmental concerns into their activities.[78]

As part of the 1986 Appropriations Bill, the Senate Foreign Operations Subcommittee adopted ten requirements to reform lending policies in the form of instructions to the secretaries of State and Treasury. They took up many of the same points made by the House, sometimes in greater detail.

These actions fulfilled the objectives of the environmental groups which were adept at linking these values to congressional concerns for human rights, domestic economic protection, and to its traditional hostility to international assistance programs. An administration better known for its hostility to environmental questions found in this acceptance a convenient way of attacking an institution of which it had been extremely critical, of justifying static or declining contributions, and pressing for administrative and programmatic reforms. Thus, in 1986, the U.S. alternate executive director voted against a $500 million loan to Brazil, calling the project a "folly" and an "environmental disaster."[79]

Constraints on the Policy

In spite of several disastrous experiences with indigenous populations and tropical deforestation projects (Philippines, Brazil), the Bank went on funding similar projects elsewhere (Indonesia). What has made it difficult for the Bank to learn from its errors? What explains the apparent failure of the Bank to develop and implement a broader and more consistent environmental policy? From the leader among international organizations in the early 1970s, it became the prime target for criticism in the 1980s. Why was the Bank so slow to respond to this criticism and especially to the set of recommendations Congress adopted in 1985?

One major element lies in its past success in adapting to its environment and shaping it to its advantage. The development of its own economic expertise, the use of economic criteria, and the creation of "enclaves" in the developing countries provided effective protection against a disturbing external environment, but also made change more difficult. In essence, the organization became bureaucratized.

A second factor is its dependence on external resources: projects and political support from its clientele, money for the IDA from the donor countries. To maintain good business relations with borrowers, it must take into account their development agencies' positions. Moreover, in the absence of opposition from its major donors, the Bank finds it difficult not to support projects that are high on a recipient's agenda (as in the case of Indonesia's transmigration program).

In 1972, Caldwell identified three important road-blocks to international environmental cooperation: the lack of international instruments, the prevalence of the sovereignty principle, and a definition of development without reference to the environment.[80] The lack of instruments has been somewhat remedied through the creation of UNEP, the elaboration of a growing corpus of international environmental laws, and, within the Bank, the routinization of environmental review. Sovereignty remains a problem.

Overcoming sovereignty has been considered crucial for international organizations if they want to achieve their goals.[81] The problem of the Bank has been to avoid giving the impression that it was interfering with national autonomy. Rather, it sought to reconcile global environmental concerns with national sovereignty over the exploitation of these resources. Chapter 4 showed that many of the implementation strategies that the Bank uses are precisely designed to overcome the sovereignty obstacle. Sanctions, coalitions, linkage, and co-optation contribute to weakening that principle. Conscious of their vulnerability, many countries have denounced the Bank's attempts to impose certain choices on them.

In the face of mounting pressures, Brazil and the other Amazonian region countries reacted by emphasizing unity and stressing the principle of sovereignty over natural resources embodied in the 1974 *Charter of Economic Rights and Duties of States*. Unity was achieved through the Amazonian Cooperation Treaty, and the 1980 Belem Declaration which reaffirmed the principle of national sovereignty while paying lip service to the environment.[82] What is the Bank to do in that context?

The Bank cannot do much to change this attitude. Issues are much more difficult to solve when they are transformed into matters of principle.[83] The Bank's leverage over a large borrower like Brazil or Indonesia is minimal: first, because the organization has an important stake in that country and needs it as an outlet for its large infrastructural projects; second, because sanctions may jeopardize the little environmental good it is doing (when it supports water pollution control projects in São Paulo, for example, or attaches soil conservation components to agricultural loans); and third, because Brazil can always turn away from the Bank and rely on other sources of financing to support the same project. Although the financial difficulties of major borrowers and the development of structural adjustment loans seemed to point to an increase in the Bank's influence, the very vulnerability of these countries increased the need for large and regular financial transfers, which major donors strongly supported.

The turbulence of the international environment also hindered greater progress. Environmental protection is best approached in times of plenty. At the same time several Third World countries (Thailand, Nigeria, the Philippines, Kenya, Ivory Coast, Colombia, Ecuador) requested greater assistance for forest protection, the developed countries were seeking to slow down the growth of the Bank's environmental protection activities until growth had returned.[84] Thus, while the international and domestic environmental commitment of the rich countries was declining, greater efforts were demanded from the poor countries already in precarious financial positions.

The arguments used by the Bank's critics also posed problem. Many criticisms advanced by environmental organizations either seemed to seek to impose American standards and values on other countries or reflected overt political goals that recipients may have found objectionable. For example, many organizations acted as spokespersons or arranged for the testimony of groups for whom environmental issues were inherently linked to larger political ones. Statements—such as "Recipient countries' objections to the open formulation of development projects should be strongly resisted, so that projects do not institutionalize undemocratic forces"[85]— seek to tie environmental and ethnological issues to concern for human rights. Although they play well in Congress, to borrowers they confirm that the promotion of environmental issues is only a device to achieve unrelated political goals, while serving external interests or contributing, however unwillingly, to national disintegration. Opposition to POLONOROESTE was justified, according to several witnesses, because such projects made it easier for the Brazilian government to ignore or postpone land reform in the northeast or to reconsider the cash crop orientation of the southern agriculture.[86] As a Brazilian environmentalist exclaimed to Congress: "In our fight for ecological sanity, we must always keep in mind that social justice and a healthy environment go together."[87] Not only would that statement contradict much of the experience of the industrialized countries, it is also bound to create suspicion. Emphasis is also placed on the need to include local citizen groups in the preparation and implementation of development plans. Rather than decentralizing decision-making, however, the first objective of most developing countries is precisely to strengthen the state and integrate society through centralization. These groups want the Bank to play a political role that its close relations with the state make it difficult to adopt. By echoing these arguments or even facilitating these testimonies, American environmentalists and Congressmen in fact ally themselves with the political opponents of the regimes in question.

The tactic of seeking congressional legislation to force the United States, in turn, to pressure the organization made it more difficult to yield to it without being castigated as a tool of U.S. interests or of U.S. domestic politics. American criticisms of the treatment of indigenous populations are considered to interfere with sovereignty and smack of hypocrisy. And the threat to hold IDA hostage clearly indicated to the Bank and developing countries that environmental groups were at heart against the poor.

Also, from its own perspective, the Bank has already done a lot in favor of the environment. Even though performance has been problematic at times, it has accomplished much more than comparable institutions, has become a leader of sorts, and has incurred diplomatic costs in the process. Moreover, although the Bank's performance seems contradictory (supporting several environmental conservation projects while funding destructive ones), these contradictions reflect not only internal divisions but also divisions within its recipients. Finally, many recipients lack the institutions to generate, support, implement, or enforce environmental protection measures. Even when the Bank requires them, institutional deficiencies will make them dead letters. The Bank believed that its presence within controversial projects might still help mitigate their negative consequences. This argument was used to justify support for the Indonesian transmigration program and POLONOROESTE. If the Bank did not fund the latter, it would fund projects elsewhere and thus free up resources that the Brazilian government could use to implement POLONOROESTE with even fewer restraints.[88]

Indiscriminate dramatization and uncertain scientific knowledge impeded a more forceful promotion of environmental values. Between the immediate certainty of starvation, poverty, or social unrest, and the distant uncertainty of ecological catastrophes, governments and development oriented agencies must choose to prevent the former. Blaming starvation on the destruction of the basic environmental resource base is highly conjectural and ignores political and social causes. Deforestation reports have been exaggerated and condemned in principle, as if deforestation, like population growth, were inherently bad.

Finally, not only is the Bank subjected to greater and greater demands, it also seeks conflicting objectives that its members have placed upon it. For example, the goal of poverty alleviation may interfere with the protection of tropical forests. This illustrates the proposition of organization theory that as the milieu becomes more complex, the organization's goals become more diverse, and internal conflicts increase. But, the organization cannot concentrate on one value at the expense of others. Rather, it can only try to minimize the trade-offs between the main values it seeks (development, alleviation of poverty) and environmental degradation. Yet, many INGOs would like it to be a new and more powerful UNEP. Others a new UNDP, or UNIDO, or UNESCO. These demands are bounds to engender frustration. As one observer exclaimed:

> The things that the people in the MDB's are really worried about is that over the years they have been encumbered by their donors and by their

client governments with a whole series of procedures. So they have to worry about the role of women in development, income distribution. Now they have got the environment. Then they have got appropriate technology. You have got all these special interest groups all lined up outside the door of a planning process that is very long and very cumbersome and very elaborate. And the real fear at the end of the day, particularly amongst the agricultural development people who are very committed in my experience, is that another one of these guys coming in the door is going to make the process another two years longer. And it is too damn long already.[89]

This last point again underlines the various contradictions the Bank faces: contradictions between its development policies and the environment; contradictions among the strategies it uses to implement its environmental concern; contradictions between the training of the staff and an ecological perspective; contradictions between its reward system and that of OESA; between incentives and environmental values; between its role as a banker and transferer of resources and the protection of the environment; and between its various goal, basic needs, infrastructrual projects, and environmental protection.

6

Looking toward the Future

"The IMF and the World Bank Group have contributed enor-
mously to the spread of hope—to a better life throughout the
world community. In the process, they have proven themselves
capable of change, of adapting to new circumstances and to the
needs of new members.
—Ronald Reagan

What are the prospects for change? This concluding chapter reviews the
reforms that were instituted in response to external criticisms and internal
contradictions and assesses the conditions and limits of their efficacy.

The 1987 Reforms

January 1987 marked the beginning of a profound organizational reform
of the Bank's operations, necessitated, President Conable said, by complaints of inefficiency and "drifting" from its donors (chiefly the United
States), and from borrowers faulting the Bank for its perceived lack of
responsiveness to their needs. Staffing reductions and programmatic
changes generated much controversy and uncertainty within the organization, and the manner with which the reforms were conducted raised
criticisms from Bank employees as well as a few executive directors. Several well-respected senior officers left the organization, and so did James
Lee, the environmental adviser since 1970.

The reforms were intended to strenthen the links with the organization's
clientele by decentralizing the operations of the Bank toward the developing countries, increasing the transparence of its operations and improving
the links between the organization and each borrower. At the same time,
to satisfy American complaints, staff reductions were implemented and
certain policy changes instituted.

Two new vice presidencies were created, including one for Policy, Planning, and Research headed by the former head of the Bank's South East
Asia office who had witnessed the impact of deforestation and had attempted to alert the organization to a problem that was causing increasing
concerns among these countries.

A narrower hierarchical structure gave overall responsibility to forty-seven directors who will be able to integrate all Bank activities concerning each country. Although the hope was to improve communication among Bank units and with its clients, this decentralization also threatened to accentuate the tendency of boundary-spanners to become advocates of their clients.

Barber Conable took advantage of these major changes to modify the place of environmental review and meet some of the criticisms that the organization had been facing from public interest groups in developed countries, from the United States government, and from several borrowers. Other donor countries—apart from Norway, which had sponsored the 1987 United Nations report on environment and development—had expressed few concerns about the Bank's environmental policy, while most developing countries gave the environment little consideration in the face of the economic problems they confronted.

In a major speech to the World Resources Institute (WRI) in May 1987, Barber Conable sought to regain the initiative for an embattled organization and to meet the criticisms of the Bank's environmental performance. He outlined major initiatives designed to make up a "charter for a new day at the World Bank."[1]

Barber Conable acknowledged that the Bank had "stumbled," and called POLONOROESTE "a sobering example of an environmentally sound effort which went wrong."[2] Not the rationale or the appraisal methods used in support of the project, but solely poor implementation and monitoring were to blame. The "lessons" learned did not address the wisdom of such projects or the capacity of the Bank to review them adequately and enforce whatever environmental provisions it requires. The Bank believed the problem solely lay in a misplaced confidence in the inadequate enforcement capacities of the country, and this conforted its belief that non-involvement meant no influence.

First, Conable announced several organizational reforms:

A new "top-level Environment Department" with the equivalent of thirty full-time staff members was established. Its role is to help identify the direction of Bank policy, planning, and research work and promote the environmental "dialogue" with borrowers. Its high hierarchical position will give environmental criteria greater visibility, and may enable it to arbitrate effectively among competing sectors. Sectoral conflicts can be identified and resolved in the early stages of the project cycle. Better information is also expected to flow to the Executive Directors.

New offices in the four regional technical departments will review all projects and oversee the implementation of environmental measures included in Bank-supported projects. They will also identify promising advances in resource management, and help with institution-building through close contact with national environmental officials.

Second, apart from strengthening existing policy (withholding support in case of non-compliance, putting a premium on conservation), a series of new initiatives were announced:

Country-by-country environmental assessments will be performed (presumably building on existing USAID work). This initiative followed plans devised in 1986 when the Bank acquired remote sensing capabilities and secured technical support from NASA. It also started working with UNEP's Global Resources Information and Data System which makes worldwide data available to the Bank. Sub-Saharan Africa and other countries presently experiencing severe environmental constraints will be targeted first. Of course, how these studies will be used really matters here. USAID's efforts have often been criticized as perfunctory, rather than leading to the inclusion of new elements into a country's aid planning. Many developing countries are also suspicious of attempts to gather data on their natural resources and of the uses to which they could be put. The Bank intends this information to be disseminated to other development banks, IGOs and national aid agencies, and form the basis of a policy dialogue with the host country.

The Bank will actively support a global program to promote tropical forest conservation. We have seen how actively involved it had been in earlier efforts to sensitize and encourage countries to protect these resources. It now plans to triple funding for "environmentally-sound forestry projects" from $138 million in FY 1986 to $350 million in FY 1989. This corresponded to the priorities of American groups and governmental agencies which emphasized the design and management of irrigation projects and the protection of tropical forests. In 1986, the World Resources Institute released its report, *Tropical Forests: A Call for Action*, whose rationale Barber Conable endorsed in his address. It stimulated FAO to develop an action plan in this area and led to the July 1987 Bellagio Conference to which the Bank's new vice president for Policy Planning contributed actively. At this meeting, international organizations (FAO, UNDP, IBRD), non-governmental organizations, and multinational corporations released the Bellagio Declaration urging radical measures to stop what, in effect, these organizations had been doing. International agencies and governments were urged to prevent slash-and-burn practices, limit highway construction in forested areas, control the activities of lumber companies, and institute reforestation programs.

Another initiative sought to balance this concern for tropical moist forests with more attention to anti-desertification, an issue of great concern to UNEP and to several donors with scientific expertise or a political interest in the Sahel (such as France). With a primary focus on Africa, it will entail identifying regional as well as national protection projects. This would be a significant shift in policy, away from the strict national project-by-project approach, and could considerably improve the Bank's ability to promote international cooperation, one of its five original objectives. How the constraints recognized in chapters 2 and 3 will be overcomed remained unclear, however.

Finally, the Bank will also participate in a program to protect the Mediterranean, thus enabling the continuation of the Action Plan that UNEP was scheduled to stop funding, and which the countries of the region were eager to maintain.

Clearly, donors and borrowers could support this package because it gave everybody a measure of satisfaction. Developing countries saw in it a means to increase resource transfers as well as responding to their wishes; the concern of European donors for desertification and the Mediterranean were met; and the United States' main concerns (deforestation, national surveys, internal reorganization) provided the main focus of the reforms. Although these measures addressed several issues raised by American environmental organizations, their role was to remain limited. Instead of being included in the decision-making process as they had wished, they were encouraged to develop citizen involvement in environmental protection measures and training, and to support the Bank's environmental goals in each country. Rather than utilizing them as forces of decentralization, local participation and grass-roots development, Conable urged them to act on behalf of the Bank's objectives and to use their influence with other actors (e.g., the U.S. Congress) to support the work of the Bank.

The creation of forty-seven country directorates illustrates that as the organization attempts to control its milieu, it will increase its boundary-spanning activities.[3] The decision to place environmental units in four regional offices, rather than environmental officers in each of the forty-seven country directorates will not suppress internal conflicts since the latter will tend to reflect the borrower's perspective on environmental issues. Unless the political will of the Bank leadership is very strong, which previous chapters suggest will not be the case, the success of this new policy will rest on borrowers' acceptance. Education and INGO support then remain crucial. The relative modesty of the initiatives announced suggested that the Bank will proceed cautiously and first seek to respond to the concerns of its borrowers. Much will also depend on the quality of the new forty-seven directors whose qualifications quickly provoked substantial infighting upon their nominations.

What Future for the Policy?

Can the Bank's environmental policy move toward sustainable management and consistent protection of natural resources without alienating the support of its constituencies further? Or can it use environmental values to regain prestige and autonomy? Improvements in the Bank's performance will rest on the removal of certain internal and external constraints, on the understanding of others, as well as on the full exploitation of existing opportunities.

The environmental record of the Bank will necessitate a close reexamination of the methods used to appraise projects. Although the OESA endeavored in 1986 to pay more attention to improving the methodology of natural resources economics, the broader scope of the policy will cause disturbance within the organization. Its basic impulse is to function smoothly, not only because it is dependent on external resources, but also because it relies on certain types of projects and on a methodology with which it is familiar. The scope of cost-benefit analyses could be broadened and the discount rates used lowered since high discount rates work against environmental improvement projects whose benefits are not visible for a long time. At the very least, the political nature of project appraisal would be made more visible. But in the absence of a well-developed methodology that can replace the old one, the implementation of the new policy will be very difficult.

The effect of macroeconomic policy recommendations also needs studying. For example, the removal of price controls, a common condition for Structural Adjustment Lending, may encourage environmental degradation. Units of the Bank (such as the Economic Research Staff) and some donors (such as the United States) have actively promoted their faith in price adjustments and in a minimal role for the state. Although they argue that price control may exacerbate environmental degradation, the opposite may be as likely.[4] Higher prices may encourage farmers to exhaust soils rapidly to take advantage of them. Less subsidized rural credit, that is higher interest rates, may persuade people to put immediate financial gains before long-term environmental benefits.[5] At the national level, countries such as Indonesia, Thailand and the Ivory Coast may be pressured to increase timber sales to maximize their immediate income.

The experience of the Bank in Indonesia and Brazil pointed up the importance of creating the institutional and technical conditions necessary for the success of the project. This often requires a long-term commitment to a certain program, to training, and to experimental projects whose immediate economic returns may also be uncertain. The Bank funded isolated conservation projects which had little impact, whereas a series of cumulated projects may affect national policies over time. For example, eighteen irrigation-rehabilitation projects in Indonesia influenced governmental guidelines regarding the operation and maintenance of irrigation systems.[6]

Crucial impetus must also come from management. The Bank traditionally has been dominated by its top officers, and its operations have usually reflected the philosophies and capacities of its top management. McNamara provided the most salient illustration of the difference that creative leadership can make.[7] The departure of many senior officials and the appointment of at least one supportive vice president may facilitate the capacity of the organization again to adapt creatively to a changing milieu.

The leadership of the United States has been crucial in the past and will remain so. An active environmental policy will require sustained American support for the organization as a whole and for the forms that environmental protection projects may take. Indiscriminate attacks on the organization must cease. It is difficult to understand why the United States objects to the size of the Bank staff when the organization's administrative budget comes only from its own profits. Yet, American officials, while supporting an increase in the number of environmental specialists, have also argued against expanding the staff. Reliance on ideological arguments must also decrease. Free markets may or may not have beneficial environmental consequences. The task of the Bank can be to determine the conditions under which they do.

American support can take several forms. The United States can propose and support a special fund for the protection of tropical forests or other environmental plans, to be administered by the Bank and used to compensate countries for the additional expenditures incurred (a return to the compensation principle proposed at Founex). It could mobilize other developed countries behind the goal of supporting the Bank's environmental priorities. There were indications that other donors, although interested, would not move unless the United States did. It could bear a larger share of the costs of providing developing countries with commercial incentives to protect their ecosystems.

An enhanced U.S. role depends on support from the American Congress. It was able to influence the Bank's environmental activities significantly because of the difficulties the organization was experiencing under the twin challenges from the United States and a turbulent international economic environment. But the hearings it has held on these questions have been far from balanced. Members of Congress will have to demonstrate that their concern for the environment is not a convenient way to justify protectionist measures or gain quick electoral dividends. This evolution must include greater appreciation for the political context of the policy, rather than limit itself to the problem as it is defined by environmental activists.

Chapter 2 described the limitations attached to the Bank's project focus. The growth of policy-based lending in the 1980s may help alleviate the problems of linking the disbursement of project-related funds to policy issues on which the success of its activities depend. Structural and sectoral adjustment loans constituted about 30 percent of lending in 1986. But heavier policy orientation also led to some uneasiness on the part of recipients weary of the Bank's interference in politically sensitive areas, although Conable's managerial reforms may now help alleviate these misgivings. Certainly, the experience of sub-Sahara Africa underscored the necessity of integrating project lending and policy reforms. Both the Bank and WRI blamed poor macroeconomic policies for the economic difficulties and the famine many of these countries experienced.

As Please has pointed out, the Bank holds a comparative advantage in handling policy issues by virtue of its analytical resources, commitment to development, and autonomy from national interest groups.[8] Yet, it has not been very successful in improving policies, which became evident in the record of its environmental involvement in Brazil. It often found itself prisoner of the development agencies it helped build. As the organization itself recognized in 1982: "On the basis of experience, it would be reasonable to conclude that individual projects in general are inefficient instruments for inducing policy-change."[9] The development of structural adjustment lending may help strengthen its capability to enforce policy covenants.

SAL or policy-oriented loans are not viewed sympathetically by the environmental critics of the Bank chiefly because they are convinced that local projects can be better targeted to serve the local population and minimize centralized decision-making and politicization. On the other hand, regardless of the governments' interests in strengthening the central apparatus, SALs will prove indispensable instruments in transferring enough resources to Third World countries to enable the Bank to maintain its preeminent position as a lender, protect its previous investments and the capacities of these countries to service their debts to the Bank, and to fend off criticisms by the recipients that the largest development organization's financial receipts have surpassed its disbursements. Expansion, as noted in chapter 4, is not only an adaptation to changing values or to a more complex task-environment, it is also an organizational imperative.

For the Bank to broaden its policy initiatives, an agreement over the environmental problems facing a particular country and the measures to address them must be reached. The development of the Bank's remote-sensing capacities and its willingness to undertake national environmental studies will facilitate the collection of basic data. This is, however, an inherently political exercize. The determination of what constitutes an environmental problem and which solution should be used depends on each country's cultural values, political and economic priorities, and social resources; and on the Bank's need to secure the support of its clientele. The opposition that often exists between the militancy of American environmentalists and the perspective of local environmental groups illustrates the need to cast the environmental dialogue squarely in its political context, lest the Bank be perceived as the tool of narrow interests. INGOs' pressures on the Bank to change its development philosophy by focusing on the resource base first—and turning away from traditional infrastructural projects, export-oriented agriculture, and deforestation for resettlement and lumber exports—either betray a poor evaluation of the context of the problem or seek to impose politically-unacceptable solutions. Any definition of the problem will require compromises with other objectives (e.g., poverty alleviation or export-led development) as well as strong support from donors behind the provision of positive inducements to reform the environmental practices of these countries.

Many elements identified in the preceding chapter will limit the Bank's ability to improve its policy along these lines. Its effectiveness in removing other internal and external constraints and in promoting this new environmental commitment will depend on the degree to which the organization's decisions are supported by its milieu. In that sense, it refers to what has been called institutionalization in the organization theory literature.[10] Three variables affect institutionalization: ideology, autonomy, and elite constituency.

The crisis in the Bank's environmental policy reflected its ideological uncertainty. In the 1970s, McNamara's reforms responded to the priorities of the developing countries as well as to changing concerns among donor countries for the human targets of their aid programs. The early 1980s saw two other attacks on the developmental philosophy of the Bank. One came from the Reagan administration and strict liberal economists who sought to de-emphasize the state and systemic factors. The other came from environmentalists who sought to change the focus of development toward small decentralized projects aimed at improving a country's ability to provide for its own needs whild protecting the environment. With these latest reforms, the Bank has now tried to accommodate both views without reneging on McNamara's legacy. Although a skillful use of its ideology enabled the Bank to expand its functional scope in the late 1940s and to redefine its development policies in light of evolving developmental thinking in the 1970s, it has been unable to show similar creativity in the 1980s. As we have seen, this past success proved a liability in the case of the environment and forced OESA to frame its concerns *within* the prevalent economic paradigms, both within and outside the organization. Moreover, its environmental ideology has been constrained by its members' concern with human resources and transfers of international financial resources, and by the diversity of the goals the organization was pursuing. Without a coherent vision of its task, the Bank remains hostage to the contradictory demands that emanate from its milieu, and will experience great difficulties in pursuing consistent and independent objectives. Libby's earlier claim that "the Bank's ability to resolve environmental crises by reformulating its ideology to adjust to a threatening environment suggests that it has attained a degree of autonomy," seems no longer valid.[11]

The World Bank has long been considered unique among international organizations for the extent of its autonomy.[12] Mason and Asher have contended that the World Bank owed its success to a source of revenues independent of both the UN and governments.[13] But IDA provided governments with new leverage over the organization's policies. The evolution of its operations demonstrated that rather than freeing itself from its milieu, the Bank attempted to meet more pressures and counter-pressures.[14] Its policies themselves have not shown much independence from those implemented by national agencies.

Organizational theorists have suggested that a trade-off exists between milieu certainty and organizational autonomy.[15] As the organization moves from strategies of competition to bargaining, cooptation, and coalition, it loses autonomy while gaining certainty. Terreberry also argued that organizations are becoming less and less autonomous because they are involved more and more with other organizations in their environment.[16] This observation, however, applies to relatively stable milieux. Cox and Jacobson have shown that an increase in the complexity of the international organizations' milieu—when new states arrived suddenly on the international scene after World War II—complicated coalition-building instead of increasing their latitude.[17] In a turbulent international milieu, the Bank failed to gain much certainty while losing considerable autonomy. Bargaining and coalition originally defined its environmental policy. The various strategies the organization used helped it adapt successfully to its milieu. But its failure to transform it, and international turbulence, precluded the evolution of the policy and prevented the organization from shielding itself from mounting pressures. Yet, to say that the Bank is at the ultimate mercy of the states is not to deny it any freedom from control or any policy influence. When states have difficulties defining clearly their development and environmental objectives, the organization is free to promote its own or, at the very least, can frame the decisions that its members will have to make by defining the issues at stake and the means to address them.

The existence of support for segments of the task-environment within the organization, as well as support for segments of the organization within the task-environment, also affected the organization's effectiveness. We have seen that intra-organizational support for environmental parameters was weak and that the OESA had devoted much resources toward improving it. The regional offices remained reluctant to follow OESA's lead and the economists' and engineers' professional inclinations took them away from environmental concerns. External support in developing countries existed among environmental ministries but little appeared among planning agencies or financial ministries. Conable's managerial reforms may help the organization secure support both from donors and borrowers, but an extensive implementation of its environmental reforms will prove controversial. Ultimately, the success of its policy rests on strong government commitment. Without it, the best projects will be neglected once the Bank withdraws.

The last decade of the twentieth century will see a world readjustment to ecological scarcity. Whether it is prepared to do it or not, whether it likes it or not, whether developed and developing countries are ready to acknowledge it or not, the World Bank will have to play a crucial role during this transition period. Even though the Bank's mandate is not the promotion of environmental values per se, it cannot escape this new role once it is recognized that it will be impossible to achieve development goals without taking ecological variables into account. Its potential role in the formation of international environmental policy is considerable. The wide variety of strategies it can use, its unique access to national decision-making centers, and its ability to demonstrate technically the value of environmental protection can greatly complement the activities of other IGOs in that area and enable it to impose its definition of the problem upon all actors in its task-environment. The Bank has demonstrated a strong ability to change in the past. Despite the internal and external constraints that impinge on its policy, the last organizational shake-up may have reduced its bureaucratization sufficiently to enable it to respond to the economic and ecological challenges of the coming years, thereby fulfilling both sides of President Reagan's tribute.

Appendix A
Declaration of Environmental Policies
and Procedures Relating to Economic Development

(adopted at New York, 1 February 1980)

Whereas, economic and social development is essential to the alleviation of major environmental problems by providing for an integral relationship between societies and their environment, realizing also that economic development and social goals should be pursued in such a manner as to avoid or minimize environmental problems peculiar to it,

Recognizing that, the major environmental problems of the developing countries are not necessarily of the same nature as those of developed countries in that they are problems which often reflect the impact of poverty which not only affects the quality of life but life itself,

Convinced, that in the long run environmental protection and economic and social development are not only compatible but interdependent and mutually reinforcing,

Acknowledging, that the need for environmentally sensitive and responsible development has become more important and urgent in light of increasing population and concomitant pressures on the earth's resources and life-supporting ecological systems in some areas,

Acknowledging, the sovereign right of governments, to determine their own priorities and development patterns,

Recalling, that the States which adopted the Declaration of the United Nations Conference on the Human Environment (Stockholm, 1972) stated their common conviction (principle 25) that they will ensure that the international organizations play a co-ordinated, efficient and dynamic role in the protection and improvement of the environment,

Considering, furthermore that international development assistant [sic] institutions have, along with their member governments, a responsibility to ensure the sustainability of the economic development activities financed by them,

Therefore, the undersigned declared that they:

I. *Reaffirm* their support for the principles and recommendations for action of the United Nations Conference

II. *Will*, to the best of their abilities, endeavour to:

1. *Institute* procedures for systematic examination of all development activities, including policies, programmes and projects, under consideration for financing to ensure that appropriate measures are proposed for compliance with section I above;

2. *Enter* into co-operative negotiations with governments and relevant international organizations and agencies, to ensure integration of appropriate environmental measures in the design and implementation of economic development activities;

3. *Provide* technical assistance, including training, on environmental matters to developing countries, at their request, thus developing their indigenous capacity, and facilitating technical co-operation between developing countries.

4. *Give* active consideration and, if appropriate, support project proposals that are specially designed to protect, rehabilitate, manage or otherwise enhance the human environment, the quality of life, and resources thereto related;

5. *Initiate* and/or otherwise co-operate in research and studies leading to improvement or project appraisal, implementation and evaluation methodologies, including cost-benefit analysis, of environmental protection measures;

6. *Support* the training and informing of operational staff in the environmental dimension of economic development;

7. *Prepare*, publish and disseminate documentation and audiovisual material providing guidance on the environmental dimension of economic development activities.

Adopted at New York on 1 February 1980.

Signed by:

The African Development Bank (Kwame Donkor Fordwor, President)

The Arab Bank for Economic Development in Africa (Chadli Ayari, President)

The Asian Development Bank (Taroichi Yoshida, President)

The Caribbean Development Bank (William Demas, President)

The Inter-American Development Bank (Antonio Ortiz Mena, President)

The World Bank (Robert S. McNamara, President)

The Commission of the European Communities (Roy Jenkins, President)

The Organization of American States (Alejandro Orfila, Secretary-General)

The United Nations Development Programme (Bradford Morse, Administrator)

The United Nations Environment Programme (Mostafa K. Tolba, Executive Director)

Appendix B
Recommendations Regarding Environmental Concerns Associated with Multilateral Development Bank Activity

Recommendations of the Subcommittee on International Development Institutions and Finance of the House Banking, Finance and Urban Affairs Committee, adopted December 1984.

(1) A representative from the Council on Environmental Quality or, alternatively, from the State Department's Bureau of Oceans and International Environment and Scientific Affairs, should be designated as a member of the Working Group on Multilateral Affairs (WGMA). As the staffing agency for the WGMA, Treasury should initiate the necessary procedures to achieve such representations.

(2) A permanent Treasury Department staff position should be established within the Office of Multilateral Development Banks to monitor environmental aspects of bank activities, to facilitate constructive U.S. involvement in assuring that sound environmental policies are implemented by multilateral lending agencies supported by the U.S., and to expedite the flow of information between the banks and the U.S. Congress, other relevant federal agencies and the public regarding environmental considerations.

(3) Within the Inter-American Development Bank (IDB), a staff position should be established to serve as the environmental coordinator for bank activities.

(4) An environmental coordinator position should be established at the African Development Bank.

(5) A staff member of each of the World Bank's six regional offices should be assigned full time responsibility for environmental issues.

(6) The Economic Development Institute (EDI) of the World Bank should be expanded with the addition of a component which provides training in environmental and natural resource planning and program development.

(7) A renewed effort should be made through the Committee of International Development Institutions on Environment (CIDIE) to obtain joint

support for creation of the EDI environmental component, making courses available to all participating institutions. The Subcommittee urges the World Bank, IDB, ADB, and AfDB to join in pressing such action.

(8) Each of the multilateral development banks should do its utmost to foster expanded environmental awareness in recipient and member countries.

(9) The development banks should, wherever possible, contract with conservation NGOs to provide their services during pre-project planning and during project implementation phases for purposes of local information gathering and dissemination so as to achieve maximum local input and participation in the assessment of planning for projects.

(10) Each of the multilateral development banks should press their borrower countries to actively involve environment and/or health ministers or comparable representatives in bank-supported country program planning and strategy sessions.

(11) In accordance with Title VIII of the International Financial Institutions Act of 1977, appropriate or light capital technology should be incorporated, to the maximum extent possible, into bank project operations.

(12) Country program planning and strategy activities of each of the development banks should reflect and conform to the 1980 World Conservation Strategy forged by the International Union for the Conservation of Nature and Natural Resources (IUCN) and the United Nations Environment Programme (UNEP). Where programs deviate from the precepts of the World Conservation Strategy program, documentation should be provided justifying the need for deviation.

(13) The Declaration of Environmental Policies and Procedures Relating to Economic Development to which nine international development organizations subscribed in 1980 complements the World Conservation Strategy. It was signed by the World Bank, IDB, ADB, and AfDB. The signatories to the Declaration should, as a matter of course, adhere to the guidance which the Declaration provides.

(14) There are a number of criteria which should be applied by the U.S. Executive Directors for the World Bank and regional banks to determine whether environmental considerations should impel the United States to work for changes to project proposals or, failing this, to oppose projects when they come before each organization's Executive Directors. The Subcommittee recommends that the U.S. Executive Directors oppose any project which, in its final form:

(a) results in using natural resource harvests (such as forest, fish, grassland, or wildlife) at an unsustainable level within a population or ecological unit;

(b) threatens to cause species extinction or to endanger species survival;

(c) causes environmental degradation beyond recipient country boundaries unless and until agreement is obtained from the impacted country;

(d) is expected to significantly convert or degrade those minimal and already overtaxed designated natural areas including national parks, wildlife reserves, world heritage sites and biosphere reserves which serve as the last vestiges of sanctuary for many forms of life;

(e) threatens to significantly impair the land and resource base upon which indigenous people depend; and/or

(f) fails to adequately provide for management and control of pesticide use. Adequate provision would include, specifically, that assessment of risks be conducted prior to project evaluation, loan stipulations be included which prevent use of pesticides classified as extremely or highly hazardous by the World Health Organization and that agricultural projects not be undertaken without providing adequate training for pesticide use or adequate monitoring mechanisms.

(15) Given the magnitude of global environmental problems and the need for aggressive leadership in the international development community regarding environmental and natural resource issues, and given the leadership which the United States has taken on many aspects of environmental protection, the U.S. Executive Directors should exert a leadership role in each of the multilateral lending institutions to promote a strong and effective environmental program.

(16) The Department of the Treasury should prepare a report to Congress annually presenting the activities of the World Bank Group, the Inter-American Development Bank and Fund for Special Operations, the Asian Development Bank and Fund and the African Development Bank and Fund which address environmental impacts and environmental protection so that Congress may have the opportunity to review such activities. This Subcommittee will be interested in examining the Treasury Department's report most immediately to ascertain the degree to which efforts have been undertaken to implement these recommendations and would hope that a first report would be voluntarily presented by March 1985.

Notes

Introduction

1. The concept of "task-environment" refers to the "parts of the [organizational] environment which are relevant to goal setting and goal attainment." (This is William Dill's definition; *see* James D. Thompson, *Organizations in Action* [New York: McGraw-Hill, 1967], 27.) Since this book is a study of the environmental policy of the World Bank (that is, of its policy regarding the protection of natural resources and the preservation of a healthy living and working environment), I shall restrict the use of the term "environment" to this sense. What organization theorists have called the organizational "environment" will here be called "milieu" in order to avoid any confusion. I shall, however, retain the term "task-environment" which does not lend itself so easily to misinterpretation.

2. Edward Buehrig, "The Resolution-Based International Agency," *Political Studies* 29, no.2 (1981): 2171–31.

3. Throughout this study, the expression "the World Bank" (or more simply, the Bank) refers to the International Bank for Reconstruction and Development (IBRD) and to its affiliate, the International Development Association (IDA). "World Bank Group" also includes IBRD's second affiliate, the International Finance Corporation (IFC). The IBRD was created in 1945. It finances its operations from its own borrowings in world capital markets, from its retained earnings, and from repayments on its loans, which have a twenty-year maturity (with a five-year grace period) and variable interest rates. The IDA, created in 1960, focuses on the poorer developing countries. The funds it lends, called "credits" to distinguish them from IBRD's "loans," come mostly from general replenishments by the Bank's donor countries, and transfers from IBRD's earnings. Lending terms are much "softer": forty-year maturities (with a ten-year grace period) at virtually no interest. The IFC, established in 1956, lends to the private sector of the developing countries' economies.

4. Ronald T. Libby, "International Development Association: A Legal Fiction Designed to Secure an LDC Constituency," *International Organization* 29, no.4 (1975):1065–72.

5. For an economic analysis and general evaluation of the changing scope of the Bank's activities in the 1970s, see Bettina Huerni, *The Lending Policies of the World Bank in the 1970s* (Boulder, Colo.: Westview Press, 1980). For discussions of its record, see Art Van de Laar, *The World Bank and the Poor* (Boston: Nijhoff, 1980), Cheryl Payer, *The World Bank: A Critical Analysis* (New York and London: Monthly Review Press, 1982), and Robert L. Ayres, *Banking on the Poor: The World Bank and World Poverty* (Cambridge and London: The MIT Press, 1983). The history by Edward S. Mason and Robert E. Asher, *The World Bank since Bretton Woods* (Washington D. C.: The Brookings Institution, 1973) is unsurpassed in its thoroughness.

6. For details on the application of organization theory to international organizations, *see* inter alia, Philippe Le Prestre, "A Problematique for International Organizations," *International Social Science Journal* 107 (1986): 127–38.

Chapter 1. Defining an Environmental Policy

1. See Lester B. Pearson, *Partners in Development: Report on the Commission on International Development* (New York: Praeger, 1969). This special commission was formed at the instigation of Presidents George Woods and Robert McNamara of the World Bank to "study the consequences of 20 years [of economic development policies], assess the results, clarify the errors and propose the policies which will work better in the future" (Preface, p. vii). Other noteworthy reports include: Sir Robert Jackson, *A Study of the Capacity of the United Nations Development Systems* (the Jackson Report) U.N. Doc. OP15, 2 vols. (Geneva: United Nations, 1969); and Raúl Prebisch, "Change and Development: Latin America's Great Task" (Report submitted to the Inter-American Development Bank, July 1970).

2. *See* Barbara Ward (Lady Jackson), et al. eds., *The Widening Gap: Development in the 1970s* (New York: Columbia University Press, 1971).

3. Robert McNamara, "Address to the Board of Governors, Washington, D.C., Sept. 29, 1969," in *The McNamara Years at the World Bank* (Baltimore: Johns Hopkins University Press, 1981), 69–94.

4. Ibid., 87. Along with a real GNP growth rate of 6 % in developing countries, the main objective of the second development decade, as finally proclaimed by the United Nations General Assembly that same year, was to reach a net annual transfer of external resources of 1% of the Developed Countries' GNP, with at least 70% of that amount on concessional terms going through official channels (the famous 0.7% GNP in foreign aid). See United Nations, International Development Strategy: Action Programme of the General Assembly for the Second United Nations Development Decade, St/ECA/1939 (New York: United Nations, 1970).

5. Robert McNamara, "Address to the United Nations Economic and Social Council"(Mimeograph, Washington, D.C.: The World Bank, 1970), 3–6.

6. While acknowledging the failures of the "trickle down" argument of economic development, this strategy was designed to complement classical development approaches by "channeling more of the benefits of that growth toward meeting the basic human needs of the absolute of the poor." Thus, by emphasizing redistributive policies as well as non-growth-oriented targets of development, the Bank was entering a new area involving a country's social development. The Bank also recognized the potential political obstacles that it would face: "The problem is that doing this requires changes in both developed and developing countries which may cut across the personal interests of a privileged minority who are more affluent and more politically influential" (Robert McNamara, "Address to the Board of Governors, Sept. 26, 1977" [Washington, D.C.: The World Bank, 1977], 12). For detailed historical and analytical accounts of this policy change, see Escott Reid, *Strengthening the World Bank* (Chicago: Adlai Stevenson Institute, 1973); Aart van de Laar, *The World Bank and the World Poor* (Boston: Nijhoff, 1980); Bettina Huerni, *The Lending Policies of the World Bank in the Nineteen-Seventies: Analysis and Evaluation* (Boulder, Colo.: Westview Press, 1980).

7. The new emphasis on the agricultural sector and the increase in the volume of lending it entailed did not force the Bank to alter its reliance on the inflow of capital and on the expansion of the export sector. The larger volume of lending allowed it to increase its support to traditional and non-traditional projects alike.

8. McNamara, "Address to ECOSOC," (1970), 5.

9. For a general overview of the growth of the environmental movement and the various theses that were debated, *see* Tim O' Riordan, *Environmentalism* (London: Pion, 1976). For an account of the international efforts to devise a new en-

vironmental regime, *see* Lynton K. Caldwell, *In Defense of Earth: International Protection of the Biosphere* (Bloomington: Indiana University Press, 1972) and *International Environmental Policy: Emergence and Dimensions* (Durham, N.C.: Duke University Press, 1984). *See* also *International Organization* 26, no. 2 (Spring 1972). For a more legal perspective, *see* Ludwig A. Teclaff and Albert Utton, *International Environmental Law* (New York: Praeger, 1974) and Jan Schneider, *World Public Order and the Environment* (Toronto: Toronto University Press, 1979). Finally, for an appraisal of the ecological damages to spaceship earth, *see* Department of State and Council on Environmental Quality, *Global 2000. Entering the Twenty-First Century*, 2 vols (Washington, D.C.: Government Printing Office, 1980), Nicholas Polunin, ed., *Growth Without Ecodisasters?* (New York: Wiley, 1980), and International Institute for Environment and Development and World Resources Institute, *World Resources 1987* (New York: Basic Book, 1987).

10. *See,* for example, Taghi Farvar and John Milton, eds., *The Careless Technology* (Garden City, N.Y.: Natural History Press, 1972).

11. Initially the Office of Environmental and Health Affairs (OEHA), it became the Office of Environmental Affairs (OEA) soon thereafter, and the Office of Environmental and Scientific Affairs (OESA) in the early 1980s. The latest name, OESA, will be used as often as possible to avoid confusion.

12. World Bank, *Environment and Development* (Washington, D.C.: The World Bank, 1979), 6.

13. World Bank, *The World Bank and the World Environment* (Washington, D.C.: The World Bank, 1971), 6.

14. World Bank, *Annual Report 1971* (Washington, D.C.: The World Bank, 1971), 23.

15. Ezra Mishan, *The Cost of Economic Growth* (Harmondsworth, U.K.: Penguin Books, 1967).

16. Farvar and Milton, *Careless Technology.*

17. *See* David Hart, *The Volta River Project: A Case Study in Politics and Technology* (Edinburgh: University Press, 1980).

18. Brent Blackwelder and Barbara Bramble, in U.S., House, Committee on Banking, Finance and Urban Affairs, *Environmental Impact of Multilateral Development Bank-Funded Projects, Hearings before the subcommittee on International Development Institutions and Finance.*, 98th Congress, 1st session, 1983 (Patterson, 83).

19. James Lee, "Environmental Considerations in Development Finance," in *World Eco-crisis*, eds. David A. Kay and Eugene B. Skolnikoff (Madison: The University of Wisconsin Press, 1972), 181.

20. David A. Kay and Harold K. Jacobson, *Environmental Protection: the International Dimension* (Totowa, N.J.: Allanheld, Osmun, 1983); R. M. M'Gonigle and M. W. Zacher, *Pollution, Politics and International Law: Tankers at Sea* (Berkeley: University of California Press, 1979).

21. United Nations General Assembly Resolution 2398 (XIII) adopted December 3, 1968.

22. *See* for example, Caldwell, *In Defense of Earth*; Maurice Strong, "One Year After Stockholm." *Foreign Affairs* vol. 51, no.4 (July 1973), pp. 690–707; *see also International Organization* 26, no. 2 (Spring 1972).

23. Ernst B. Haas, Mary Pat Williams, with Don Babai, *Scientists and World Order* (Berkeley: University of California Press, 1977), 182. UNESCO, for example, had taken an early lead with the 1968 Biosphere Conference and the launching of the Man and Biosphere Programme (MAB).

24. Barbara Ward and René Dubos, *Only One Earth* (New York: Norton, 1972).

25. Roland Bird, "Barbara Ward," *The Economist*, June 6, 1981, 38.

26. She withdrew from the presidency in 1980 to become Chairman of its council and called on William Clark, then Vice-President of the World Bank for External Affairs, to replace her at the head of the organization.

27. *See* Mahbub ul Haq, "The Limits to Growth: A Critique," *Finance and Development* 9, no. 4 (December 1972): 2–8; Nicholas Carter, "Population, Environment, and Natural Resources: A Critical Review of Recent Models," Staff Working Paper, No. 174 (Washington, D.C.: The World Bank, 1974).

28. William Clark in International Institute for Environment and Development (IIED), *1980 Annual Report* (London and Washington, D.C.: IIED, 1980), 8.

29. World Bank, *Environment and Development* (Washington, D.C.: The World Bank, 1975), p. 8.

30. *See* Aart Van der Laar, "The World Bank: Which Way?" *Development and Change* 7 (1976), 67–97; James A. Lee, "Environment and Development: Choices for the 3rd World," paper prepared for presentation at the 12th technical meeting of the IUCN, Banff, Canada, September 11–16, 1972, 12.

31. World Bank, *World Environment*, 5.

32. Robert McNamara, quoted in *International Journal of Environmental Studies* 3 (1972), 298.

33. Michael Hoffman, "Development Finance and the Environment," *Finance and Development* 7, no. 3 (1970), 2–6.

34. James Lee, "Environmental Considerations," 172.

35. *Ibid.*, 174.

36. Robert McNamara, "Address to the United Nations Conference on the Human Environment," Stockholm, Sweden, June 8, 1972 (Washington, D.C.: The World Bank, 1972), (Stockholm Address).

37. *See*, World Bank, *World Environment*, 4.

38. World Bank, *Annual Report 1985* (Washington, D.C.: The World Bank), 74.

39. McNamara, "Stockholm Address," 6.

40. The World Bank, *Environmental Health and Human Ecologic Considerations in Economic Development Projects* (Washington, D.C.: The World Bank, 1974); Idem, *Environmental Considerations for the Industrial Development Sector* (Washington, D.C.: The World Bank, 1979); Idem, *Environmental Considerations for the Pulp and Paper Industry* (Washington, D.C.: The World Bank, 1980); Idem, *Guidelines for Identifying, Analyzing, and Controlling Major Hazard Installations in Developing Countries* (Washington, D.C.: The World Bank, 1984); Idem, *Manual of Industrial Hazard Assessment Techniques* (Washington, D.C.: The World Bank, 1985); James Lee, *The Environment, Public Health, and Human Ecology Considerations for Economic Development* (Baltimore and London: The Johns Hopkins University Press for the World Bank, 1985), a new edition of the 1974 publication.

41. See chapter 5.

42. World Bank, *Annual Report 1985*, 74.

43. Charles Weiss and Nicolas Jequier, *Technology, Finance, and Development. An Analysis of the World Bank as a Technological Institution* (Lexington, Mass.: Lexington Books, 1984).

44. World Bank, "The World Bank's Environmental Activities, an Overview," Information and Public Affairs Department and Office of Environmental and Scientific Affairs, mimeograph (Washington, D.C.: 1986), 2.

45. Robert Goodland, *Tribal Peoples and Economic Development* (Washington, D.C.: The World Bank, 1982)
46. Alden W. Clausen, "Sustainable Development: The Global Imperative," (Fairfield Osborn Memorial Lecture in Environmental Science, Washington, D.C., Nov. 12, 1981), in Idem, *The Development Challenge of the Eighties. Major Policy Addresses, 1981-1986* (Washington, D.C.: The World Bank, 1986), 23–35; and Idem, "Address to the Board of Governors," Seoul Korea, Oct. 8, 1985 (Washington, D.C.: The World Bank).

Chapter 2. Internal Determinants of the Policy

1. *See*, for example, Sir Arthur Lewis, *The Evolution of the International Economic Order* (Princeton: Princeton University Press, 1978); Gilbert T. Brown, "Agricultural Pricing Policies in Developing Countries," in *Distortions of Agricultural Incentives*, ed. Thedore W. Schultz (Bloomington: Indian University Press, 1978), 84–113.
2. *See* Keith Griffin, *The Political Economy of Agrarian Change* (Cambridge: Harvard University Press, 1974).
3. Bettina Huerni, *The Lending Policies of the World Bank in the 1970s: Analysis and Evaluation* (Boulder, Colo.: Westview Press, 1980), 21.
4. *See*, for example, John Adler, "Development Theory and the Bank's Development Strategy: A Review," *Finance and Development* 14, 4 (1977), 31–4.
5. Paul Streeten, "Basic Needs: Premises and Promises," *Journal of Policy Modeling* 1 (1979), 136.
6. The World Bank, *Toward Sustained Development in Sub-Sahara Africa. A Joint Program of Action* (Washington, D.C.: The World Bank, 1984), 1.
7. *See* Robert Lavalle, *La banque mondiale et ses filiales, aspects juridiques et fonctionnement* (Paris: Librairie générale de droit et de jurisprudence, 1972), 150.
8. *See* Raymond Barre, *Economie politique* (Paris: Presses universitaires de France, 1956), 302.
9. Robert McNamara, "Address to the Economic and Social Council," mimeograph (Washington, D.C.: The World Bank, 1970), 5; *see also* World Bank, "Environment and Development," (Washington, D.C.: The World Bank, 1979), pp. 3–4.
10. The first project for environmental training was approved in FY 1981 in Indonesia.
11. Escott Reid, *Strengthening the World Bank* (Chicago: Adlai Stevenson Institute, 1973), 44.
12. World Bank, *Annual Report 1984*, 25; Idem, *Annual Report 1986*, 29.
13. In FY 1986, 16.9% of IBRD and IDA foreign exchange disbursements were procured in Japan. The United Kingdom accounted for 14.6%, France 10.8%, West Germany 8.3% and the United States 8.1% (World Bank, *Annual Report 1986*, 31)
14. Reid, *Strengthening*, 44.
15. *See* Albert O. Hirschman, *Development Projects Observed* (Washington, D.C.: The Brookings Institute, 1967).
16. Mason and Asher define a program loan as "a loan [designed] to finance the importation of raw materials, intermediate products, and equipment related to a national development program," whereas project loans "are limited to the financing of specific and independent productive installations". They hasten to say,

however, that the distinction is not as clear in practice, and it turns out that program loans have been given a larger scope. *See* Edward S. Mason and Robert E. Asher, *The World Bank Since Bretton-Woods* (Washington, D.C.: The Brookings Institution, 1973), 230.

17. Quoted in Robert E. Asher, "Comment: The Leopard's Spots," in *The World Bank Group, Multilateral Aid, and the 1970s*, eds. John Lewis and Ishan Kapur (London: Lexington Books, 1973), 25. The answer, of course, lies in the Bank's conception of its role in development and international relations, and in its relations with its task-environment.

18. Teresa Hayter. *Aid as Imperialism* (Harmondsworth, UK: Penguin Books, 1971), 78.

19. "Aid givers should adapt the form of aid to the needs and level of development of the receiving country and recognize the great value, in many cases, of many program aid. . . . IDA should undertake program lending whenever appropriate, seeking, if necessary, statutory change to make this possible." in Lester B. Pearson, *Partners in Development* (New York: Praeger, 1969), 190.

20. World Bank, *Annual Report 1986*, 47.

21. Peter Wright, "World Bank Lending for Structural Adjustment," *Finance and Development* 17, no. 3 (1980), 21.

22. Stanley Please, *The Hobbled Giant* (Boulder, Colo.: Westview, 1984), chaps. 3, 4.

23. The criteria the Bank considers when assessing creditworthiness are: per capita income and potential; savings rate and vehicles of saving; foreign exchange position; sources of borrowing; tax base; terms of trade and prospects; population growth; reliance on commodity imports; tariff structure; reliance on food and energy imports; overall economic health; and the relative commitment of resources to productive and unproductive projects. Eugene Rotberg, *The World Bank: A Financial Appraisal* (Washington, D.C.: The World Bank, 1978), 8.

24. Huerni, *Lending Policies*, 106.

25. Henderson estimates the grant element of IDA loans in the early 1970s to have been 86%, as opposed to an average of 20% for Bank loans. See P. D. Henderson, "Terms and Flexibility of Bank Lending," in Lewis and Kapur, eds., *World Bank Group*, 65–76.

26. A quick computation of the number of loans and credits with an environmental component between 1977 and 1986 shows a slight advantage in favor of IDA credits as vehicles for environmental components (mostly because rural development projects were involved).

27. Henderson, "Terms."

28. Warren C. Baum, "The Project Cycle," *Finance and Development* 7, no. 2 (1970), 2–13.

29. Huerni, *Lending Policies*, 235.

30. Baum, "Project Cycle," 6.

31. Mason and Asher, *The World Bank*, 299.

32. *See* Robert E. Stein and Brian Johnson, *Banking on the Biosphere?* (Lexington, MA: Lexington Books., 1979).

33. Warren C. Baum, "The Project Cycle," *Finance and Development* 15, no. 4 (1978), 13.

34. Ibid. Baum mentions that "the Bank regional missions in East and West Africa were established primarily to supplement the limited capabilities of governments in those regions to identify and prepare sound projects."

35. Huerni, *Lending Policies*, 109.

36. The Bank's publication destined for the financial community (Rotberg, *Financial Appraisal*) did not mention that environmental aspects are also reviewed during appraisal.

37. Michael S. Baram, "Cost-Benefit Analysis: An Inadequate Basis for Health, Safety, and Environmental Regulatory Decisionmaking," *Ecology Law Quarterly* 8, 473–531.

38. Anandarup Ray and Herman G. van der Tak, "A New Approach to the Economic Analysis of Projects," *Finance and Development* 16, no. 1 (1979) 28–32.

39. Baram, "Cost-Benefit Analysis." *See also* Yusuf J. Ahmad, *The Economics of Survival: The Role of Cost-Benefit Analysis in Environmental Decision-Making* (UNEP, 1981); Maynard Hufschmidt et al., *Environment, Natural Systems, and Development: an Economic Valuation Guide* (Baltimore and London: The Johns Hopkins University Press, 1983); A. Myrick Freeman III, *The Benefits of Environmental Improvement. Theory and Practice* (Baltimore and London: The Johns Hopkins University Press, for Resources For the Future, 1979).

40. World Bank, *Environment and Development* (Washington, D.C.: The World Bank, 1979), 23. *See also* Charles B. Pearson and Anthony Prior, *Environment: North and South. An Economic Interpretation* (New York: Wiley, 1978), chap. 4.

41. *See* Michael Hoffman, "Development Finance and the Environment," *Finance and Development* 7, no. 3 (1970), 2–6.

42. *See*, for example, the controversy over the Cananea copper mine and smelter project in Mexico which mixed protectionist and environmental arguments. *See* U.S. Congress, House, Committee on Interior and Insular Affairs, *US Assistance to Foreign Copper Producers and the Effects on Domestic Industries and Environmental Standards. Hearings before the subcommittee on Mining, Forest Management, and Bonneville Power Administration*, 98th Cong., 1st sess., 1983.

43. Huerni, *Lending Policies*, 68.

44. Ibid. 71.

45. Ahmed, *Economics of Survival*, 44; OESA did it using national experiences.

46. See chap. 1, note 40.

47. AID which had been sued by four environmental groups in 1975 for failing to comply with the EIS requirement of NEPA, resolved the issue (which contains numerous political ramifications) by agreeing to perform programmatic environmental impact statements or EIS only for projects which are likely to have global ecological incidence. Simple assessments are sufficient for other projects.

48. The following account is taken from David Price in U.S. Congress, House, Committee on Banking, Finance and Urban Affairs, *Environmental Impact of Multilateral Development Bank-Funded Projects, Hearings before the subcommittee on International Development Institutions and Finance*, 98th Cong., 1st sess., 1983, 480–94 (Patterson 1983).

49. Ibid. 480.

50. Robert Goodland, *Tribal Peoples and Economic Development. Human Ecologic Considerations* (Washington, D.C.: The World Bank, 1982).

51. The Bank preferred relying on independent scholars (whom it supported) to evaluate project failures very generally (*see* Hirschman, *Development Projects Observed*).

52. Stein and Johnson, *Banking*, 21.

53. A. van de Laar, *The World Bank and the Poor* (Boston: Nijhoff, 1980), 235.

54. Lynton K. Caldwell, "Alabama Lectures," mimeograph, Indiana University, 1981, 38.

55. Bruce Rich in U.S. Congress, House, Committee on Banking, Finance and Urban Affairs, *A Review of Multilateral Bank Environmental Policies. Hearing before the subcommittee on International Development Institutions and Finance*, 99th Cong., 2nd sess., 1986, 73 (Lundine 1986).

56. *See* John A. King, "Reorganizing the World Bank," *Finance and Development* 11, no. 1 (1974), 5–8.

57. *See* Anthony Downs, *Inside Bureaucracy* (Boston: Little, Brown, 1966), 11.

58. *See* James D. Thompson, *Organizations in Action* (New York: McGraw-Hill, 1967), 138–9; William Asher, "Adaptations to New International Strategies: the World Bank and the IMF," paper presented at the 1981 annual meetings of the American Political Science Association, New York, 1981.

59. *See* Walter Heller, *Economic Growth and Environmental Quality: Collision or Conscience?* (Morristwon, NJ: General Learning Press, 1973); Peter Passell and Leonard Ross, *The Retreat from Riches: Affluence and its Enemies* (New York: Viking, 1973).

60. Garrett Hardin, "The Tragedy of the Commons," *Science*, 162(1968): 1243–1248; Gerald Alonzo Smith, "The Teleological View of Wealth: A Historical Perspective," in *Economic, Ecology, Ethics: Essays Toward a Steady-State Economy*, ed. Herman Daly (San Francisco: W. H. Freeman, 1980).

61. Kenneth A. Dahlberg, *Beyond the Green Revolution* (New York: Plenum Press, 1979), 16–18.

62. *See*, for example, William Ophuls, *Ecology and the Politics of Scarcity* (San Francisco: W. H. Freeman, 1977), 156–64.

63. T. O'Riordan, *Environmentalism* (London: Pion, 1976), 12.

64. *See* Lynton K. Caldwell, "Strategies and Alternatives: The Ethics and Politics of Survival," mimeograph, Indiana University, 1980, 10.

65. Keith Griffin, *The Political Economy of Agrarian Change* (Cambridge: Harvard University Press, 1974), 54.

66. Personal interview, October 1980.

67. U.S. Congress, House, Committee on Banking, Finance and Urban Affairs, *Draft Recommendations on the Multilateral Banks and the Environment, Hearings before the subcommittee on International Development Institutions and Finance*, 98th Cong., 2nd sess., 1984, 148 (Patterson 1984b).

68. *See* Judith Tendler, *Inside Foreign Aid* (Baltimore: The Johns Hopkins University Press, 1978).

69. Mason & Asher, *The World Bank*, 468–9.

70. Reid, *Strengthening*, 35.

71. Van de Laar, *The World Bank*, 215.

72. This was apparent in OESA's attempts to disseminate a greater concern for the welfare of native populations; see Patterson 1983.

73. USAID played a significant role in the development of Bank policy (see chapter 3).

74. Ronald T. Libby, "The Ideology of the World Bank" (Ph.D. diss., University of Washington, 1975), 2.

75. The voting power of the five appointed executive directors in 1986 was (IBRD%/IDA%): United States, 20.13/18.74; Japan, 5.98/8.40; United Kingdom, 5.70/6.50; France, 5.36/3.78; Federal Republic of Germany, 5.03/7.06; Total for the big five: 42.2/44.48. In 1971, the US shares were 23.84/25.14 and the five countries' total voting power was 46.80/46.99 (*Annual Report 1986*, p. 217, *Annual Report 1971*, p. 115)

76. Reid, *Strengthening*, 23.

77. U.S. Congress, Senate, Committee on Governmental Affairs, *U.S. Partici-*

pation in the Multilateral Development Banks, 96th Cong., 1st sess., 1979, 40 (hereafter *Sen. G. A.* 1979).

78. Maluca M. Besteliu, "The Procedure of Consensus in the Adoption of Decision by the IMF and the IBRD," *Revue Roumaine d'Etudes Internationales* 38 (1977), 516–26.

79. Personal interview, October 1980.

80. James W. Conrow, in Patterson 1984b, 22.

81. John Negroponte, in U.S., Congress, Senate, Committee on Appropriations, *International Concerns for Environmental Implications of Multilateral Development Bank Projects, Special hearing before the subcommittee on Foreign Operations*, 99th Cong., 2nd sess., 1986, 13 (Kasten 1986).

82. *Sen. G. A.* 1979, 40.

83. Michael Hoffman, "The Challenges of the 1970s and the Present Institutional Structure," in Lewis and Kapur, *World Bank Group*, 16.

84. Ibid.

85. Ernst B. Haas, *Beyond the Nation-State* (Stanford, Calif.: Stanford University Press, 1964), 127.

86. David A. Kay and Harold K. Jacobson, eds., *Environmental Protection. The International Dimension* (Totowa, NJ: Allanheld, Osmun, 1983); Robert W. Cox, "The Executive Head: An Essay on Leadership in the ILO," *International Organization* 23, no. 1 (1969), pp. 205–29.

87. *See* Tendler, *Inside Foreign Aid*.

88. Van de Laar, *The World Bank*, 233.

89. Bruce Rich in, Patterson 1984b, 150–1.

90. Tendler, *Inside Foreign Aid*, 109.

Chapter 3. External Constraints on Bank Policy

1. An organization-set refers to the network of organizations in the focal organization's milieu. *See* William Evan, *Organization Theory: Structure, Systems and Environments* (New York: Wiley, 1976), 122.

2. F. E. Emery and E. C. Trist, "The Causal Texture of Organizational Environments," *Human Relations*, 18 (1965), 21–32.

3. Yves Laulan, *Le tiers-monde et l'environnement* (Paris: Presses Universitaires de France, 1976).

4. Dennis L. Meadows, et al., *The Limits to Growth* (New York: Universe Books, 1972).

5. Indian Prime Minister Indira Gandhi at Stockholm, quoted in Laulan, *Le tiers-monde*, 27.

6. Edward Goldsmith and Robert Alein, "Blueprint for Survival," *The Ecologist*, January 1972.

7. United Nations, *Report of the United Nations Conference on the Human Environment—Summary proceedings*, 82.

8. Brazil at UNCHE, quoted in Laulan, *Le tiers-monde*, 30.

9. USAID, *Environment and Natural Resources Management in Developing Countries—A Report to Congress*, vol. 1 (Washington, D.C.: U.S. Government Printing Office, 1979), 16.

10. Robert Boardman, *International Organization and the Conservation of Nature* (Bloomington: Indiana University Press, 1981), 15.

11. United Nations, *Report of the United Nations Conference on the Human*

222
NOTES

Environment, Stockholm, 5–16 June 1972, A/CONF.48/14/Rev. 1 (New York: United Nations, 1973): 4; (hereafter, *UNCHE*).

12. George Chambers, Governor of the Bank from Trinidad and Tobago, in World Bank, *Summary Proceedings 1972 Annual Meetings* (Washington, D.C.: The World Bank, 1972), 142.

13. M. Banda, Governor from Malawi, 1970 Annual Meetings of the World Bank Group and the International Monetary Fund, quoted in Cyrill Davies, "The Annual Meetings," *Finance and Development* 7, no. 4 (December 1970), 37.

14. *See also* UNCHE principle 21 (*UNCHE*, 5).

15. Joao Augusto de Araujo Castro, "Environment and Development: the Case of the Developing Countries," in *World Eco-crisis*, eds., David A. Kay and Eugene B. Skolnikoff (Madison: University of Wisconsin Press, 1972), 248.

16. *UNCHE*, 4 (principle 11).

17. Ibid., 26. For a detailed explanation and analysis of this concept, *see* Shadia Schneider-Sawiris, *The Concept of Compensation in the Field of Trade and Environment*, Environmental Policy and Law Paper, No. 4 (Morges, Switzerland: IUCN., 1973).

18. *See* Mahbub Ul Haq, *The Poverty Curtain* (New York: Columbia University Press, 1976), 110–115.

19. *UNCHE*, p. 26 (recommendation 103).

20. Mexico, for example, ran advertisements to lure industries from the United States through its more lenient environmental regulations; *see* Jeffrey James, "Growth, Technology and the Environment in Less Developed Countries: A Survey," *World Development* 6 (July/Aug. 1978), 937–65.

21. The Cameroons at UNCHE, quoted in Laulan, *Le tiers-monde*, 35.

22. Ibid., 36.

23. M. Ozorio de Almeida, et al., "Environment and Development. The Founex Report," *International Conciliation*, No. 586 (1972), 22; (hereafter, "Founex").

24. *See* Charles Pearson and Anthony Pryor, *Environment North and South: an Economic Interpretation* (New York: Wiley, 1978), 238.

25. "Founex," 10–11.

26. *See* Biplab Dasgrupta, "Some Awkward Questions," *Mazingira*, 3/4 (1977), 62–7.

27. Araujo Castro, "Environment," 252.

28. "Founex," 13.

29. Ibid., 34 (recommendation 7).

30. Ibid., (recommendation 9).

31. *UNCHE*, 6.

32. Ul Haq, *Poverty Curtain*, 110; this was an actual Bank example.

33. These were Gamani Corea (Chairman of UNCTAD), Ignacy Sachs, Jan Tinbergen, Mahbub ul Haq, and Samir Amin.

34. Republic of Kenya, "National Report on the Human Environment in Kenya," prepared for UNCHE, 56, and Laulan, *Le tiers-monde*, 33–34.

35. Professor Adebayo Adedeji, quoted in *International Journal of Environmental Studies* 3 (1972), 297.

36. *World Development Report* 3 (5 Dec. 1977), 3.

37. *See* Theodore Cohn, "Influence of the Less Developed Countries in the World Bank Group," (Ph.D. diss., University of Michigan, 1973), 376, 381.

38. "Founex," 31.

39. World Bank, *1972 Proceedings*, 8.

40. *See* Boardman, *Conservation*; Ernst B. Haas, et al., *Scientists and World Order* (Berkeley: University of California Press, 1977), 180.

41. UNCTAD, "The Impact of Environmental Issues on Development and International Economic Relations," Research Memorandum, 53, (UNCTAD/RD/114 [1976]).

42. Ibid., 5.

43. United Nations General Assembly, 35th session, "Development and International Economic Co-operation," A/35/592/Add. 1 (1980), 38–9.

44. Ibid., 39.

45. UNCTAD, "Impact," 16.

46. UNEP/INFO/79 (23 Dec. 1980), p.1.

47. These interrelationships were formally examined in 1978 and 1979 by the United Nations at the initiative of Sweden; *see* ECOSOC/1979/75 (6 June 1979).

48. United Nations, *Economic Cooperation*, 11–12.

49. Ibid., 38.

50. Daniel T. Arap Moi, President of Kenya, at the opening ceremony of the UNEP Governing Council Session of Special Character, Nairobi, 10 May 1982.

51. AID, *Environmental*, 17.

52. Raymond Dasmann in *IUCN Bulletin*, (1977), 23.

53. Alden W. Clausen, "Sustainable Development: The Global Imperative," (Fairfield Osborn Memorial Lecture in Environmental Science," Washington, 12 Nov. 1981, in World Bank, *The Development Challenge of the Eighties. A. W. Clausen at the World Bank, Major Policy Addresses, 1981–1986* (Washington, D.C.: The World Bank, 1986), 25.

54. Arap Moi, 1982.

55. AID, *Environmental*, 2.

56. UNEP, "Environmental Machinery in Africa," *Uniterra* (March 1977), 2.

57. Aid, *Environmental*, 85, 88.

58. Ibid. 112–115.

59. *See*, for example, U.S. Congress, Senate, Committee on Appropriations, *International Concerns for Environmental Implication of Multilateral Development Bank Projects, Special Hearing before the subcommittee on Foreign Assistance and Related Programs*, 99th Cong., 2nd sess., 1986; (hereafter Kasten *1986*).

60. *See* Brian Johnson, "The United Nations Institutional Response to Stockholm: A Case Study in the International Politics of Institutional Change," in *World Eco-Crisis*, eds. David A. Kay and Eugene B. Skolnikoff (Madison: University of Wisconsin Press, 1972), 91.

61. Marvin Soroos, "Trends in the Perception of Environmental Problems in the United Nations General Debates," paper presented at the Annual Meetings of the International Studies Association, Toronto, March 1979.

62. World Bank, *Annual Meetings of the Boards of Governors* (Washington, D.C.: The World Bank, 1970), 97.

63. Cohn, "Influence," 236.

64. World Bank, *Environment and Development* (Washington, D.C.: The World Bank, 1975), 11.

65. The World Bank, *1972 Meetings*, 84.

66. Jacobson and Kay, "Environmental," 52. The U.S. is nevertheless still instrumental in raising issues (e.g., tropical deforestation).

67. Cohn, "Influence," 384.

68. World Bank, *Annual Report 1986*, 209; Escott Reid, *Strengthening the World Bank* (Chicago: Adlai Stevenson Institute, 1973), 13.

69. Reid, *Strengthening*, 15.

70. Ibid., 19.

71. *Congressional Quarterly*, Weekly Reports, 1980, 362.

72. *Congressional Quarterly*, Weekly Reports, 18 April 1981.

73. *See* Robert L. Ayres, "Breaking the Bank," *Foreign Policy* 43 (Summer 1981), 104–20.

74. *See* U.S., Congress, Senate, Committee on Governmental Affairs, *U.S. Participation in the Multilateral Development Banks*, 96th Cong., 1st sess., 1979, 29.

75. U.S., Congress, House, Committee on Appropriations, *Foreign Assistance and Related Appropriations for 1980, Part 2, International Financial Institutions, Hearings before the subcommittee on Foreign Operations and Related Programs*, 96th Cong., 2nd sess., 1980, 483 (Edward Fried, U.S. Executive Director).

76. U.S., Congress, House, Committee on Foreign Affairs, *Review of the Global Environment 10 years after Stockholm, Hearings before the Subcommittee on Human Rights and International Organizations*, 97th Cong., 2nd sesss., 1982, 89 (A. Alan Hill, Chairman of CEQ) (Bonkers 1982).

77. *See* Walter A. Rosenbaum, *The Politics of Environmental Concern*, 2nd ed. (New York: Praeger, 1977).

78. This close relationship is formally stipulated in the Bank's *Articles of Agreement* (IBRD, III, 2). Succeeding the National Advisory Council on International Monetary and Financial Policies in 1977, the Interagency Working Group on Multilateral Assistance (WGMA) includes the Departments of Treasury and State, USAID, the U.S. Trade Representative, the Federal Reserve Board, and the Departments of Agriculture, Commerce, Interior, and Labor. Environmental aspects of projects are sometimes discussed by representatives of the State Department's Bureau of Oceans and International Scientific and Environmental Affairs.

79. This prompted the recommendation that USAID be given primary responsibility over the executive director's instructions. This reform, which would require an amendment of the *Articles of Agreement*, would likely benefit environmental criteria greatly.

80. U.S. Congress, House, Committee on Banking, Finance and Urban Affairs, *U.S. Participation in Multilateral Development Institutions. Hearings before the Subcommittee on International Development Institutions and Finance*, 95th Cong., 2nd sess., 1978, 176 (Gonzales 1978).

81. In 1986, the United States opposed a $500 million loan to Brazil because it would go toward subsidizing agricultural competitors of U. S. farmers (even though Brazil was also being urged to increase its export earnings to service its debt). The Brazilian government agreed to reduce subsidies to soybean farmers, and the loan was approved. (*Facts on File*, July 1986).

82. Reid, *Strengthening*: 122. *See also* John P. Lewis and Ishan Kapur, eds., *The World Bank, Multilateral Aid and the 1970s* (London: Lexington Books, 1973), chap. 3. The environment is, of course, a prime example of that influence, but dramatic ones have also been the development of the energy exploration and development sector, and the renewed emphasis on the role of the private sector.

83. Alfonso Inostroze, Governor of the Bank for Chile in, The World Bank, *1972 Annual Meetings of the Boards of Governors* (Washington, D.C.: The World Bank, 1972), 57.

84. Bank lending is constrained not by its capacity to borrow but by the size of its capital, a limitation of one-to-one. The Bank was expected to reach its latest

$15 billion ceiling in 1987, and has sought support for another increase. These re-negotiations provide an opportunity for donors to modify the allocation of their voting power which is tied to the size of their contributions. Japan, for example, which is pressured to contribute more to international assistance, will see its voting power double to about eleven percent.

85. *See* Stephen Krasner, "Power Structures and Regional Development Banks," *International Organization* 35, no. 2 (Spring 1981), 303–28; Sanford, "American Foreign Policy."

86. The following remark typifies this attitude. Referring to Congressional efforts to improve the environmental record of the Bank, Senator Kasten exclaimed: "What we are establishing here is an effort, through the funding by the legislative bodies of our country, to impose or to establish that [direct] accountability. The accountability is to the elected representatives who are appropriating the dollars, and those elected representatives have an accountability to who [sic] they represent. This is what we are trying to do." in Kasten 1986, 106.

87. Krasner, "Power Structures and Regional Development Banks," 320.

88. Quoted in Reid, *Strengthening*, 18.

89. *See* Cohn, "Influence," 378.

90. *Wall Street Journal*, 7 Nov. 1980.

91. Aart van der Laar, "The World Bank: Which Way?" *Development and Change* 7(1976), 75.

92. The approval in June 1986 of two $500 million loans to Brazil within a week fulfilled this function.

93. Richard H. Demuth, "Relations with other Multilateral Agencies," in *World Bank Group*, eds., Lewis and Kapur, 133.

94. Tendler, *Inside Foreign Aid*, 90.

95. UNEP/GC.8/7 (February 1980), 19.

96. The Jackson Report showed that inter-agency conflicts were very prominent and impaired the system's capacity to function effectively: *see* Sir Robert Jackson, *A Study of the Capacity of the United Nations Development System*, UNDOC/DP/5, vol. 2 (Geneva: United Nations, 1969), 76.

97. Reid, *Strengthening*, p. 135.

98. Ibid., 139.

99. Statement by Mostafa K. Tolba (UNEP's executive director) to the sixth meeting of the Committee on International Development Institutions on the Environment (CIDIE), Washington, D.C., 3 June 1985, 3–4.

100. For greater detail, *see* Richard L. Clinton, "Ecodevelopment," *World Affairs*, 10 (Fall 1977), 111–26; Ignacy Sachs, "Environnement et styles de développement," *Annales*, No. 3 (Mai–Juin 1974), 553–70.

101. The "Cocoyoc Declaration" adopted by the participants in the UNEP/UNCTAD symposium on "Patterns of Resource Use, Environment and Development Strategies," Cocoyoc, Mexico, 8–12 October 1974 (Reprinted in full in *International Organization* 29, 893–901).

102. *See* Lynton K. Caldwell, *In Defense of Earth* (Bloomington: Indiana University Press, 1972).

103. *See* U.S., Congress, House, Committee on Banking, Finance and Urban Affairs, *A Review of Multilateral Development Bank Environmental Policies. Hearing before the Subcommittee on International Development Institutions and Finance*, 99th Cong., 2nd sess., 1986, 86–90 (Lundine 1986).

104. *See* Boardman, *Conservation*, 177.

105. As more environmental organizations pressed for changes in the IUCN, the

organization redefined its concern for conservation in the context of development and of a rational management or protection of natural resources, away from strict scientific, aesthetic or ethical criteria. *See* Haas, et al., *Scientists*, 180.

106. IIED, *Annual Report 1979–1980* (London and Washington, D.C.: IIED, 1980).

107. Robert E. Stein and Brian Johnson, *Banking on the Biosphere? Environmental Procedures and Practices of Nine Multilateral Development Agencies* (Lexington, Mass.: Lexington Books, 1979).

108. Brian Johnson, "Response," 92.

109. AID, *Environmental.*

110. See, U.S., Congress, House, Committee on Banking, Finance, and Urban Affairs, *Environmental Impact of Multilateral Development Bank-Funded Projects. Hearings before the Subcommittee on International Development Institutions and Finance*, 98th Cong., 1st sess., 1983 (Patterson 1983); Idem, *Draft Recommendations on the Multilateral Banks and the Environment. Hearings before the Subcommittee on International Development Institutions and Finance*, 98th Cong., 2nd sess., 1984 (Patterson 1984b); U.S., Congress, House, Committee on Foreign Affairs, *U.S. International Environmental Policy. Hearings before the Subcommittee on Human Rights and International Organizations*, 98th Cong., 2nd sess., 1984 (Yatron 1984); Kasten 1986.

111. *See* Kasten 1986, 35. Indian non-governmental environmental groups have contacted U.S. organizations to request assistance and information concerning the World Bank-financed Narmada River Irrigation and Area Development Program which involved the forced relocation of nearly 100,000 individuals. Brazilian non-governmental environmental and indigenous peoples rights groups have provided U.S. environmental groups with information on North-West settlement and road construction projects supported by the Bank. U.S. organizations engineered the testimony of several representatives of foreign INGOs to a congressional subcommittee discussing proposed recommendations to the Department of Treasury and the World Bank. They have also tried forming a coalition of Western executive directors of the Bank in support of the 1984 draft recommendations, with little success (see Kasten 1986, 30–8).

112. Patterson 1984, 109; see also, U.S. Congress, House, Committee on Appropriations, *Foreign Assistance and Related Programs Appropriations Bill, 1987. Report to Accompany H.R. 5339*, 99th Cong., 2nd sess., 1986 (Obey 1986).

113. The World Bank, *Annual Report 1986* (author's calculations).

114. This does not mean that there is no cooperation in the field. Apart from co-financing, the Bank can agree to finance only a part of a massive multi-project development scheme (e.g., road construction, segments of which are funded by different agencies), and the AID agree to fund a project designed to extend the component of a Bank project (e.g., technical training).

115. For example, cooperation with the French in Africa has been difficult at times according to USAID representatives. USAID however cooperates with the French and others agencies within the Club du Sahel (*see* Yatron 1984, p. 104).

116. Reid, *Strengthening*, 161; Robert L. Ayres, *Banking on the Poor* (Cambridge and London: MIT Press, 1983), 9.

117. For an overview of USAID's environmental activities, *see* Robert Blake, et al., *Aiding the Environment* (Washington, D.C.: Natural Resources Defense Council, 1980).

118. Ibid., 76.

119. Ibid., 225.

120. *See* USAID, *Environmental.*

121. *See* Stephen Krasner, "Transforming International Regimes: What the Third World Wants and Why," *International Studies Quarterly* 25, no. 1 (March 1981), 119–48.

122. Emery and Trist, "Causal Texture."

123. Libby, "Ideology," chap. 1.

124. These demands were formally articulated in these terms at the seventh special session of the United Nations (UNSS–VII) in 1974 but had been around since the 1950s; *see* Alfred G. Moss and Herry N. M. Winton, comps., *A New International Economic Order: Selected Documents, 1945–1974*, 2 vols., UNITAR Document Service, no. 1 (New York: United Nations Institute for Training and Research, n.d.).

125. "Cocoyoc Declaration," 894–5.

126. Ibid., 897.

127. "Charter of Economic Rights and Duties of States," General Assembly Resolution 3281 (XXIX) of 12 Dec. 1974 (UNGA, OR, 29th Sess., Supp no. 31 (A/9631).

128. U.S. contribution requests, for example, were diminished several years in a row only to be restored by Congress. *See* U.S., Senate, Committee on Appropriations, *Foreign Assistance and Related Programs Appropriations, FY 1980, pt. 1. Hearings before the subcommittee on Foreign Operations Appropriations,*, 96th Cong., 1st sess., 1980, 1103–1125.

129. For a response, *see* Ayres, "Breaking the Bank".

130. The United States joined this facility almost a year later under congressional pressure which led to the appropriation of $71 million (in part to overcome procurement restrictions) despite opposition by the administration. Treasury delayed payment of the U.S. contribution in violation of U.S. law until it fell under the sequestration provision of the Gramm-Rudman Deficit Reduction Act in 1986. Recommended appropriations were reduced to $64 million for FY 1987, again with no request from the administration (*see* Obey 1986, 42–3).

131. Barber Conable, Address to the Annual Meetings of the Board of Governors, Washington, 1986 (Washington, D.C.: The World Bank, 1986), 17.

132. Ibid., 17–8.

133. Lundine 1986, 52–3 (statement by Barbara Bramble).

134. IUCN, *World Conservation Strategy: Living Resource Conservation for Sustainable Development* (Morges, Switzerland: IUCN, 1980). *See also* John McCormick, "The Origins of the World Conservation Strategy," *Environmental Review* 10, no. 3 (Fall 1986), 177–87; Lee Talbot, "The World Conservation Strategy," in Francis Thibodeau and Hermann Field, eds., *Sustaining Tomorrow: A Strategy for World Conservation and Development* (Hanover and London: University Press of New England for Tufts University, 1984).

135. U.S., Council on Environment Quality and Department of State, *The Global 2000 Report to the President. Entering the Twenty-First Century*, 3 vols. (Washington, D.C.: Government Printing Office, 1980); Idem, *Global Future: Time to Act* (Washington, D.C.: Government Printing Office, 1981), xi.

136. United Nations, Economic and Social Council, "The Study of Interrelationships Between Population, Resources, Environment and Development," Report of the Secretary General, E/1979/75 (United Nations, 1979).

137. Alden W. Clausen, "Global Interdependence in the 1980s," Remarks before the Yomiuri International Economic Society, Tokyo, January 1982 (Washington, D.C.: The World Bank, 1982), 10.

138. Uma Lele, "Rural Africa: Modernization, Equity, and Long Term Development," *Science* 211 (1981), 547–53.

Chapter 4. Controlling the Milieu

1. *See* James Lee, "Environmental Considerations in Development Finance," *International Organization* 26, no. 1 (1972), 337–47.

2. Robert Dahl, *Modern Political Analysis* (Englewood Cliffs, NJ: Prentice-Hall, 1963), 40.

3. Stephen Krasner, "What the Third World Wants and Why," *International Studies Quarterly* 25, no. 1 (1981) 122.

4. Ibid. (author's emphasis).

5. Michel Crozier and Ehrardt Friedberg, *L'acteur et le système* (Paris: Seuil, 1977).

6. Escott Reid, *Strengthening the World Bank* (Chicago: Adlai Stevenson Institute, 1973) 133.

7. *See* Ronald T. Libby, "The Ideology of the World Bank" (Ph.D. diss., University of Washington, 1975); Barbara Crane and Larry Finkle, "Organizational Impediments to Development Assistance: The World Bank's Population Programme," *World Politics* 23, no. 2 (1981), 516–53.

8. James D. Thompson, *Organizations in Action* (New York: McGraw-Hill, 1967); Charles Perrow, *Organizational Analysis: A Sociological View* (Belmont, Calif.: Wadsworth, 1970).

9. Michael M'Gonigle and Mark Zacher have emphasized this point with respect to ocean oil pollution; *see* their *Pollution, Politics and International Law—Tankers at Sea* (Berkeley: University of California Press, 1979), 260.

10. The distinction between competitive and cooperative strategies is from Thompson, *Organizations*, 32–4.

11. *See* Robert H. Miles, *Macro-organizational Behavior* (Santa Monica, Calif.: Goodyear, 1980), 320.

12. J. D. Thompson and W. McEwen, "Organizational Goals and Environment: Goal-setting as an Interaction Process," *American Sociological Review* 23 (1958), 23–31.

13. David Whetten and Howard Aldrich, "Organization-set Size and Diversity—People Processing Organizations and their Environments," *Administrative Science Quarterly* 11 (1979), 251–81.

14. For example, Ernst B. Haas, et al., *Scientists and World Order* (Berkeley, Calif.: University of California Press, 1977).

15. James Lee, "Development and Environment: A Post-Stockholm Assessment" (Paper presented at the Columbia University Seminars on Pollution and Water Resources, Washington, D.C., 1972), 9.

16. Lee, "Environmental Considerations," 345.

17. The World Bank, *Environment and Development* (Washington, D.C.: The World Bank, 1979), 4.

18. *See* Jacques Tixhon, "World Bank Involvement in Occupational Safety and Health," mimeograph, 1979, 15.

19. World Bank, *Environment and Development* (Washington, D.C.: The World Bank, 1975), 3.

20. World Bank, "Environmental Aspects of World Bank Group Projects, Some Questions and Answers," mimeograph, 1973. *See also*, Robert Stein and Brian Johnson, *Banking on the Biosphere?* (Lexington, Mass.: Lexington Books, 1979).

21. James Lee, "Environment and Development: The World Bank Experi-

ence" (Paper prepared for presentation at the international briefing sponsored by the Center for International Environmental Information, New York, 14 Oct. 1976).

22. Mahbub ul Haq, *The Poverty Curtain* (New York: Columbia University Press, 1976), 109–110.

23. *See* Jeffrey Pfeffer and Gerald Salancik, *The External Control of Organizations* (New York: Harper and Row, 1978), chap. 5.

24. Ibid.; R. Cyert and J. March, *A Behavioural Theory of the Firm* (Englewood Cliffs: Prentice-Hall, 1963); Thompson, *Organizations in Action.*

25. *See* U.S., Congress, Senate, Committee on Foreign Relations, *U.S. Policy and the Multilateral Banks: Politicization and Effectiveness*, by J. Stanford, subcommittee on Foreign Assistance, 95th Cong., 1st sess., 1977; World Bank, *Annual Report* (Washington, D.C.: The World Bank, 1979).

26. *See* Kenneth Boulding, "The Economics of the Coming Spaceship Earth," in *Economics, Ecology, Ethics: Essays Toward a Steady-State Economy*, ed. Hermann Daly (San Francisco: W. H. Freeman, 1980), 261.

27. Robert Boardman, *International Organization and the Conservation of Nature* (Bloomington: Indiana University Press, 1981), 151.

28. Quoted in Lee, "Experience," 8.

29. *See* John Spears and Montague Yudelman, "Forests in Development," *Finance and Development* 16, no. 4 (1979), 41–4.

30. *See* Council on Environmental Quality and Department of State, *Global 2000: Entering the Twenty-First Century. Volume II: The Technical Report* (Washington, D.C.: Government Printing Office, 1980).

31. Alden W. Clausen, "Sustainable Development: The Global Imperative," Fairfield Osborn Memorial Lecture in Environmental Science, World Resources Institute, Washington, D.C., 1981, in *The Development Challenge of the Eighties. A. W. Clausen at The World Bank* (Washington, D.C.: The World Bank, 1986), 29, 35.

32. World Bank, *Annual Report* (Washington, D.C.: The World Bank, 1985), 72.

33. *See*, for example U.S., Congress, House, Committee on Banking, Finance, and Urban Affairs, *U.S. Participation in Multilateral Development Institutions. Hearings before the Subcommittee in International Development Institutions and Finance*, 95th Cong., 2nd sess., 1978 (Gonzales 1978).

34. Edward S. Mason and Robert E. Asher, *The World Bank since Bretton Woods* (Washington, D.C.: The Brookings Institution, 1973), 509.

35. I. P. M. Cargill, "Efforts to Influence Recipient Performance: Case Study of India," in *The World Bank Group: Multilateral Aid and the Seventies*, eds., John P. Lewis and Ishan Kapur (London: Lexington, 1973), 95.

36. L. K. Jha, "Comment: Leaning Against Open Doors," in Lewis and Kapur, *World Bank Group*, 99.

37. *See*, for example, C. P. Bhambri, *World Bank and India* (New Delhi: Vikas, 1980).

38. Richard H. Demuth, "Relations with other Multilateral Agencies," in Lewis and Kapur, *World Bank Group*, 133–8.

39. Reid, *Strengthening*, 150.

40. Crane and Finkle, "Impediments," 540–1.

41. World Bank, *Health*, 58.

42. *See* "The World Conservation Strategy," *Nature and Resources* 16 (January–March 1980), 2–4; chap. 3, note 134.

43. Bettina Huerni points up the growing rivalry in the 1970s between the Bank and regional banks; *see The Lending Policies of the World Bank in the 1970s* (Boulder, Colo.: Westview, 1980), 106.

44. Current members include the Asian Development Bank (ADB), the Arab Bank for Economic Development in Africa (ABEDA), the Commission of the European Communities, the World Bank, UNDP, UNEP, the Organization for America States (OAS), the Inter-American Development Bank (IDB), the African Development Bank (AfDB), the Caribbean Development Bank (CDB), and the European Investment Bank.

45. Lundine 1986: 80–1; Mostafa K. Tolba (Statement to the 6th meeting of the CIDIE," Washington, D.C., 1985), 3–4.

46. Reid, *Strengthening*, 143.

47. Roger A. Horstein, "Cofinancing of Bank and IDA Projects," *Finance and Development* 14, no. 2 (1977), 40.

48. *See* M. Burke Knapp, *IBRD Co-Financing* (Washington, D.C.: The World Bank, 1975), 41; World Bank, *Co-Financing* (Washington, D.C.: The World Bank, 1980).

49. Knapp, *Co-Financing*, 10.

50. Huerni, *Lending Policies*, 92.

51. World Bank, *Co-Financing*, p. 2; *Annual Report 1987*, 34.

52. A. W. Clausen, "Address to the Board of Governors," Washington, D.C.: 1982, 15; *Annual Reports 1982,* 14 and *1986*, 28.

53. Knapp, *Co-Financing*, 15.

54. U.S. Congress, House, Committee on Banking, Finance, and Urban Affairs, *Draft Recommendations on the Multilateral Banks and the Environment. Hearings before the Subcommittee on International Development Institutions and Finance*, 98th Cong., 2nd sess., 1984 (Patterson 1984b), 151 (statement by Bruce Rich).

55. Boardman, *Conservation*, 15.

56. World Bank, *Health*.

57. World Bank, *Annual Report 1979*, 28.

58. *See also*, Stein and Johnson, *Banking*, 16.

59. *See* T. O'Riordan, *Environmentalism* (London: Pion, 1976).

60. J. P. Barde and E. Gerelli mention two techniques that rely on Guttman scales and the development of priority scaling, evaluators, and simulation techniques; *see* their *Economie et politique de l'environnement* (Paris: P.U.F., 1977); *See also* Maynard M. Hufschmidt et al., *Environment, Natural Systems, and Development. An Economic Valuation Guide* (Baltimore & London: The Johns Hopkins University Press, 1983).

61. Eugene B. Black, *The Diplomacy of Economic Development* (New York: Atheneum, 1963), 83.

62. A. A. Fatouros, "The World Bank," in *The Impact of International Organizations on Legal and Institutional Change in the Developing Countries* (New York: International Legal Center, 1977), 2–79.

63. Thompson, *Organizations in Action*, 30.

64. Ibid., 32.

65. Robert McNamara, *One Hundred Countries, Two Billion People: The Dimensions of Development* (New York: Praeger, 1973), 20.

66. Frank Vibert, "The Process of Replenishing IDA Finances," *Finance and Development* 14, no. 5 (1977), 40.

67. Quoted in Pierre Uri, ed., *Towards a North-South Dialogue* (Paris: P.U.F., 1976), 41.

68. World Bank, *Policies and Operations* (Washington, D.C.: The World Bank, 1973), 96; *Annual Report 1972*, 71.

69. E. H. Rotberg, *The World Bank: A Financial Appraisal* (Washington, D.C.: The World Bank, 1981), 14; *Annual Report 1986*: 172.

70. V. H. Oppenheim, "Whose World Bank?" *Foreign Policy* 19 (1975), 99–108; R. McNamara, "Address to the Board of Governors," in *The McNamara Years at the World Bank: Major Policy Addresses of Robert McNamara, 1968–1981*, (Baltimore: Johns Hopkins University Press for the World Bank, 1981), 274.

71. Ronald T. Libby, "International Development Association: a Legal Fiction Designed to Secure and LDC Constituency Constituency," *International Organization* 29, no. 4 (1975), 1065–72.

72. Crane and Finkle, "Impediments," 15.

73. For example, Richard E. Feinberg, "An Open Letter to the World Bank's New President," in idem, ed., *Between Two Worlds: The World Bank's Next Decade* (Washington, D.C.: Overseas Development Council, 1986), 3–30.

74. The PLO was eventually refused an observer seat at the 1981 and 1982 annual meetings of the Bank and the Fund, promoting fears that OPEC members would renege on their pledges in retaliation. They did not.

75. Lynton K. Caldwell, *In Defense of Earth* (Blommington: Indiana University Press, 1972), 228.

76. *See*, for example, Taghi Favar and John Milton, eds., *The Careless Technology* (Garden City, N.Y.: Natural History Press, 1972).

77. *Environment Reporter* 8 (9 Aug. 1977), 615; World Bank, *Environmental, Health and Human Ecologic Considerations of Economic Development Projects* (Washington, D.C.: The World Bank, 1974).

78. *See* chapter 1, note 40.

79. World Bank, *Health*, 16.

80. World Bank, *Forestry* (Washington, D.C.: The World Bank, 1978), 24.

81. In 1984, eight American environmental organizations sent a letter to Alden Clausen detailing these criticisms, suggesting changes, and claiming for themselves the right to review future sector policy papers dealing with natural resources. *See* U.S., Congress, House, Committee on Banking, Finance and Urban Affairs, *U.S. Participation in the International Development Association Seventh Replenishment, Hearings before the Subcommittee on International Development and Institutions and Finance*, 98th Cong., 2nd sess., 1984, 241–56 (Patterson 1984a).

82. International Development Association, *Articles of Agreement*, V, 5(v).

83. Art Van de Laar, *The World Bank and the Poor* (Boston: Nijhoff, 1980), 212.

84. Mason and Asher, *The World Bank*, 316; Van de Laar, *World Bank*, 241.

85. Jacques Tixhon, "World Bank Involvement in Occupational Safety and Health," mimeograph, 1979, 7.

86. R. W. van Wegenen, "Training as an Element in Bank Group Projects," *Finance and Development* 9, no. 3 (1972), 34–9.

87. World Bank, *Forestry*, 48.

88. Daniel Katz and Robert Kahn, *The Social Psychology of Organizations*, 2nd ed. (New York: Wiley, 1978), 646.

89. World Bank, *Forestry*, 45.

90. *See*, for example, Eugene Black, *The Diplomacy of Economic Development* (New York: Atheneum, 1963).

91. Reid, *Strengthening*, 83.

92. U.S., Congress, Senate, Committee on Environment and Public Works, *International Wildlife Conservation*, 96th Cong., 2nd sess., 1980, 33.

232 NOTES

93. USAID, *Environmental and National Resources Management in Developing Countries. A Report to Congress*, vol. 1 (Washington, D.C.: Government Printing Office, 1979), 112.

94. Black, *Diplomacy*, 153.

95. Michael Kaufman, "World Bank Loan to India is Held Up," *New York Times*, 6 Jan. 1981, D-11.

96. Teresa Hayter, *Aid as Imperialism* (Harmondsworth, U.K.: Penguin, 1971), 80–1.

97. Ronald T. Libby, "The Ideology of the World Bank," (Ph.D. diss., University of Washington, 1975), 164; Whether the Bank's action was the sole cause or only a pretext of this disgrace is unclear. The long-time ruler of Tunisia was prone suddenly to eliminate apparent political heirs whose growing power he feared.

98. Changing the borrower's attitude was, in fact, secondary in the minds of the supporters of sanctions to changing the Bank's willingness to promote its environmental pledge forcefully.

99. Reid, *Strengthening*, 84.

100. Van de Laar, *World Bank*, 130.

101. Caldwell, *In Defense of Earth*, 6.

102. Philip Selznick, *TVA and the Grass Roots* (New York: Harper & Row, 1966), 13.

103. Naomi Caiden and Aaron Wildavsky, *Planning and Budgeting in Poor Countries* (New York: Wiley, 1974), 61.

104. Idem, 144.

105. The World Bank, *Annual Meetings 1959. Summary Proceedings* (Washington, D.C.: The World Bank, 1959), 8.

106. Libby, "Ideology," 100.

107. Albert O. Hirschman, *Development Projects Observed* (Washington, D.C.: The Brookings Institution, 1967), 167.

108. Libby, "Ideology," 118.

109. Reid, *Strengthening*, 95.

110. International Union for the Conservation of Nature and Natural Resources, *I.U.C.N. Bulletin*, (November–December 1980), 104.

111. Peter Haas, "Regional Cooperation for Pollution Control: The Mediterranean Action Plan" (Paper presented at the annual meetings of the International Studies Association, Atlanta, 27–31 March 1984).

112. Pfeffer and Salancik, *External Control*, 189.

113. Harold N. Leaves, Jr., "The Bank as an International Mediator: Three Episodes," in Mason and Asher, *The World Bank*, 595–643.

114. Alden W. Clausen, "Address to the Board of Governors," (Washington, D.C.: The World Bank, 1982), 5–6.

115. William Clark, "Interview," *Finance and Development* 17 no. 2 (June 1980), 6.

116. World Bank, *Annual Meetings 1980—Summary Proceedings* (Washington, D.C.: The World Bank, 1980), 355. Its official name is "Joint Ministerial Committee of the Boards of Governors of the Bank and the Fund on the Transfer of Real Resources to Developing Countries."

117. Ibid., 362. In 1988, the Development Committee discussed the importance of environmental issues, especially those raised by the 1987 Brundtland report on environment and development.

118. Arnold Nachmanoff (deputy assistant secretary of the Treasury for developing nations), in U.S. Congress, House, Committee on Banking, Finance, and Urban Affairs, *U.S. Participation in the Multilateral Development Institutions*.

Hearings before the Subcommittee on International Development Institutions and Finance, 95th Cong., 2nd sess, 1978, 189.

119. World Bank, *Annual Report* (Washington, D.C.: The World Bank, 1978), 21.

120. Jan Schneider, *World Public Order and the Environment* (Toronto: University of Toronto Press, 1979).

121. Libby, "Ideology," 164.

Chapter 5. The Art of the Possible

1. Council on Environmental Quality and Department of State, *Global 2000: Entering the Twenty-First Century*, vol. 1 (Washington, D.C.: Government Printing Office, 1980), 23, 26.

2. World Resources Institute, *Tropical Forests: A Call for Action* (Washington, D.C.: World Resources Institute, 1985).

3. For further discussion and references, *see* Spears (1983), CEQ (1980), Ledec (1985), Myers (1980). The rate of tropical deforestation has generated controversy. Myers and CEQ reported a high estimate of 20 million hectares for tropical moist forests deforestation. In 1982, the FAO (*Tropical Forest Resources*, Forestry Paper No. 30) estimated the loss of tropical moist forests at 6 million hectares and total tropical deforestation at 11.2 million hectares. Moreover pressure on the virgin forests, as opposed to secondary growth, is much lower. Thus, although the total picture that emerges is cause for great concern, the situation may not be as dramatic as was initially portrayed (*see* letter by Roger Sedjo, in U.S. Congress, House, Committee on Foreign Affairs, *U.S. International Environmental Policy. Hearings before the Subcommittee on Human Rights and International Organizations*, 98th Cong., 2nd sess., 1984, 222–3 (Yatron 1984).

4. Norman Myers and Richard Tucker, "Deforestation in Central America: Spanish Legacy and North American Consumers," *Environmental Review* 11, no. 1 (1987), 63.

5. Philippe Lena, "Aspects de la Frontière Amazonienne," *Cahiers des Sciences Humaines* 22, nos. 3–4 (1986), 319–43; Myers and Tucker, "Deforestation in Central America."

6. Daniel Dobry, "Comment enrayer la disparition des forêts tropicales," *Le Monde Diplomatique* (February 1987), 30–1.

7. John Spears, "Saving the Tropical Forest Eco-system. A Discussion Paper," The World Bank, mimeograph, (June 1983) in Patterson 1983, 395.

8. Nurul Almy Halfid, in U.S. Congress, Senate, Committee on Appropriations, *International Concerns for Environmental Implications of Multilateral Development Bank Projects. Special Hearing before the Subcommittee on Foreign Operations*, 99th Cong., 2nd sess., 1986 (Kasten 1986), 122.

9. James D. Nations and Daniel I. Komer, "Rainforests and the Hamburger Society," *Environment* 25, no. 3 (1983), 12–20; Michael Nelson, *The Development of Tropical Lands: Policy Issues in Latin America* (Baltimore: The Johns Hopkins University Press, 1973).

10. Lena, "Aspects de la Frontière Amazonienne."

11. Myers and Tucker, "Deforestation in Central America," 63.

12. Nicholas Guppy, "Tropical Deforestation: A Global View," *Foreign Affairs* 62, no. 4 (1984), 941.

13. Roger Sedjo, in Yatron 1984, 141.

14. Simon Commander, "Managing Indian Forests: A Case for the Reform of Property Rights," *Development Policy Review* 4, no. 4 (1986), 325–44.

15. Roger A. Sedjo, in Yatron 1984, 141–2.

16. Lena, "Aspects de la Frontière Amazonienne."

17. Roger A. Sedjo, in Yatron 1984, 142; Guppy, "Tropical Deforestation," 943.

18. John Spears and Montague Yudelman, "Forests in Development," *Finance and Development* 16, no. 4 (1979), 41.

19. World Bank, *Forestry Sector Policy Paper* (Washington, D.C.: The World Bank, 1978), 45.

20. World Bank, *Annual Reports, 1980–1986*.

21. James Conrow, U.S. Congress, House, Committee on Banking, Finance and Urban Affairs, *A Review of Multilateral Development Bank Environmental Policies. Hearing before the Subcommittee on International Development Institutions and Finance*, 99th Cong., 2nd sess., 1986, 12 (Lundine 86).

22. *See* Robert Asher, "Comment: The Leopard's Spots," in *The World Bank Group, Multilateral Aid, and the 1970s*, eds. John P. Lewis and Ishan Kapur (London: Lexington Books, 1973), 21.

23. *See* John Spears, "Rehabilitation of Watersheds," *Finance and Development* 19, no. 1 (March 1982): 30–33; *see also*, U.S., Congress, House, Committee on Foreign Affairs, *Tropical Deforestation. Hearings before the Subcommittee on International Organizations*, 96th Cong., 2nd sess., 1980, 158–72 (Bonder 1980).

24. *See* note 3, and Yatron 1984, 130.

25. Spears, "Saving the Tropical Forest Eco-system."

26. *See* Antoon de Vos, *Africa: The Devastated Continent? Man's Impact on the Ecology of Africa* (The Hague: Dr. W. Junk, 1975).

27. Nurul Almy Hafild, in Kasten 1986, 117–8.

28. Idem, 120.

29. Much of this information comes from Marcus Colchester in Kasten 1986, 74–81.

30. Idem, 120–1.

31. Office of Environmental Affairs, "Environmental Aspects of Transmigration," mimeograph, The World Bank, 1979.

32. Charles Secrett, "The Environmental Impact of Transmigration," *The Ecologist* 16, no. 2/3 (1986), 85.

33. Idem, 87.

34. *See* the 1986 letter to Alden Clausen by Rovin Hanbury-Tenison, President Survival International and endorsed by 28 other organizations, in Kasten 1986, 88–91.

35. Marcus Colchester, "Banking on Disaster: International Support for Transmigration," *The Ecologist* 16, no. 2/3 (1986), 66.

36. Secrett, "The Environmental Impact of Transmigration," 87.

37. Idem, 86.

38. *See* a special issue of *The Ecologist* 16, no. 2/3 (1986).

39. Robert Goodland, "Brazil's Environmental Progress in Amazonian Development," in *Change in the Amazon Basin*, vol. 1, ed. John Hemming (Manchester, UK: Manchester University Press, 1985), 5–35.

40. Martin Coy, "Développement régional à la périphérie amazonienne," *Cahiers des Sciences Humaines* 22, no. 3–4 (1986), 382–83.

41. Ibid.; Goodland, "Brazil's Environmental Progress."

42. Cheryl Payer, *The World Bank: A Critical Analysis* (New York: Monthly Review Press, 1982), 346–7.

43. Brent Millikan, in U.S. Congress, House, Committee on Science and Technology, *Tropical Forests Development Projects: Status of Environmental and Agricultural Research. Hearings before the Subcommittee on Natural Resources, Agriculture Research and Environment*, 98th Cong., 2nd sess., 1984, 182. (Scheuer 1984).

44. Idem, 183.

45. Scheuer 1984, 25.

46. Jack Anderson and Joseph Spear, "Malaria Scourges World Bank Project," *Washington Post*, 1 May 1986, Maryland edition, 11.

47. *See* statement by Brent Millikan, in Scheuer 1984, 173.

48. Philip M. Fearnside and Eneas Salati, "Explosive Deforestation in Rondonia, Brazil," *Environmental Conservation* 12, no. 4 (1985), 355–6.

49. These examples come from the testimony of Mary Allegretti (anthropologist and environmental coordinator of the Brazilian NGO, the Institute for Socio-Economic Research, an organization concerned with human rights issues in Brazil) in Kasten, 1986, 129–130.

50. Anderson, "Malaria."

51. Robert W. Kasten, Jr., "Development Banks: Subsidizing Third World Pollution," *Washington Quarterly* 9, no. 3 (Summer 1986), 109–14.

52. James Lee, "Environmental Considerations in Development Finance," *International Organization* 26, no. 1 (1972), 343.

53. Barbara Bramble, in U.S. Congress, House, Committee on Banking, Finance and Urban Affairs, *Environmental Impact of Multilateral Development Bank-Funded Projects. Hearings before the Subcommittee on International Development Institutions and Finance*, 98th Cong., 1st sess., 1983, 99 (Patterson 1983).

54. Penny Lernoux, "Ecological Disaster Threatens Colombia's Hydroelectric Projects," *Environment Report*, 5 Dec. 1977, in Patterson 1983, 173.

55. *See* World Bank, Office of Environmental Affairs, "Case Study: A Lead Smelter and Refinery," mimeograph, 1977; Idem, "Case Study: A Pesticide Manufacturing Plant," mimeograph, 1979.

56. *See* J. L. Tixhon, "Occupational Health and Safety," mimeograph, The World Bank, 1979.

57. *See*, for example, Emmanuel de Kadt, ed., *Tourism: Passport to Development*, a joint World Bank/UNESCO study (New York: Oxform U. Press, 1979).

58. The World Bank, *Agricultural Land Settlements* (The World Bank, 1978), 47 (author's emphasis).

59. Ibid., 9.

60. *See* Mahbub ul Haq, *The Poverty Curtain* (New York: Columbia University Press, 1976), chap.6.

61. Andrew M. Karmack, *The Tropics and Economic Development* (Baltimore: Johns Hopkins University Press, 1976).

62. *See* Emilio Moran, *Developing the Amazon* (Bloomington, Indiana University Press, 1981), chap.2.

63. *See* David Leonard, *Reaching the Peasant Farmer* (Chicago: University of Chicago Press, 1977); C. Leys, ed., *Politics and Change in Developing Countries* (London: Cambridge University Press, 1969); E. P. Morgan, ed., *The Administration of Change in Africa* (New York: Dunellen, 1974).

64. *See* D. Plucknett and N. J. H. Smith, "Agriculture Research and Third World Food Production," *Science* 217, no. 4556 (1982), 215–20.

65. *See* Robert Keohane, "The International Energy Agency: State Influence and Transgovernmental Politics," *International Organization* 32, no.4 (1978), 930.

66. Robert E. Stein and Brian Johnson, *Banking on the Biosphere? Environmental Procedures and Practices of Nine Multilateral Development Agencies* (Lexington, Mass.: Lexington Books, 1979).

67. As an amendment to the U.S. State Department authorization act, the 1983 U.S. International Environmental Protection Act directed USAID to "Assist countries in protecting and maintaining wildlife habitats and in developing sound wildlife management and plant conservation programs. Special efforts should be made to establish and maintain wildlife sanctuaries, reserves, and parks; to enact and enforce anti-poaching measures; and to identify, study, and catalog animal and plant species, especially in tropical environment."

68. Kasten, "Development Banks."

69. Brent Blackwelder in Patterson 1983, 36–37.

70. Ziauddin Sardar, "Dam Threatens Malaysia's National Park," *New Scientist*, 6 May 1982, 339.

71. Barbara Bramble in Patterson 1983, 98.

72. Ibidem.

73. "Minutes of the Operational Policy Subcommittee Meeting of March 9, 1984," reproduced in part in Secrett, "Environmental Impact of Transmigration," 86.

74. Leonard Ortolano, "Integrating Environmental Considerations into Infrastructure Planning," in *Integrated Impact Assessment*, eds. Frederick A. Rossini and Alan L. Porter (Boulder, Colo.: Westview Press, 1983), 125.

75. *See* Griffin, *The Political Economy of Agrarian Change* (Cambridge: Harvard University Press, 1975).

76. Brazil, for example, decided to proceed with road construction through reserves and national parks, even before POLONOROESTE. *See* R.J.A. Goodland and H.S. Irwin, *Amazonian Jungle: Green Hell to Red Desert?* (New York: Elsevier, 1975), 57.

77. *See* A. de Vos, *Africa*: 46; Douglas L. Johnson, "Pastoral Nomadism in the Sahel Zone," in *Eco-social Systems and Ecopolitics*, ed., Karl Deutsch (Paris: UNESCO, 1977), 169–85; Richard W. Franke and Barbara M. Chasin, *Seeds of Famine* (Montclair, NJ: Allenheld, Osmun, 1980).

78. U.S. Congress, House, Committee on Appropriations, *Foreign Assistance and Related Programs Appropriations Bill, 1987*, Report to accompany H.R. 5339, 99th Cong., 2nd sess., 1986, 29 (Obey 1986).

79. Shabecoff, "World Lenders," 1, D24.

80. Lynton K. Caldwell, *In Defense of Earth* (Bloomington, Indiana University Press, 1972), 145.

81. *See* A. J. R. Groom, "The Advent of International Institutions," in *International Organizations. A Conceptual Approach*, eds., Paul Taylor and A. J. R. Groom (New York: Nichols, 1978), 22.

82. *Environment Policy and Law* 7 (1981), 46.

83. *See* Kal J. Holsti, "Resolving International Conflicts: A Taxonomy and Some Figures on Procedures," *Journal of Conflict Resolution* 10 (1966), 272–96.

84. Norman Myers, in *Environment* 25, no. 5, 44.

85. Marcus Colchester in Kasten 1986, 79.

86. *See*, for example, testimony by Jose Lutzenberger, in Scheuer 1984, 22.

87. Idem, p. 242.

88. Payer, *The World Bank*, 351.

89. Runnalls, in Patterson 1984b, 106–7.

Chapter 6. Looking toward the Future

1. Gus Speth, President of the World Resources Institute, quoted in Philip Shabecoff, "World Bank Offers Environmental Projects," *New York Times*, 6 May 1987, A14.

2. Barber B. Conable, "Address to the World Resources Institute," Washington, D.C., 1987 (mimeograph, The World Bank).

3. David Whetten and Howard Aldrich, "Organization-Set Size and Diversity: People Processing Organizations and their Environment," *Administrative Science Quarterly* 11 (1979), 252–81.

4. World Bank, *World Development Report* (Oxford: Oxford University Press, 1986).

5. *See* Michael Lipton, "Limits of Price Policy for Agriculture: Which Way for the World Bank?" *Development Policy Review* 5, no. 2 (1987), 197–215.

6. Montague Yudelman, "The World Bank and Agricultural Development: An Insider's View," (Washington, D.C.: World Resources Institute, 1985).

7. *See* the short, laudatory, but telling account in William Clark's memoirs, *From Three Worlds* (London: Sidgwick and Jackson, 1986): chap. 9.

8. Stanley Please, *The Hobbled Giant* (Boulder, Colo.: Westview Press, 1984).

9. World Bank (Operations Evaluation Department), "8th Annual Review of Project Performance Audit Report," (Washington, D.C., 1982), par. 306 (quoted in Please, *Hobbled Giant*, 27).

10. Hans Michelman, "Organizational Effectiveness in A Multinational Bureaucracy: the Commission of the European Communities," (Ph.D. thesis, Indiana University, 1975); J. L. Price, *Organizational Effectiveness* (Homewood, IL: R. D. Irwin, 1968).

11. Ronald T. Libby, "The Ideology of the World Bank," (Ph.D. diss., University of Washington, 1975), 15.

12. Organization autonomy can be defined as "the amount and variety of strategic decisions made by the members of the organization." *See* Jerald Hage, *Theories of Organizations: Forms, Processes, and Transformation* (New York: Wiley, 1980), 387. Thus an organization with few decisions to make would have little autonomy.

13. Edward Mason and Robert Asher, *The World Bank since Bretton Woods* (Washington, D.C.: The Brookings Institution, 1973).

14. *See also* William Clark, "McNamara at the World Bank," *Foreign Affairs* 60, no. 1 (1981), 167–84.

15. Philip Selznick, *TVA and the Grass Roots* (New York: Harper & Row, 1966); James D. Thompson, *Organizations in Action* (New York: McGraw-Hill, 1967); Howard Aldrich, *Organizations and Environment* (Englewood Cliffs, NJ: Prentice-Hall, 1979).

16. Shirley Terreberry, "The Evolution of Organizational Environments," *Administrative Science Quarterly* (1968), 590–613.

17. Robert W. Cox and Harald K. Jacobson. *The Anatomy of Influence: Decision-Making in International Organizations* (New Haven, Conn.: Yale University Press, 1973).

Bibliography

Adams, Patricia, and Lawrence Solomon. *In the Name of Progress: The Underside of Foreign Aid.* New York: Doubleday, 1985.

Alder, John H. "Development Theory and the Bank's Development Strategy: A Review." *Finance and Development* 14 (December 1977): 31–34.

Agency for International Development. "Environmental and Natural Resource Management in Developing Countries." In *A Report to Congress. Vol. I Report.* Washington, D.C.: Department of State, February 1979.

Ahmad, Yusuf J., ed. *The Economics of Survival. The Role of Cost-Benefit Analysis in Environmental Decision-making.* Nairobi: United Nations Environment Programme, 1981.

Aldrich, Howard. *Organizations and Environments.* Englewood Cliffs, N.J.: Prentice-Hall, 1979.

Allen, M. P. "The Structure of Interorganizational Elite Cooptation." *American Sociological Review* 39 (1974): 393–426.

Anderson, Charles W. "The Place of Principles in Policy Analysis." *American Political Science Review* 23, no. 3 (1979): 711–723.

Anderson, Jack, and Joseph Spears. "Malaria Scourges World Bank Project." *Washington Post*, 1 May 1986.

Ansari, Javed A. "Environmental Characteristics and Organizational Ideology: UNCTAD and the Lessons of 1964." *British Journal of International Studies* 4 (July 1978): 135–60.

Araujo Castro, Joao Augusto de. "Environment and Development: The Case of the Developing Countries." in *World Eco-crisis*, 237–52. Edited by David A. Kay and Eugene B. Skolnikoff. Madison: University of Wisconsin Press, 1972.

Ascher, William. *The World Bank and the IMF.* Mimeograph, 1981.

———. "New Development Approaches and the Adaptability of International Agencies: the case of the World Bank," *International Organization* 37, no. 3 (1983): 415–40.

Asher, Robert. "Comment: The Leopard's Spots," in *The World Bank Group: Multilateral Aid, and the 1970s.* Edited by John P. Lewis and Ishan Kapur. London: Lexington Books, 1973.

Ayres, Robert L. "Breaking the Bank." *Foreign Policy* 43 (1981): 104–20.

Ayres. Robert L. *Banking on the Poor: The World Bank and World Poverty.* Cambridge and London: MIT Press, 1983.

Bahmbhri. C. P. *World Bank and India.* New Delhi: Vikas, 1980.

Baram, Michael S. "Cost-Benefit Analysis: An Inadequate Basis for Health, Safety, and Environmental Regulatory Decisionmaking," *Ecology Law Quarterly*, 8 (1980): 473–531.

Barde, Jean-Philippe, and Emilio Gerelli. *Economie et politique de l'environnement.* Paris: Presses universitaires de France, 1977.

Barre, Raymond. *Economie politique*. Paris: Presses universitaires de France, 1956.

Baum, Warren C. "The Project Cycle." *Finance and Development* 7 (June 1970): 2–13.

———. "The Project Cycle." *Finance and Development* 15 (December 1978): 10–17.

Bello, Walden F., David Kinley, and Elaine Elinson. *Development Debacle. The World Bank in the Philippines*. San Francisco: Institute for Food and Development Policy, 1972.

Besteliu, Maluca Mija. "The Procedure of Consensus in the Adoption of Decisions by the IMF and the IBRD." *Revue roumaine d'études internationales* 38 (1977): 516–26.

Bird, Roland. "Barbara Ward." *The Economist*, 6 June 1981.

Black, Eugene R. *The Diplomacy of International Development*. New York: Atheneum, 1963.

Blake, Robert O., et al. "Aiding the Environment: A Study of the Environmental Policies, Procedures, and Performance of the United States Agency for International Development." Washington, D.C.: Natural Resources Defense Council, 1980.

Boardman, Robert. *International Organization and the Conservation of Nature*. Bloomington: Indiana University Press, 1981.

Boulding, Kenneth. "The Economics of the Coming Spaceship Earth." In *Economics, Ecology, Ethics: Essays Toward a Steady-state Economy*, 253–63. Edited by Herman E. Daly. San Francisco: W. H. Freeman, 1980.

Brinkerhoff, Merlin B., and Philip R. Kunz, eds. *Complex Organizations and Their Environment*. Dubuque, Iowa: William Brown, 1972.

Buehrig, Edward. "The Resolution-Based International Agency." *Political Studies* 29, 2 (1981): 217–31.

Bureau of National Affairs. "World Bank Committed to Protecting Environments of Underdeveloped Countries." *Environment Reporter*, Special Report (1977): 615–19.

Burke, Knapp M. "New Directions in the World Bank Group Policies." In *Toward a North-South Dialogue*. Edited by Pierre Uri. Paris: Presses Universitaires de France, 1976.

Burki, Shahid Javed. "The Prospects for the Developing World: A Review of Recent Forecasts." *Finance and Development* 18 (March 1981): 20–24.

Bussow, Whitman. "The Third World: Changing Attitudes Toward Environmental Protection." *Annals of the American Academy of Political and Social Science* 444 (July 1979): 112–20.

Caiden, Naomi, and Aaron Wildavsky. *Planning and Budgeting in Poor Countries*. New York: Wiley, 1974.

Caldwell, Lynton K. *In Defense of Earth*. Bloomington: Indiana University Press, 1972.

———. "Strategies and Alternatives: the Ethics and Politics of Survival." Mimeograph, 1980.

———. *International Environmental Policy: Emergence and Dimensions*. Durham, N.C.: Duke University Press, 1984.

Cargil, I. P. M. "Efforts to Influence Recipient Performance: Case Study of India." In *The World Bank Group: Multilateral Aid and the 1970s*. Edited by John P. Lewis and Ishan Kapur. London: Lexington Books, 1973.

Carter, Nicholas. "Population, Environment and Natural Resources : A Critical Review of Recent Models." Bank Staff Working Paper, No. 174. Washington, D.C.: The World Bank, 1974.

Child, John. "Organizational Structure, Environment, and Performance: The Role of Strategic Choices." *Sociology* 6 (1972): 1–22.

Clark, William. "Interview." *Finance and Development* 17 (June 1980): 5–6.

———. "McNamara at the World Bank." *Foreign Affairs* 60 (1981): 167–84.

———. *From Three Worlds*. London: Sidgewick & Jackson, 1986.

Clausen, A.W. "Address to the Board of Governors." September 1982. Washington, D.C.: The World Bank, 1982.

———."Sustainable Development: The Global Imperative." Fairfield Osborne Memorial Lecture in Environmental Science in *The Developmental Challenge of the Eighties; A. W. Clausen at the World Bank*. Washington, D.C.: The World Bank, 1986.

———. "Global Interdependence in the 1980s." Address before the Yomiuri International Economic Society, Tokyo, Japan, January 1982. Washington, D.C.: The World Bank, 1982.

Clinton, Richard L. "Ecodevelopment." *World Affairs* 140 (1977): 111–26.

The Cocoyoc Declaration. Adopted by the participants in the UNEP/UNCTAD symposium on "Patterns of Resource Use Environment and Development Strategies," Cocoyoc, Mexico, 8–12 October 1974. Reprinted in full in *International Organization* 29 (Summer 1975): 893–901.

Cohn, Theodore H. "Influence of the Less Developed Countries in the World Bank Group." Ph.D. diss., University of Michigan, 1972.

Colchester, Marcus. "Banking on Disaster: International Support for Transmigration." *Ecologist* 16, no. 2/3 (1986): 61–70.

Commander, Simon. "Managing Indian Forests: A Case for the Reform of Property Rights." *Development Policy Review* 4, no. 4 (1986): 325–44.

Council on Environmental Quality and Department of State. *Global 2000: Entering the Twenty-First Century*, 3 vols. Washington, D.C.: Government Printing Office, 1980.

Council on Environmental Quality and Department of State. *Global Futures: Time to Act. Report to the President on Global Resources, Environment and Population*. January 1981.

Cox, Robert W. "The Executive Head: an Essay on Leadership in the ILO." *International Organization* 23, no. 1 (Spring 1969): 205–29.

———. and Harold K. Jacobson. *The Anatomy of Influence: Decision-Making in International Organizations*. New Haven, Conn.: Yale University Press, 1973.

Coy, Martin. "Développement régional à la périphérie amazonienne." *Cahiers des Sciences Humaines* 22, no. 3–4 (1986): 371–88.

Crane, Barbara, and Larry Finkle. "Organizational Impediments to Development Assistance: The World Bank's Population Program." *World Politics* 23 (1981): 516–53.

Crozier, Michel, and Ehrardt Friedberg. *L'Acteur et le Système*. Paris: Seuil, 1977.

Cyert, R. M., and J. G. March. *A Behavioral Theory of the Firm.* Englewood Cliffs: Prentice-Hall, 1963.

Dahl, Robert A. *Modern Political Analysis.* Englewood Cliffs: Prentice-Hall, 1963.

Dahlberg, Kenneth A. *Beyond the Green Revolution.* New York and London: Plenum Press, 1979.

Dasgrupta, Biplab. "Some Awkward Questions." *Mazingira* 3/4 (1977): 62–67.

Dasmann, Raymond F., et al. *Ecological Principles for Economic Development.* New York: Wiley, 1973.

Demuth, Richard H. "Relations with Other Multilateral Agencies." In *The World Bank Group: Multilateral Aid and the 1970s.* Edited by John P. Lewis and Ishan Kapur. London: Lexington Books, 1973.

Dobry, Daniel. "Comment enrayer la disparition des forêts tropicales," *Le Monde Diplomatique*, Fevrier 1987: 30–31.

Dogra, Bharat. "World Bank vs. The People of Bastar—Reforestation or Deforestation?" *Ecologist* 15, no. 1/2 (1985).

Douglas, Mary and Aaron Wildavsky. *Risk and Culture: an Essay on the Selection of Technical and Environmental Dangers.* Berkeley: University of California Press, 1982.

Downs, Anthony. *Inside Bureaucracy.* Boston: Little, Brown and Co., 1966.

Ehrlich, Paul, and Anne Ehrlich. *Population, Resources, Environment: Issues in Human Ecology.* San Francisco: Freeman, 1972.

Emery, F. E., and E. C. Trist. "The Causal Texture of Organizational Environments." *Human Relation* 18 (1965): 21–32.

Emery, F. E., and E. C. Trist. *Organization Theory: Structures, Systems and Environments.* New York: Wiley, 1976.

Farvar, Taghi, and John P. Milton, eds. *The Careless Technology.* Garden City, N.Y.: Natural History Press, 1972.

Fatouros, A. A. "The World Bank." In *The Impact of International Organizations on Legal and Institutional Change in the Developing Countries.* New York: International Legal Center, 1977.

Fearnside, Philip M. "Environmental Change and Deforestation in the Brazilian Amazon." In *Change in the Amazon Basin*, vol. I. Edited by John Hemming. Manchester, U.K.: Manchester University Press, 1985: 70–89.

Fearnside, Philip M., and Eneas Salati. "Explosive Deforestation in Rondonia, Brazil." *Environmental Conservation* 12 no. 4 (1985): 355–6.

Franke, Richard W., and Barbara M. Chasin. *Seeds of Famine. Ecological Destruction and the Development Dilemma in the West African Sahel.* Montclair, NJ: Allanheld, Osmun, 1980.

Freeman, A. Myrick, III. *The Benefits of Environmental Improvement.* Baltimore and London: Johns Hopkins University Press for Resources for the Future, Inc., 1979.

Galbraith, John K. *The New Industrial State.* 3rd ed. Boston: Houghton-Mifflin, 1978.

Goodland, Robert. "Brazil's Environmental Progress in Amazonian Development," in *Change in the Amazon Basin*, vol. I. Edited by John Hemming. Manchester U.K.: Manchester University Press, 1985: 5–35.

Goodland, Robert, and H. S. Irwin. *Amazon Jungle: Green Hell to Red Desert.* New York: Elsevier, 1975.

Graves, Harold N. "The Bank as an International Mediator: Three Episodes." In *The World Bank Since Bretton Woods*. Edited by E. S. Mason and R. E. Asher. Washington, D.C.: The Brookings Institution, 1973.

Griffin, K. *The Political Economy of Agrarian Change*. Cambridge: Harvard University Press, 1974.

Groom, A. J. R. "The Advent of International Institutions." In *International Organizations: A Conceptual Approach*. Edited by Paul Taylor and A. J. R. Groom. New York: Nichols, 1978.

Guppy, Nicholas. "Tropical Deforestation: A Global View." *Foreign Affairs* 62, no. 4 (1984): 928–65.

Haas, Ernst B. *Beyond the Nation-State*. Stanford, Calif.: Stanford University Press, 1964.

———. "Turbulent Fields and the Theory of Regional Integration." *International Organization* 30 (1976): 173–212.

Haas, Ernst B., and Mary Pat Williams; with Don Babai. *Scientists and World Order: The Uses of Technical Knowledge in International Organizations*. Berkeley: University of California Press, 1977.

Hage, Jerald. *Theories of Organizations: Form, Processes, and Transformations*. New York: Wiley, 1980.

Hall, Richard H. *Organizations: Structure and Process*. Englewood Cliffs, N.J.: Prentice-Hall, 1972.

Haq, Mahbub ul. "The Limits to Growth: A Critique." *Finance and Development* 9 (December 1972): 2–8.

———. *The Poverty Curtain*. New York: Columbia University Press, 1976.

Hardin Garett. "The Tragedy of the Commons." *Science*, 162 (1968): 1243–1248.

———. "The Ethics of a Lifeboat." *Bioscience* 26 (October 1979): 561–8.

Hart, David. *The Volta River Project: A Case Study in Politics and Technology*. Edinburgh: University Press, 1980.

Hayter, Teresa. *Aid as Imperialism*. Harmondsworth, U.K.: Penguin Books, 1971.

Heller, Walter. *Economic Growth and Environmental Quality: Collision or Conscience?* Morristown, N.J.: General Learning Press, 1973.

Hemming, John, ed. *Change in the Amazon Basin*. vol. I. Manchester, U.K.: Manchester University Press, 1985.

Henderson, P. D. "Terms and Flexibility of Bank Lending." In *The World Bank Group: Multilateral Aid and the 1970s*. Edited by John P. Lewis and Ishan Kapur. London: Lexington Books, 1973.

Hirsch, P. M. "Organizational Effectiveness and the Institutional Environment." *Administrative Science Quarterly* 20 (1975): 327–44.

Hirschman, Albert O. *Development Projects Observed*. Washington, D.C.: The Brookings Institution, 1967.

Hirschman, Albert O., and C. E. Lindblom. "Economic Development, Research and Development, Policymaking: Some Convergent Views." *Behavioral Science* 7 (1962): 211–22.

Hoffman, Michael. "Development Finance and the Environment." *Finance and Development* 7 (September 1970): 2–6.

———. "The Challenges of the 1970s and the Present Institutional Structure." In *The World Bank Group: Multilateral Aid and the 1970s*. Edited by John P. Lewis and Ishan Kapur. London: Lexington Books, 1973.

Holsti, K. J. "Resolving International Conflicts: A Taxonomy and Some Figures on Procedures." *Journal of Conflict Resolutions* 10 (1966).

Horberry, John. "The Accountability of Development Assistance Agencies: The Case of Environmental Policy," *Ecology Law Quarterly* 12 (1985): 817–69.

Hornstein, Roger A. "Cofinancing of Bank and IDA Projects." *Finance and Development* 14 (June 1977): 40–43.

Huerni, Bettina. *The Lending Policies of the World Bank in the 1970s: Analysis and Evaluation*. Boulder, Colo.: Westview, 1970.

Hufschmidt, Maynard M., David E. James, Anton D. Meister, T. Blair Bower, and John A. Dixon. *Environment, Natural Systems, and Development. An Economic Valuation Guide*. Baltimore and London: Johns Hopkins University Press, 1983.

International Institute for Environment and Development. *1980 Annual Report*. London & Washington: IIED, 1980.

International Institute for Environment and Development and World Resources Institute. *World Resources 1987*. New York: Basic Books, 1987.

Jackson, Sir Robert. "A Study of the Capacity of the United Nations Development System." 2 vols. UN/Doc/DP/5. Geneva: United Nations, 1969.

Jacobson, Harold K., and David A. Kay. "The Environmental Protection Activities of International Organizations: An Appraisal and Some Suggestions." Paper delivered at the Annual Meeting of the American Political Science Association. Washington, D.C., 31 August to 3 September 1979.

James, Jeffrey. "Growth Technology and the Environment in Less Developed Countries: A Survey." *World Development* 6 (July–August 1978): 937–65.

Jequier, Nicolas, ed. *Les organizations internationales entre l'innovation et la stagnation*. Lausanne: Presses Polytechniques Romandes, 1985.

Jha, L. K. "Comment: Leaning Against Open Doors?" In *The World Bank Group: Multilateral Aid and the 1970s*, Edited by John P. Lewis and Ishan Kapur. London: Lexington Books, 1973.

Johnson, Brian. "The United Nations' Institutional Response to Stockholm: A Case Study in the International Politics of Institutional Change." In *World Ecocrisis*. Edited by David Kay and Eugene B. Skolnikoff. Madison: University of Wisconsin Press, 1972.

Johnston, Brian. "The New Direction of World Bank Policy." *Journal of Social and Political Studies* 3 (Fall 1978): 347–52.

Johnston, Brian, and Robert O. Blake. "The Environmental and Bilateral Aid: The Environment Policies, Programs and Performance of the Development Assistance Agencies of Canada, the Federal Republic of Germany, the Netherlands, Sweden, the United Kingdom, and the United States." Washington, D.C.: International Institute for Environment and Development, 1980.

Juda, Lawrence. "International Environmental Concern: Perspectives of, and Implications for, Developing States." In *The Global Predicament: Ecological Perspectives on World Order*. Edited by David W. Orr and Marvin S. Soroos. Chapel Hill: University of North Carolina Press, 1979.

Kadt, Emmanuel de, ed. *Tourism: Passport to Development?* (a joint World Bank/UNESCO study) New York: Oxford University Press, 1979.

Kamarck, Andrew M. *The Tropics and Economic Development*. Baltimore & London: Johns Hopkins University Press, for the World Bank, 1976.

Kasten, Robert W., Jr. "Development Banks: Subsidizing Third World Pollution," *The Washington Quarterly* 9, no. 3 (1986): 109–14.

Katz, Daniel, and Robert Kahn. *The Social Psychology of Organizations.* New York: Wiley, 1978.

Kay, David A., and Eugene B. Skolnikoff, eds. *World Eco-crisis: International Organizations in Response.* Madison: University of Wisconsin Press, 1972.

Kay, David A., and Harold K. Jacobson. *Environmental Protection: The International Dimension.* Totowa, N.J.: Allanheld, Osmun, 1983.

Keohane, Robert W. "The International Energy Agency: State Influence and Transgovernmental Politics." *International Organization* 32, no. 4 (Fall 1978).

Keohane, Robert W., and Joseph S. Nye. "Transgovernmental Relations and International Organizations." *World Politics* 21 (October 1974): 39–62.

Keohane, Robert W., and Joseph S. Nye. *Power and Interdependence.* New York: Little, Brown, 1978.

King, John A. "Reorganizing the World Bank." *Finance and Development* 11 (March 1974): 5–8.

Knorr, Klaus. *The Power of Nations: The Political Economy of International Relations.* New York: Basic Books, 1975.

Krasner, Stephen D. "Power Structures and Regional Development Banks." *International Organization* 35 (1981): 303–28.

———. "Transforming International Regimes: What the Third World Wants and Why." *International Studies Quarterly* 25 (1981): 119–48.

Laar, A. van de. "The World Bank and the World's Poorest." *World Development* 4 (1976): 837–51.

———. "The World Bank: Which Way?" *Development and Change* 7 (1976): 67–97.

———. *The World Bank and the Poor.* Boston: Nijhoff, 1980.

Laulan, Yves. *Tiers-monde et crise de l'environnement.* Paris: Presses Universitaires de France, 1974.

Lavalle, Robert. *La banque mondiale et ses filiales: Aspects juridiques et fonctionnement.* Paris: Librairie générale de droit et de jurisprudence, 1972.

Lawrence, Paul, and Jay W. Lorsch. *Organizations and Environment: Managing Differentiation and Integration.* Boston: Harvard School of Business Administration, 1967.

Ledec, George. "The Political Economy of Tropical Deforestation." In *Divesting Nature's Capital: The Political Economy of Environmental Abuse in the Third World.* Edited by H. Jeffrey Leonard. New York & London: Holmes & Meier, 1985.

Lee, James. "Environmental Considerations in Development Finance," *International Organization* 26, no. 1 (1972): 343. Also in *World Eco-crisis.* Edited by David A. Kay and Eugene B. Skolnikoff. Madison: University of Wisconsin Press, 1973.

———. "Environment and Development: Choices for the Third World." Paper prepared for presentation at the 12th Technical Meeting of the IUCN. Banff, Canada, 11–16 September 1972.

———. "Development and Environment: A Post-Stockholm Assessment." Paper presented at the Columbia University Seminars on Pollution and Water Resources, Washington, D.C., 13 December 1972.

——. "Environment and Development: The World Bank Experience." Paper prepared for presentation at the international briefing sponsored by the Center for International Environmental Information, New York, 14 October 1976.

——. *The Environment, Public Health, and Human Ecology Considerations for Economic Development.* Baltimore and London: The Johns Hopkins University Press for the World Bank, 1985.

Lele, Uma. "Rural Africa: Modernization, Equity, and Long Term Development." *Science* 211 (6 February 1981): 547–53.

Leonard, David. *Reaching the Peasant Farmer: Organization Theory and Practice in Kenya.* Chicago, University of Chicago Press, 1977.

Lena, Philippe. "Aspects de la Frontière Amazonienne." *Cahiers des Sciences Humaines* 22, no. 3–4 (1986): 319–43.

Le Prestre, Philippe G. "A Problematique for International Organizations." *International Social Science Journal* no. 107 (1986): 127–38.

Lewis, Sir Arthur. *The Evolution of the International Economic Order.* Princeton: Princeton University Press, 1978.

Lewis, John P., and Ishan Kapur, eds. *The World Bank Group: Multilateral Aid, and the 1970s.* London: Lexington Books, 1973.

Leys, C., ed. *The Politics of Change in Developing Countries: Studies in the Theory and Practice of Development.* London: Cambridge University Press, 1969.

Libby, R. T. "The Ideology of the World Bank." Ph.D. diss., University of Washington, 1975.

——. "International Development Association: Legal Fiction Designed to Secure an LDC Constituency." *International Organization* 29 (1975): 1065–72.

Lipton, Michael. "Limits of Price Policy for Agriculture: Which Way for the World Bank?." *Development Policy Review* 5, no. 2 (1987): 197–215.

Mason, Edward S., and Robert E. Asher. *The World Bank Since Bretton Woods.* Washington, D.C.: The Brookings Institution, 1973.

Maybury-Lewis, David. "Multilateral Development Banks and Indigenous Peoples," *Cultural Survival Quarterly* 10, no. 1 (1986): 1–3.

McCormick, John. "The Origins of the World Conservation Strategy." *Environmental Review* 10, no. 3 (1986): 177–87.

McNamara, Robert. *One Hundred Countries, Two Billion People: The Dimensions of Development.* New York: Praeger, 1973.

——. "Address to the U.N. Economic and Social Council." mimeograph, Washington: The World Bank, 1970.

——. "Address To the Board of Governors." Copenhagen, Denmark, 21 September 1970. Washington, D.C.: The World Bank, 1970.

——. *The McNamara Years at the World Bank.* Baltimore, MD: Johns Hopkins Press, 1981.

Meadows, Dennis, et al. *The Limits to Growth: A Report for the Club of Rome's Project on the Predicament of Mankind.* New York: Universe Books, 1972.

M'Gonigle, Michael, and Mark Zacher. *Pollution, Politics and International Law: Tankers at Sea.* Berkeley: University of California Press, 1979.

Michelman, Hans. "Organizational Effectiveness in a Multinational Bureaucracy: The Commission of the European Communities." Ph.D. diss., Indiana University, 1975.

Miles, Robert H. *Macro-Organizational Behavior*. Santa Monica, Calif.: Good-year, 1980.

Mishan, Ezra N. *The Costs of Economic Growth*. Harmondsworth, U.K.: Penguin Books, 1967.

Moran, Emilio. *Developing the Amazon*. Bloomington: Indiana University Press, 1981.

Morgan, E. Philip, ed. *The Administration of Change in Africa: Essays in the Theory and Practice of Development Administration in Africa*. New York: Dunellen, 1974.

Myers, Norman. *Conversion of Tropical Moist Forests*. Washington, D.C.: National Academy of Science, 1980.

Myers, Norman, and Richard Tucker. "Deforestation in Central America: Spanish Legacy and North American Consumers." *Environmental Review* 11, no. 1 (1987): 55–71.

Nations, James D., and Daniel I. Komer. "Rainforests and the Hamburger Society," *Environment* 25, no. 3 (1983): 12–20.

Nelson, Michael. *The Development of Tropical Lands: Policy Issues in Latin America*. Baltimore: Johns Hopkins University Press, 1973.

Nicholls, Yvonne. "The Emergence of the Idea of Compensating Developing Countries for Maintaining Environmental Quality." Morges, Switzerland: IUCN, 1973.

Ophuls, William. *Ecology and the Politics of Scarcity*. San Francisco: Freeman, 1977.

O'Riordan, Tim. *Environmentalism*. London: Pion, 1976.

Oppenheim, V. H. "Whose World Bank?" *Foreign Policy* 19 (1975): 99–108.

Organization for Economic Cooperation and Development. *Interfutures: Mastering the Probable and Managing the Unpredictable*. Paris: OECD, 1979.

Orr, David W. and Marvin S. Soroos, eds. *The Global Predicament: Ecological Perspectives on World Order*. Chapel Hill: University of North Carolina Press, 1979.

Ozorio de Almeida, M., et al. "Environment and Development: The Founex Report." *International Conciliation* no. 586 (1972).

Ozorio de Almeida, M., et al. "The Confrontation Between Problems of Development and Environment." *International Conciliation* 586 (1972): 37–56.

Passell, Peter, and Leonard Ross. *The Retreat from Riches: Affluence and Its Enemies*. New York: Viking, 1973.

Payer, Cheryl. *The World Bank: A Critical Analysis*. New York and London: Monthly Review Press, 1982.

Pearson, Charles S., and Anthony Pryor. *Environment, North and South: An Economic Interpretation*. New York: Wiley, 1978.

Pearson, Charles S., and Anthony Pryor. *Organizational Analysis: A Sociological View*. Belmont: Wadsworth, 1970.

Pearson, Lester B. *Partners in Development*. Report of the Commission on International Development. New York: Praeger, 1969.

Pfeffer, Jeffrey, and Gerald R. Salancik. *The External Control of Organizations: A Resource Dependence Perspective*. New York: Harper & Row, 1978.

Please, Stanley. *The Hobbled Giant*. Boulder, Colo.: Westview, 1984.

Plucknett, Donald, and N. H. J. Smith. "Agricultural Research and Third World Food Production." *Science* 217, no. 4556 (1982): 215–220.

Polunin, Nicholas S., ed. *Growth Without Ecodisasters?* Proceedings of the 2nd International Conference on Environmental Future (2nd ICEF). Reykjavik, Iceland, 5–11 June 1977. New York: Wiley, 1980.

Price, J. L. *Organizational Effectiveness*. Homewood, Ill.: R. D. Irwin, 1968.

Ramakhrishna, Kiliparti. "Interest Articulation by the Developing Countries in the International Environmental Movement," *International Review of Contemporary Law* 2 (1984).

———. "The Emergence of Environmental Law in Developing Countries: A Case Study of India," *Ecology Law Quarterly* 12, no.4 (1985).

Ray, Anandarup, and Herman G. van der Tak. "A New Approach to the Economic Analysis of Projects." *Finance and Development* 16 (March 1979): 28–32.

Reid, Escott. "McNamara's World Bank." *Foreign Affairs* 51 (1973): 794–810.

———. *Strengthening the World Bank*. Chicago: Adlai Stevenson Institute, 1973.

Rich, Bruce M. "The Multilateral Development Banks, Environmental Policy, and the United States," *Ecology Law Quarterly* 12, no. 4 (1985): 681–745.

Rosengren, W. R. "The Careers of Clients and Organizations." In *Organizations and Clients*. Edited by W. R. Rosengren and M. Lefton. Columbus, Ohio: Merrill, 1970.

Ross, G. Alexander. "The Emergence of Organization Sets in the Ecumenical Disaster Recovery Organizations: An Empirical and Theoretical Exploration." *Human Relations* 33 (January 1980): 23–40.

Rotberg, Eugene. *The World Bank: A Financial Appraisal*. Washington, D.C.: The World Bank, 1978.

———. *The World Bank's Borrowing Program: Some Questions and Answers*. Washington, D.C.: The World Bank, 1979.

Sachs, Ignacy. "Environnement et styles de développement." *Annales* 3 (May–June 1974): 553–70.

Sanford, Jonathan F. "American Foreign Policy and the Multilateral Banks." Ph.D. diss., The American University, 1977.

Schelling, Thomas C. *Incentive for Environmental Protection*. Cambridge: MIT Press, 1983.

Schneider, Jan. *World Public Order and the Environment*. Toronto: University of Toronto Press, 1979.

Schultz, Theodore W. ed. *Distortions of Agricultural Incentives*. Bloomington: Indiana University Press, 1978.

Schwartzman, Stephen. "World Bank Holds Funds for Development Project in Brazil," *Cultural Survival Quarterly* 10, no. 1 (1986): 25–27.

Secrett, Charles. "The Environmental Impact of Transmigration." *Ecologist* 16, no. 2/3 (1986): 77–88.

Selznick, Philip. *TVA and the Grass Roots*. New York: Harper & Row, 1966.

Shabecoff, Philip. "World Lenders Facing Pressure from Ecologists." *New York Times*, 30 Oct. 1986, 1, D24.

Smith, Gerald A. "The Teleological View of Wealth: A Historical Perspective." In *Economics, Ecology and Ethics: Essays Toward a Steady-state Economy*, Edited by Herman Daly. San Francisco: Freeman, 1980.

Soroos, Marvin S. "Trends in the Perception of Environmental Problems in the

United Nations General Debates." Paper presented at the Annual Meeting of the International Studies Association, Toronto, 21–24 March 1979.

Spears, John. "Rehabilitation of Watersheds." *Finance and Development* 19, no. 1 (1982): 30–33.

———. "Saving the Tropical Forest Eco-system. A Discussion Paper." The World Bank, mimeograph, June 1983.

Spears , John and Montague Yudelman. "Forests in Development." *Finance and Development* 16 , no. 4 (1979): 41–44.

Stein, Robert E. and Brian Johnson. *Banking on the Biosphere? Environmental Procedures and Practices of Nine Multilateral Development Agencies.* Lexington, Mass.: Lexington Books, 1979.

Streeten, Paul. "Basic Needs: Premises and Promises." *Journal of Policy Modeling* 1 (1979): 136–46.

Strong, Maurice. "One Year After Stockholm." Foreign Affairs 51 (1973): 690–707.

Teclaff, Ludwig A., and Albert E. Utton. *International Environmental Law.* New York: Praeger, 1974.

Tendler, Judith. *Inside Foreign Aid.* Baltimore and London: Johns Hopkins University Press, 1975.

Terreberry, Shirley. "The Evolution of Organizational Environments." *Administrative Science Quarterly* 12 (1968): 590–613.

Thibodeau, Francis R., and Hermann H. Field, eds. *Sustaining Tomorrow: A Strategy for World Conservation and Development.* Hanover and London: University Press of New England for Tufts University, 1984.

Thompson, James D. *Organizations in Action.* New York: McGraw-Hill, 1967.

Thompson, James D. and William J. McEwen. "Organizational Goals and Environment: Goal-Setting as an Interaction Process." *American Sociological Review* 23 (1958): 23–31.

Tixhon, J. "World Bank Involvement in Occupational Safety and Health." Mimeograph, Washington, D.C.: The World Bank, 1979.

United Nations. *International Development Strategy: Action Programme of the General Assembly for the Second Development Decade.* St/ECA/1939/Unit no. 6. New York: United Nations, 1970.

———. *Economic and Social Council.* "The Study of Interrelationships between Population, Resources, Environment and Development." Report of UN Secretary General E (979/75). New York: United Nations, 1979.

———. *Report on the UNCHE.* Stockholm, 5–16 June 1972. (A/Conf. 48/14/Rev. 1) New York: United Nations, 1973.

———. General Assembly. "Development and International Economic Cooperation." (A/35/592/Add. 1) New York: United Nations, 1980.

United Nations Conference on Trade and Development. "The Impact of Environmental Issues on Development and International Economic Relations." Research Memorandum No. 53, 23 April 1976. UNCTAD-RD-114.

———. "Implications for the Trade and Investment of Developing Countries of United States Environmental Controls." TD/B/C.2/150/Add. 1/Rev. 1. New York: United Nations, 1976.

U.S. Agency for International Development. "Environmental and National Resources Management in Developing Countries. A Report to Congress." Vol. 1: Report. Washington, D.C., 1979.

U.S. Congress. House. Committee on Appropriations. *Foreign Assistance and Related Programs Appropriations Bill, 1987. Report to accompany H.R. 5339*, 99th Cong., 2nd sess., 1986.

U.S. Congress. House. Committee on Banking, Finance and Urban Affairs. *U.S. Participation in Multilateral Development Institutions, Hearing before the Subcommittee on International Development Institutions and Finance*, 95th Cong., 2nd sess., 1978. (Gonzales 1978).

————. *Environmental Impact of Multilateral Development Bank-Funded Projects, Hearings before the Subcommittee on International Development Institutions and Finance.* 98th Cong., 1st sess., 1983.

————. *U.S. Participation in the International Development Association Seventh Replenishment, Hearings before the Subcommittee on International Development Institutions and Finance.* 98th Cong., 2nd sess, 1984. (Patterson 1984a).

————. *Draft Recommendations on the Multilateral Banks and the Environment, Hearings before the Subcommittee on International Development Institutions and Finance.* 98th Cong., 2nd sess., 1984. (Patterson 1984b).

————. *To Provide for a United States Contribution to the Special Facility for Sub-Saharan Africa Administered by the International Development Association. Hearing before the Subcommittee on International Development Institutions and Finance.* 99th Cong., 1st sess., 1985. (Lundine 1985a).

————. *A Mandate for Development: the Future of the World Bank, Hearing before the Subcommittee on International Development Institutions and Finance.* 99th Cong., 1st sess., 1985. (Lundine 1985b).

————. *A Review of Multilateral Development Bank Environmental Policies, Hearings before the Subcommittee on International Development Institutions and Finance.* 99th Cong., 2nd sess., 1986.

U.S. Congress. House. Committee on Foreign Affairs. *Tropical Deforestation, Hearings before the Subcommittee on International Organizations.* 96th Cong., 2nd sess., 1980. (Bonder 1980).

————. *Review of the Global Environment 10 Years After Stockholm, Hearings before the Subcommittee on Human Rights and International Organizations*, 97th Cong., 2nd sess., 1982. (Bonker 1982).

————. *U.S. International Environment Policy, Hearings before the Subcommittee on Human Rights and International Organizations*, 98th Cong., 2nd sess., 1984. (Yatron 1984)

U.S. Congress. House. Committee on Interior and Insular Affairs. *U.S. Assistance to Foreign Copper Producers and the Effects on Domestic Industries and Environmental Standards, Hearing before the Subcommittee on Mining, Forest Management, and Bonneville Power Administration*, 98th Cong., 1st sess., 1983. (Weaver 1983).

U.S. Congress. House. Committee on Science and Technology. *International Energy Negotiations, Hearings before the Subcommittee on Energy, Conservation and Power*, 97th Cong., 1st sess., 1981.

————. *Carbon Dioxide and Climate: the Greenhouse Effect, Hearing before the Subcommittee on Natural Resources, Agriculture Research and Environment and the Subcommittee on Investigations and Oversight.* 99th Cong., 2nd sess., 1982. (Scheuer 1982a).

————. *Deforestation: Environmental Impact and Research Needs, Joint Hearing before the Subcommittee on Natural Resources, Agriculture Research and En-*

vironment, and the Subcommittee on Human Rights and International Organizations of the Committee on Foreign Affairs. 97th Cong., 2nd sess., 1982. (Scheuer 1982b).

————. Tropical Forest Development Projects: Status of Environmental and Agricultural Research, Hearings before the Subcommittee on Natural Resources, Agriculture Research and Environment. 98th Cong., 2nd sess., 1984. (Scheuer 1984).

U.S. Congress. Senate. Appropriations Committee. Foreign Assistance and Related Programs Appropriations, FY80, pt. 1, Hearings before the Subcommittee on Foreign Operations, 96th Cong., 1st sess., 1979.

————. Foreign Assistance and Related Programs Appropriations, FY85, pt. 1, Hearings before the Subcommittee on Foreign Operations Appropriations, 98th Cong., 2nd sess., 1984.

————. Foreign Assistance and Related Programs Appropriations, FY86, pt. 1, Hearings before the Subcommittee on Foreign Operations Appropriations, 99th Cong., 1st sess., 1985.

————. Environmental Considerations in Multilateral Development Bank Projects, FY86, Special Hearings before the Subcommittee on Foreign Operations Appropriations, 99th Cong., 1st sess., 1985.

————. Foreign Assistance and Related Programs Appropriations, FY87, pt. 1, Hearings before the Subcommittee on Foreign Operations Appropriations, 99th Cong., 2nd sess., 1986.

————. International Concerns for Environmental Implications Of Multilateral Development Bank Projects, FY87, Special Hearings before the Subcommittee on Foreign Operations Appropriations. 99th Cong., 2nd sess., 1986.

U.S. Congress. Senate. Committee on Environment and Public Works. International Wildlife Conservation Hearings. 96th Cong., 2nd sess., 1980.

U.S. Congress. Senate. Committee on Foreign Relations. Subcommittee on Foreign Assistance. U.S. Policy and the Multilateral Banks: Politicization and Effectiveness. Staff Report prepared by J. Sanford. Washington, D.C., 1977.

————. Tropical Deforestation, Hearings before the Subcommittee on International Organizations, 96th Cong., 2nd sess., 1980.

————. Security and Development Assistance, Hearings. 98th Cong., 2nd sess., 1984.

U.S. Congress. Senate. Committee on Governmental Affairs. U.S. Participation in the Multilateral Development Banks. 96th Cong., 1st sess., 1979.

Uri, Pierre. Towards a North-South Dialogue. Paris: Presses Universitaires de France, 1976.

van Wagenen, R. W. "Training as an Element in Bank Group Projects." Finance and Development 9 (September 1972): 34–39.

Vibert, Frank. "The Process of Replenishing IDA Finances." Finance and Development 14 (September 1977): 25–27.

Vos, Antoon de. Africa, the Devastated Continent? Man's Impact on the Ecology of Africa. The Hague: Dr. W. Junk, 1975.

Wall, David. The Charity of Nations. London: MacMillan, 1973.

Ward, Barbara, and René Dubos. Only One Earth: the Care and Maintenance of a Small Planet. New York: Norton, 1972.

Ward, Barbara, Lenore d'Anjou, and J. D. Runnalls, eds. The Widening Gap: Development in the 1970s. New York: Columbia University Press, 1971.

Wheten, David, and Howard Aldrich. "Organization-set Size and Diversity: People Processing Organizations and their Environments." *Administrative Science Quarterly* 11 (1979): 251–81.

World Bank. *Summary Proceedings. Annual Meetings of the Boards of Governors.* Washington, D.C.: The World Bank, 1970–1986.

———. *Annual Report.* Washington, D.C.: The World Bank, 1970–1986.

———. *The World Bank and the World Environment.* Washington, D.C.: The World Bank, 1971.

———. *World Development Operations: Sectoral Programs and Policies.* Baltimore: Johns Hopkins University Press, 1972.

———. *Environmental, Health, and Human Ecologic Considerations in Economic Development Projects.* Washington, D.C.: The World Bank, 1974.

———. *Environment and Development.* Washington, D.C.: The World Bank, 1975.

———. *Rural Development.* Sector Policy Report. Washington, D.C.: The World Bank, 1975.

———. *Water Supplies and Sewerage.* Washington, D.C.: The World Bank, 1975.

———. *Policies and Operations.* Washington, D.C.: The World Bank, 1975.

———. *Agricultural Land Settlements.* Sector Policy Paper. Washington, D.C.: The World Bank, 1978.

———. *Forestry.* Sector Policy Paper. Washington, D.C.: The World Bank, 1978.

———. *Environment and Development.* Washington, D.C.: The World Bank, 1979.

———. *Environmental Considerations for the Industrial Development Sector.* Washington, D.C.: The World Bank, 1979.

———. *Health.* Sector Policy Paper. Washington, D.C.: The World Bank, 1979.

———. *Environmental Considerations for the Pulp and Paper Industry.* Washington, D.C.: The World Bank, 1980.

———. *Energy in the Developing Countries.* Washington, D.C.: The World Bank, 1980.

———. *Cofinancing.* Washington, D.C.: The World Bank, 1980.

———. *The McNamara Years at the World Bank: Major Policy Addresses of Robert McNamara, 1968–1981.* Baltimore & London: Johns Hopkins University Press, 1981.

———. *Toward Sustained Development in Sub-Saharan Africa. A Joing Program of Action.* Washington, D.C.: The World Bank, 1984.

———. *Guidelines for Identifying, Analyzing, and Controlling Major Hazard Installations in Developing Countries.* Washington, D.C.: The World Bank, 1984.

———. *Manual of Industrial Hazard Assessment Techniques.* Washington, D.C.: The World Bank, 1985.

———. *World Development Report.* Oxford: Oxford University Press, 1986.

World Bank/Information and Public Affairs and OESA. "The World Bank's Environmental Activities, an Overview." Mimeograph, 1986.

World Bank/Office of Environmental Affairs. "Case Study: A Lead Smelter and Refinery." Mimeograph, 1977. "Case Study: A Pesticide Manufacturing Plant." Mimeograph, 1979.

Wright, Peter. "World Bank Lending for Structural Adjustment." *Finance and Development* 17 (September 1980): 20–23.

Yudelman, Montague. "The World Bank and Agricultural Development—An Insider's View." Washington, D.C.: World Resources Institute, 1985.

Index